RUSSIA AND ASIA

BY

A. LOBANOV-ROSTOVSKY

Professor of History
University of Michigan

PUBLISHED BY

THE GEORGE WAHR
PUBLISHING COMPANY

ANN ARBOR, MICH.

1951

TO
MY WIFE

FOREWORD

This book was first published in 1933. In view of
the persistent demand for a work which would give
students of Russian affairs an overall view of the
problem of the relations of Russia with Asia, the
present edition is appearing revised and brought up
to date. Though in the main the views expressed by
the writer in the Conclusion have not been invalidated by the events of later years, the writer deemed
it desirable to make some modifications and shift
the emphasis in view of the rapidly changing flow
of events.

CONTENTS

RUSSIA AND ASIA

INTRODUCTION

The map reveals Russia as a vast plain stretching from the Baltic and the Black Seas to the Pacific Ocean. This plain, covering Eastern Europe and Northern Asia, is divided by a chain of mountains, the Urals, stretching north-south, and forming the geographic frontier between the two continents. But these mountains rise in gentle slopes to no greater heights than 5,500 feet, while they are intersected by valleys and easy passes at an average height of 1,000 to 2,000 feet. They therefore form no real obstacle to communication between the European and Asiatic halves of the great plain. Furthermore, they do not extend further south than the 51st parallel, leaving a vast gap of flat desert country stretching south to the Caspian Sea. Under these circumstances the whole plain must be looked upon as a single geographic entity, a sub-continent, Eurasia, the more so because along its southern border it is very definitely separated from adjoining regions by such obstacles as great mountains, deserts and inland seas, while the Arctic and Pacific Oceans limit it to the north and to the east. Thus appears the first important factor affecting the history of the inhabitants of this plain: the existence of natural boundaries limiting their expansion, namely, the two oceans and a land boundary stretching from the Black Sea to the

1

Pacific Ocean. This boundary is formed by an uninterrupted chain of mountains, deserts and inland seas, i.e., the Caucasian Mountains, the Caspian Sea, the Ust Urt Desert, the Aral Sea, the Kizil Kum Desert, the Hindu Kush, the Pamirs, the Tian Shan ranges, the Gobi Desert and the Khingan Mountains to the Pacific Ocean. From the west, the access to the Eurasian plain is free, but in Asia it is limited to four gateways: through the lowlands of Turkestan from Persia and Afghanistan, through the difficult trails of the lower Tian Shan and through the valley of the Ili River in the Northern Tian Shan from Western China, through the Khingan Mountains from Manchuria and the Far Eastern countries beyond. The plain itself is divided into two distinct zones: the forest zone in the north and the steppe zone in the south, and this will be the second important geographic factor to influence history. As the steppe zone is contiguous to the gateways into the plain, it will lure the nomadic invaders, whereas the forest zone will serve as a place of hiding and refuge for the people fleeing from these invasions. The last important factor to be considered is the net of marvellous waterways, broad rivers flowing majestically for thousands of miles, very different in their breadth and calm from the streams of Western Europe. Unfortunately they all flow in directions which make them of little use as connections with the outside world. The rivers of European Russia flow into closed seas, the White Sea, the Baltic Sea, the Black Sea and the Caspian; the Siberian rivers, except for the Amur, fall into the icebound Arctic Ocean, and the Central Asian rivers flow into the inland sea of Aral or lose themselves in the great sandy desert. Nevertheless with all their tributaries they form an exceptionally convenient system of inland waterways, and they will be the main channels for the spreading of colonization and civilization, particularly in the earlier periods of Russian history.

Already at the very dawn of Russian history the sharp distinction between the forest and steppe zones had become evident; the forest zone was inhabited by scattered Finnish tribes on the lowest scale of civilization, and its history started only when Gothland invaders in the 3rd and 4th centuries A.D. built up a powerful though shortlived empire, the first organized state in Russian history. In the steppe, a succession of invading tribes from Asia can be traced to several centuries before our era. These tribes, the Simerians and Scythians in the days of Herodotus, and the Sarmatians (3rd century B.C.) were of Indo-Iranian stock, hence susceptible to civilizing influence. The Scythians particularly came under the influence of Greek colonies, which sprang up along the coasts of the Black Sea from the 6th century B.C. These tribes were followed by numerous others, such as the Yazigi, the Roxalani, the Alani (all of Sarmatian stock), the Bastarni, the Dacians, and the Getae, all rolling in from Asia and each one forcing the other to move westward, particularly when the decaying Roman Empire offered such temptations for loot.

At this time and for a few centuries to come, Russia formed a great vacuum, sucking in the influences from neighbouring civilizations and races. Rome, though it

was too far away in the west to be a direct influence, affected Russia's destinies by acting as the great magnet which attracted barbarian invasions from Asia. But Rome's semi-oriental version, Byzantium, was to have a very strong influence on Russian history. Further to the east along the southern border of the Eurasian plain, we find two more great centers of civilization, Persia and China. On the edge of these two countries a vast and scattered mass of Turko-Mongol tribes, warlike and restless, formed a dangerous reserve of man-power ready at any time to change the course of history by the pressure of their masses.

These races produced no great civilizations. Their elements were war, plunder and destruction, but they had the virile qualities required for building great empires and they were to come to dominate Asia and half of Europe. However, they appropriated from neighbouring China and Persia some general elements of culture and they were a channel for transmitting Chinese ideas into Persia and Persian ideas of education into China. Though they carried on this work of transmission for practically ten centuries from 600 to 1600, they themselves remained extraordinarily free from these ideas of which they were the vehicles. When in an elementary way they did come under certain cultural influences, they lost their military virtues and gradually disappeared. This family of Turko-Mongol tribes was scattered over a tremendous area, the Finnish populations of European Russia forming the limit of their westward settlement in the forest zone from the Urals to Scandinavia and the White

Sea. At the other end of the Eurasian plain the Manchus, the Koreans, the Yakuts and the primitive tribes
along the Behring Sea formed the most eastern branch
of this family. But it is essentially the Turkish and
Mongol tribes inhabiting Central Asia and the region
of the Gobi with which we are concerned.

They alone were sufficiently dynamic to play a rôle
in history. The vast and undefined region west and
north of China and east of Persia, which may be considered their home, was in the first centuries of our era
in a state of constant flux for several reasons. China,
already a great empire under the Han dynasty was
concerned with exportations of her staple industry, silk,
to Rome and Byzantium. The most convenient road
was the one mentioned by Ptolemy via Kashgar and
Ferghana to the Oxus and from there through Persia.
In or about 138 B.C. the Chinese general, Chang Chien
"The Road Opener," set out on an official mission to
the West from the Emperor Wu. He reached as far
as Bokhara but was captured by Turko-Mongol tribes.
He succeeded in escaping, however, and returned to
China after an absence of thirteen or fourteen years,
bringing back a detailed report of these tribes. He also
succeeded in smuggling in, hidden in a cloak, seeds of
the grape, the walnut, and hemp, the culture of which
he thus introduced into China. Chinese embassies now
began following his itinerary in an endeavour to reach
the West. Some fell into the hands of the nomads,
with the result that punitive expeditions followed. This
protection of trade routes led to expansion. In 104 B.C.
a Chinese expedition sent to avenge the murder of an

embassy, suffered a heavy disaster in the desert of Gobi. A new expedition of 60,000 men was sent, well organized and well supplied. This one succeeded in crossing the desert and mountains and subjecting Ferghana. In the 1st century A.D., Pan C'hao, "the greatest of the soldier-statesmen who ever served China's Central Asian policy," extended his conquests beyond the Pamirs and entered into relations with Parthia. His lieutenant, Kang Yin, reached the Syrian border of Byzantium in 97 A.D. and pushed as far as the Persian Gulf. The result of this activity on the part of the Chinese was to set the Turko-Mongol tribes in motion.

Here was the actual beginning of a kind of human whirlwind which gradually swelling, reached Russia. At first the nomads, pressed by the Chinese, started moving westward, but they broke against the resistance of Persia. Persia, in the meanwhile, was expanding in the opposite direction, also at the expense of the Turko-Mongols. After Alexander the Great had extended his Empire right into the very heart of Central Asia, founding the city of Alexandria Eschate near present-day Khokand, thus making the Greek Empire contiguous to the Chinese, the Persians had five centuries of Parthian rule. Then the greatest national dynasty in the history of Persia arose, the Sassanides. During the rule of the third monarch of this dynasty, Shapur II, The Great, Persia was menaced by the invasion of the Turko-Mongol tribe of the White Huns. The Persians achieved a brilliant victory said to be due to a stratagem in which the Persian cavalry tied skins filled with pebbles to the necks of their horses, and so the White Huns turned away to invade India. Pressed by the double advance of Chinese and Persians, other Turko-Mongol tribes sought the line of least resistance, marched north into the great wastes beyond the Caspian Sea, and invaded Russia. The great Hunnish invasion swept over Russia and under Attila pushed as far as France and Northern Italy, while the Bolgars, a closely related tribe, settled on the lower Volga and the Don. Pressed in their turn by the Avars, they moved towards the Danube and in 679 A.D. under their khan, Asparukh, crossed the river and settled in present Bulgaria.

In the meanwhile a great Turkish Empire arose in the 5th century in the original home of the Turko-Mongols and knit together loosely various tribes from Mongolia to the Caspian. The Chinese had come to look upon these border regions as a kind of dependency. They called the tribes the Houng Niou and the region the Marshes or Routes, Pe Lou the northern route through the Tian Shan, and Nan Lou the southern route. The Empire of the Houng Niou had grown to such power that both the Chinese and the Romans sent ambassadors to the Il Khan, the Turkish ruler, and in 568 one of the Chinese emperors married the Il Khan's daughter. The emergence of this power was naturally a serious menace to China, hence a constant effort was made by China to subdue the Houng Niou, crowned finally by a partial success. This drove more tribes to start moving westward.

In the 7th century a great catastrophe occurred. The

Persian Empire crumbled under the terrific impact of the Arabs spreading the Muslim faith with the sword. In the caliphate of Walid I the new faith was spread by Qutaiba ibn Muslim, and in a holy war in Central Asia, Bokhara, Khoresm, Tashkent and Ferghana, the lands of the Il Khan up to the Tian Shan, were conquered. It was these events which accounted for the fact that the seething masses in Central Asia could not settle down and new tribes kept following those who had started their westward drive and so new invasions continued to splash over the great Russian plain.

Thus after the Avars had established a great empire from the Don to the Adriatic Sea during the 5th, 6th and 7th centuries, the Khazars followed, driving them out. These settled down, losing their nomadic character. We will have to deal later in more detail with their attempt to develop a civilization. They were followed in the 9th century by the savage and bloodthirsty nomads, the Pechenegues and the Black Bolgars, but in their turn they had to give place to the Polovtsy or Cumans in the 11th century. Two centuries later, when Chengiz Khan restored the power of the Houng Niou Empire and spread it over the greater part of the world as it was then known, the conquest of Russia by his orderly armies came as a final climax to this long list of invasions.

Thus for eighteen centuries in an ever-recurring regular rhythm, Asia aggressively dominated the steppe zone. This period came to an end only when the Russians, reversing the current of expansion, from west to east, were to become finally not only strong enough to stem the Asiatic tide but actually to sweep across Asia in their turn. So far no mention is found of these future masters of the Eurasian plain, the Slavs, later known as Russians. Up to the 7th century they did not come into the picture at all. The first mention we have in history of the Slavs is as subjects of the Kingdom of the Dacians on the middle Danube. This kingdom was destroyed by the Roman Emperor Trajan, and the Slavs then moved towards the Carpathian Mountains. In the 5th century a part of these tribes, forming a loose military union, moved back to the Balkans and attacked the Byzantine Empire. During the 6th and 7th centuries Byzantine historians mention great unrest amongst the Slavs, after which no more is heard of them from the Greeks until an attack on Constantinople in the 9th century when they are already spoken of as Russians.

In this interval the Slavs had moved back to the Carpathians and to Central Europe, whence they started radiating in various branches, the western one pushing as far as the Elbe, another branch moving eastward into Russia and colonizing the Dnieper region. This division into branches took place in the 7th century. As the unrest mentioned by the Byzantine historians coincided with the attacks on the Slavs by the Avars, it is obvious that these movements were an attempt on the part of the Slavs to escape the harsh domination of the Avars, who reduced them to slavery, making them fight their wars for them and then taking the booty in case of victory. Hence the march eastward was an attempt to avoid the nomads by going into the forest and scattering in the zone between the Dnieper and the Don, impassable with marshes and forests. It is important, therefore, to notice that the Russians came into Russia from the west and that their history was to be a continuous movement of colonization of the great plain from west to east.

This movement was somewhat similar to the movement of the American pioneers, only in the opposite direction and extended over nine centuries. Here the similarity stops. Whereas the Americans were fortunate in having two oceans separating them from powerful neighbouring races, the Russians had to engage in a long-drawn-out battle against the forces of Asia as a part of their forward movement. And when they did overcome the Asiatic invaders, invasions were to start from Europe. From the Avars and Khazars down to Charles XII of Sweden, Napoleon and the Austro-Germans of 1914, every two or three generations there was to be a death struggle with a powerful foe intruding upon Russian territory.

This penalty of a central position between two continents accounts for the continuous atmosphere of state of siege and martial law in all subsequent Russian history and also for the sporadic and uneven movement in the growth of Russian civilization. Cultural pursuits were continually interrupted by the necessity of converging all national energies in a struggle against races challenging the Russian domination of the Eurasian plain. And here it became apparent that in view of the special geographic features, in particular the river systems, no two masters could co-habit peacefully in this plain. At the beginning of Russian history it was not a⁺ all certain that there was a manifest destiny reserving to the Russian people a position of supremacy over this vast territory, but it did become apparent from the very beginning that they either had to dominate or be dominated and submerge their personality in that of a more powerful race. This accounts for the extremely bitter nature of the struggle between the Russians and the Asiatic invaders.

Under these circumstances the astonishing feature is not the backwardness of Russian culture compared with that of Western European nations more favourably located and with a cultural inheritance from Rome dating back nearly a millennium prior to the coming of the Slavs to the Dnieper, but on the contrary, the rapidity with which these Slavs built up a civilization, and the resiliency with which this civilization was reshaped after each great invasion. The Slavs, on coming into the forest region, inevitably lost what little tribal organization they had. They were a peaceful folk, and they scattered all over the great forest in search of clearings where individual families could settle down to primitive husbandry, fishing, apiculture and hunting. Some homesteads, if located on the waterways which were the only means of communication, gradually became centers of barter, and with the development of trade grew into cities.

The enormous importance of the Dnieper system with its tributaries extending into the heart of the plain and connecting the Baltic Sea with the Black Sea soon became apparent, and the two most important cities in the early period of Russian history grew up at the two ends of this great waterway: Novgorod in the north, and Kiev where the Dnieper flowed out of the forest zone. Here a Slavonic tribe, the Poliane, venturing out of the forest into the steppe, had settled and come under the domination of the Khazars, the masters of the plain at that time. The Khazar yoke was not only light but actually beneficial, for the Khazars, as has already been said, settled down themselves to peaceful pursuits. The capital of the Khazar Empire, Itil, on the lower Volga, became in the 8th century a great trading center attracting Jewish and Arab traders from the Near East. The Khazar khans came so much under their influence that they embraced the Jewish faith.

Not only did the Khazars make the Dnieper route safe to the Black Sea and thus enable the Russian traders to develop a highly lucrative trade with Constantinople, then the commercial and financial center of the world, but they also taught the Russians the existence of trade routes into the Near East. For a small toll of a tenth of the value of the goods the Russians brought their exports to Itil and shipped them further on camels into Asia. The Arabic writer Khordadbih saw Russian merchants in the bazaars of Bagdad. How lively this trade was is shown by the number of Arabic coins, dirghems, found in the burial mounds (Kurghans) in the Dnieper region. Some of these coins are of the 7th, but mostly of the 8th and 9th centuries, and archæological research has traced them right up the waterway into Scandinavia. It is obvious, therefore, that when the peaceful Khazars were overthrown by the fierce Pechenegues, this was a major catastrophe for the trading cities of the Dnieper region. Not only did the nomads close the routes to Constantinople and to Itil, but they menaced the very existence of Kiev.

This proved, however, to be a blessing in disguise. The Dnieper had long been known to the Scandinavian Vikings as the shortest way to Byzantium. Many of these adventurers settled in the cities along the route and important Varangian colonies grew up in the Russian cities. Now that these cities had to think in terms of defence against the nomads, the Vikings came to the foreground as fighters hired by the merchants. There came into being mixed Varangian and Russian armies, in which the Norsemen displayed their innate qualities of leadership. Political leadership was the next step, and by the end of the 9th century the Norsemen had provided Russia with the dynasty of Rurik (862) which, through one branch or another, ruled right down to the end of the 16th century. Under this dynasty the various territories occupied by the Russians were united into one powerful state of which Kiev, by the logic of its geographical position, became the capital.

But if the Norsemen gave the Russians their political body, it was Byzantium which gave a soul to the new nation by giving it its religion. With the Greek Orthodox Church, the influence of Byzantine culture in Russia became paramount. Kiev grew to great splendour. Thietmar von Meresburg, who visited it in its heyday, describes Kiev as a great and powerful city with four hundred churches and eight markets, and Adam of Bremen speaks of it as the "rival of the shining glory of the East," [1] i.e., Constantinople. Beautiful monuments such as the Cathedral of Saint Sophia with its marvellous mosaics, sumptuous palaces, the wealth of its citizens, and the high level of its culture justify the German travellers' enthusiasm. Russian manuscripts as well as the jewelry of the time show a high standard of artistry. The princes collected libraries and founded schools in which Latin and Greek were taught. Foreign scholars and artists were invited. The code of laws, the Russkaia Pravda, shows humane tendencies in advance of its times. There was no death penalty, monetary fines taking its place. On the other hand it was extremely elaborate in defining economic and commercial matters, going into minute detail concerning bankruptcy, dividends, etc., which shows a commercial civilization quite highly developed. Equality of women before the law and their right to own property was another remarkable aspect of Kievian life. The place this state occupied in Europe may be judged by the fact that the Grand Prince Yaroslav married his sister Mary to the King of Poland, his daughter Elizabeth to King Harold Hardrada of Norway, his second daughter Anastasie to King Andrew of Hungary, his last daughter Anne to King Henry I of France, while his son Vsevolod married the daughter of Constantine Monomakh, Emperor of Byzantium. It is on record that his brother spoke five foreign languages.

But notwithstanding this brilliant beginning, Kiev

[1] Kluchevsky, A History of Russia, Vol. I, p. 96.

was exposed to the heavy curse of the persistent menace of Asia. Even in the days of her greatest power, the nomads were only at a distance of two days' travel on foot from the city. In spite of a chain of fortified posts connected with trenches which was gradually pushed further out into the steppe, war with the nomads was a constant feature of the life of Kiev, and sapped her energy. Grand Prince Vladimir Monomakh alone signed peace with the Polovtsy nineteen times. In fighting the nomad, Kiev Russia was fulfilling her historic mission of defending Europe on her left flank against the forces of Asia, just as Spain was holding out against the Moors on the right flank. But the effort exhausted the young state.

The insecurity of the frontier provinces and the constant and terrible ravages resulting from nomadic incursions started a drift of Russian population once more away from the exposed steppe zone into the safety of the forest. Hence the center of gravity shifted northeast, and this process became so pronounced in the 12th century that the Grand Prince Andrew Bogoliubski refused to go to Kiev and moved his capital into the Rostov-Suzdal area, north of present-day Moscow. Hence Kiev, which in the subsequent civil war over this issue, suffered a sacking from which she never quite recovered, was weakened and made anæmic at the very time when a grave menace surged once more from Asia.

This was the Tartar Invasion. Though once more it was a Houng Niou wave sweeping over the steppe, its character was very different. It was not a wild horde moved by the sheer pressure of inertia, but an army carrying out a planned campaign, an army well equipped and sternly disciplined by a great military genius, an army at par or superior to the armed forces of Europe. Kiev under these circumstances had no chance of surviving.

The story of how Temujin, the son of a comparatively insignificant chieftain of a tribe of Mongols in the Gobi Desert, built up the greatest Empire known in history and has come down to posterity under the name of Chengiz Khan, "Emperor of All Men," is too well known to be retold, but some of its features are important for the understanding of what happened in Russia. It will be remembered that, hunted after the death of his father by rivals and enemies, he succeeded in regaining the leadership of his tribe, and eventually by his acquired reputation of courage and skill, in bringing under his power all the tribes of the Gobi Desert. Thus the Houng Niou Empire once more came into being, but Chengiz did not stop there. In 1206, the Great Kurultai or tribal assembly of the Mongols elected him Great Khan with the title of Chengiz Khan, and he established a capital at Karakorum in the desert. He also subdued the Karaits and Oigurs, Turko-Mongol tribes which had settled in Western Mongolia and in the region of the Tian Shan mountains. These had advanced to a sedentary mode of life and were subject to the influence of Nestorian Christianity, at that time very strong in Asia. It was through this channel that Chengiz Khan acquired a certain elementary culture which was to be so useful in building up his state.

But the decisive influence in this respect was his conquest of Northern China. He marvelled at the wonderful civilization he discovered there and understood how useful it might be to him. Hence, on returning to Karakorum, he took with him Chinese sages and technicians to instruct his people. Ye Liu Chutsai, a Manchurian prince who was a sage, astronomer, and poet, became his chancellor and gave valuable assistance in organizing his empire.

Now Chengiz turned legislator and gave his people the Yassak, the Ten Commandments of the Mongols, which remained for centuries their code of life. Among the main features were the complete obedience to Chengiz Khan, the putting to death of any officer who failed in his duty or refused to appear at the summons, and the formidable commandment which forbade the signing of peace with the enemy until he had submitted. A curious influence of Nestorianism is to be found in the first law, ordering all men to believe in one God, Creator of Heaven and earth, and in the sternness of the moral precepts making adultery punishable by death. In one respect Chengiz was more tolerant: "Get drunk only three times a month. It would be better not to do so at all, but who can abstain altogether?"

With this formidable code imposed upon his people, Chengiz Khan reorganized his military forces. According to Howorth, his invading horde was composed of 230,000 men divided into a center, right and left wings and reserves. The plan of campaign consisted in first preparing the ground and reconnoitering the enemy, then moving swiftly in several columns keep-

ing close contact between themselves and converging
to a selected goal. Special contingents equipped with
siege material were detached for taking fortresses and
cities so as not to hamper the general advance, and the
invaded country was thoroughly ravaged so as to leave
the enemy without supplies. Tactically, the favourite
moves were sweeping cavalry attacks enveloping the
flanks, and simulated retreat to draw the enemy out of
his positions. Great attention was paid to the line of
communications, and a special courier service made
swift communications with Karakorum possible. For
this purpose was organized a relay post service with
stations built at regular intervals. Later this system
was used for general postal service, and Marco Polo in
his Travels (Book 2, Chapter 26) gives us a graphic
description of its working in the days of Kublai Khan,
Chengiz's famous grandson:

"And the messenger of the Emperor in travelling from
Cambaluc, be the road whichsoever they will, find at every
twenty-five miles of the journey a station which they call
Yamb, or as we should say, the Horse Post House. . . . At
some of these stations, moreover, there shall be posted some
four hundred horses ready for the use of messengers."

To insure special rapidity the horses were provided
with bells announcing the approach of the courier so
that the station master might have a fresh horse ready.
In all there were 10,000 stations with 300,000 horses
in this service. These details are sufficient to show that
the Mongol Invasion was a very different matter from
the previous wild nomadic invasions of the steppe zone.

It was an insignificant incident which started the

Mongols on their great conquests westward: the Khan of Khoresm, the western neighbour of Chengiz, killed Chengiz's envoys sent to investigate the murder of some Mongol traders. By its portentous after effects the arrogant act of this oriental potentate must be ranked as one of the most important events in world history. Mohammed Khan, ruling a vast empire extending over Central Asia and Persia, which had come under the domination of Khoresm after the overthrow of the Seljuk dynasty, felt sufficiently strong to challenge Chengiz Khan. Consequently he put 400,000 warriors in the field and awaited the Mongols, who had declared war to avenge the slain ambassadors. He soon discovered their military strength, and after being defeated and seeing his country transformed into a desert by the invader, Mohammed perished miserably, while seeking refuge on an island in the Caspian Sea. Chengiz, pursuing Jelal u Din, the gallant son of the Khoresmian ruler who dared to oppose him, moved towards India. In the meanwhile two Mongol divisions under Subbotai and Chepe Noyon were idle, wintering, after their rapid campaign, on the borders of the Caspian Sea. Obtaining the permission from Chengiz to explore the region further afield, they marched through the Caucasus, and subduing Georgia and Circassia, entered the Russian steppe occupied by the Polovtsy.

The Prince of Kiev suddenly received an urgent appeal for help from his inveterate enemy, the Polovtsy. "Today they took our land, tomorrow they will take yours." Realizing the danger, Mstislav the Daring made a hasty alliance with other Russian princes and marched to the aid of the Polovtsy. The meeting with the Mongol divisions occurred on the Kalka, near the Azov Sea (1224). First the Polovtsy were defeated and then the isolated Russian detachments were separated from the main body which had to shut itself up in an armed camp. They eventually were overpowered, and all the Russian princes were crushed to death under planks upon which were seated the feasting Tartars.

Panic spread to Kiev, but the enemy disappeared. "Only God knows whence they came and whither they went," says the Chronicle. Actually the Mongols had turned south into Crimea, where they were storming the Genoese citadels, when the leaders received the order from Chengiz to return to a meeting of the Kurultai 2,000 miles away. On the way back, Subbotai ordered a careful investigation of the country traversed, with indications of fords, roads, mines and even a rough census of the population.

Fifteen years later in the second wave of Mongol expansion, after the death of Chengiz Khan, they came back. This time they did something no Asiatic invader had yet attempted, namely, marched north into the forest zone. One city after the other fell to them after desperate fighting. Finally Kiev was taken and so thoroughly ravaged that a few years later, when Plano Carpini passed through, he counted only 200 houses of this once magnificent metropolis remaining, and saw the fields around it strewn with bones. After a cavalry raid into Western Europe which brought them to the gates of Italy, the Mongols settled down in the desert region of the lower Volga, where the Khazars had once established themselves. Here the Golden Horde was formed with its capital Sarai, which ruled over the rest of Russia for over two centuries.

The Mongol, or as known in Russian history, the Tartar domination left an indelible mark on the subsequent development of Russia. It is, therefore, important to realize its exact historical rôle and limitations. The first thing to remember is that Russia had already had four centuries of history and had developed a strong cultural personality by the blending of Slavic, Norman, and Byzantine influences. Furthermore this culture was essentially religious, the ideals and the atmosphere of the Greek Church permeating every aspect of the national life and creating an exceptionally strong national feeling. It is this that saved Russia's culture. Had the Mongols come five centuries earlier, when the Slav tribes were still fluid and unorganized, possibly they would have been completely absorbed as were the Polovtsy, a part of which fused with the Golden Horde while the remainder migrated to Hungary where their descendants are living to-day.

But now it was too late as far as the Russians were concerned; for them the Tartars, being pagan, were "unclean," and hence objects of utmost horror. A number of curious Russian proverbs still current to-day attest to this fact, whereas the small number of Tartar words in the Russian language and those only of a technical nature, show the extremely limited cultural penetration of the Mongols. On the other hand the descendants of Chengiz Khan ruled jointly over an empire stretching from the Pacific to India and Western Europe. Their interests were concentrated in Asia, and Russia appeared as a distant outlying province or colony, by no means attractive. After such gorgeous and wealthy cities as Samarkand, Tabriz, Herat and Bagdad, the small Russian cities, mostly built of wood, offered small enticement. The country was bleak and the great forests frightened the nomads. Novgorod was saved by its surrounding marshes and forests. Hence the only interest which Russia presented for them was as possible tribute, and after the first destructive fury which was a part of their method of warfare, they understood that it was in their interest as tax collectors to restore normal life. To this must be added their indifference and tolerance of foreign religions as may be seen in the Yassak.

Hence, absorbed more and more in their domestic policies, the Khans of the Golden Horde limited their intervention to regular expeditions for the collection of tribute. Later, when confidence in the Russian princes grew, they entrusted the latter with the collecting of the money. Thus life in Russia was not very much interfered with and those princes who had remained alive after the storm continued to rule as before. The great distances in Russia made the Golden Horde a faraway country and the Mongol yoke was extremely light. Certain important effects of the domination, however, have to be examined.

On one condition the Tartars left Russia alone. That condition was interior peace. But once the danger was over, the Russian princes began quarrelling amongst themselves, competing for the coveted title of Grand Prince, which gave at least nominal power over the whole of the country. To put an end to this the Tartars established a mandatory system, the princes having to obtain from them a Yarlik, or a permission to rule. Thus new contacts apart from tax collecting were established between the local Russian governments and the Golden Horde; Sarai became a center for distribution of power which naturally attracted competing princes. Some, like Michael of Chernigov, showed great heroism in refusing to submit to the humiliation of bowing to pagan idols, and paid with his life; others were less discriminating. As time went on, relations improved and certain Mongol influences began filtering in from the top, though limiting themselves to the prince and his immediate surroundings. A great many princes, like the house of Tver, remained adamant in their hostility to the invader, but those that showed a more friendly attitude did so out of opportunism. Throughout the whole period of Tartar domination, the Mongols remained the national enemy, and as the Princes of Moscow were to discover later, the only way national unity could be fostered was by championing the cause of the deliverance from the invaders.

Under these circumstances, direct influence of the Tartars remained limited, so that many of the oriental aspects of Muscovy which surprised Europe in the 16th century and have been erroneously attributed to Tartar influence were really of Byzantine origin: the conception of autocracy, the cloistering of women, the long

dress and beards. It will be remembered that when the
Greek scholars came to Italy during the Renaissance,
bringing with them priceless treasures of learning and
works of art which had been saved from destruction
after the fall of Constantinople in 1453, their costumes
and demeanour provoked mirth on the part of the
Italians. Possibly these conceptions imported into Russia from Byzantium, and particularly the idea, new to
Russia, of unlimited power in the ruler, were further
developed as a result of the sympathetic echo which
resounded from Asia. Besides, the constant travelling
of the princes to the Golden Horde turned their attention eastward and foreshadowed the future expansion
of Russia in that direction.

But it was mainly in its indirect effects that the Mongol invasion was important. It cut Russia off from
Europe and halted for the time Russia's cultural progress. The best Russia did during these two centuries
was to conserve what she had already acquired. Hence
not only did Western European nations forge ahead of
her but when contact was reëstablished they had ceased
to understand her. This lack of understanding between
Western Europe and Russia, resulting in a flood of
derogatory literature and erroneous conceptions, is still
to-day one of the main causes of the present unrest and
uneasiness in the world. The idea that Russia's sacri-
fice in keeping back the destructive forces of Asia had
saved Europe and assured her future hegemony, has
not sufficiently entered European historical thought.

With regard to Russian history proper, the prin-
cipal result of the invasion was the change in the center

of gravity of the Russian people and the resulting rise of Moscow. As we have seen already, prior to the Mongol invasion a steady current of immigration away from the Kiev region into the safer northeastern forest region was taking place. With the destruction of Kiev by the Mongols and the depopulation of the steppe zone, the Northeastern Area became a refuge for the Russian nation, and new centers of political life arose. Here the Russians gradually recovered their forces and prepared the ultimate reconquest of the whole plain. Above all, it was here they conserved their sense of national unity. But in their coming they absorbed the peaceful aborigines; these scattered Finnish tribes not only welcomed the newcomers but fused readily by intermarriage with the Russians and acquired their higher culture. Thus came into existence a new stock, the Great Russians, in which a streak of Finnish blood altered the racial purity.

Politically, this resulted in the rise to power in this region of cities of which the most prominent were Novgorod and later Moscow. Novgorod, at the north end of the Dnieper trade route, rose at this time to great power and wealth, particularly when the Hanseatic League established a trading center there. Apart from a valuable trade in furs, timber, wax and other local products, there ended here one branch of a great trading route which came from China via Central Asia and Persia to Trebizond and thence bifurcated, one branch going to Constantinople and the Mediterranean, and the other through Russia to Novgorod. At the height of its power, Novgorod is said to have had 400,000

inhabitants, and in time it evolved a curiously democratic form of government. The Prince was reduced to
the rôle of a hired condottiere, and all power was
vested in a national assembly, the Vieche, of which all
free citizens were members. In reality this led to the
concentration of power in the hands of the Council of
the Assembly, itself controlled by the wealthiest merchant families.

These merchants assembled in a powerful guild, the
Guild of St. John the Baptist, and they were responsible for the enterprise shown in Novgorod. Half-
military, half-commercial companies financed by Novgorodian capitalists explored and colonized the vast
unknown territories stretching north to the White Sea
and the Arctic Ocean and east to the Urals. In the
11th century, a party in the service of a Novgorodian
patrician, Rogovich, reached these mountains and in
1364 an expedition from Novgorod pushed as far as
the Ob River in Siberia. A regular commercial intercourse was established between Novgorod and the people of the Iougra, on this side of the Ural. The latter
paid a tribute of furs, metals and silver, thus revealing
the great mineral riches of that mountain range.

It is, however, the stupendous rise of Moscow which
especially concerns us. First mentioned in 1147 as an
insignificant hamlet, Moscow was predestined to greatness by its geographical position. It was located at the
center of the Russian plain and also at the crossroads
of two important highways leading from the Dnieper
to the northeastern regions. Furthermore, the systems of the great Russian rivers flowing in various

directions came closest to each other in this particular region, and Moscow enjoyed the privilege of being able to profit by all the inland waterways of Russia. Lastly, because of its central position, it was padded by outlying principalities and made comparatively safe from incursions of external foes. It received refugees from more exposed principalities during the Tartar Invasion and also from the West during a war with Lithuania in 1368. Efficiently managed and well policed, Moscow attracted colonists in search of safety in those troubled times.

The growth of Moscow, however, was due not solely to natural advantages but also to the energy of a line of princes, peace-loving, without great vices or virtues but hard-working, economical, cold and calculating. Ruthlessly and patiently they labored for its greatness with astounding results. Whereas at the opening of the 14th century the Principality of Moscow measured some 500 square miles, by 1462 it had 15,000 square miles. A century later all the Russian principalities were brought under its sway, except for the Kiev region, which had been lost to Poland, and another century later, not only these territories were regained, but Muscovy had expanded right across Asia to the Pacific. The great Russian Empire had come into existence.

All methods were used for this purpose: conquests and annexations of neighbouring principalities, political and family alliances, loaning money to weaker neighbours who could not repay and hence had to cede their territories, but above all by a Machiavellian policy with regard to the Golden Horde. The Princes of Moscow, realizing the danger of arousing the suspicions of the Tartars concerning this growing power, assumed an attitude of complete submissiveness to the Mongol overlords. The arrival of the Prince of Moscow was always hailed with joy at Sarai because of the costly presents the prince brought with him for the khan's entourage. This policy so won the favour of the Tartars that the Prince of Moscow was given the Yarlik of Grand Prince and allowed to collect the taxes for the Tartars in the neighbouring principalities. This not only gave Moscow a legal power over the rest of Russia but allowed it to interfere in its neighbours' business, thus preparing their final annexation.

Then suddenly, when Moscow felt strong enough she abruptly turned against the Tartars, espousing the cause of national deliverance. Grand Prince Dimitri Donskoi openly challenged the Golden Horde by refusing to pay tribute. The ruling Khan, Mamai, understood the seriousness of this menace. After a few preliminary encounters which revealed Moscow's newly acquired military strength, Mamai decided to prepare carefully for a crushing blow. He mustered up a force of 500,000 men, partly made up of Genoese and other European mercenaries not averse to fighting against Christians on the side of the infidel. Dimitri on his side prepared for the struggle in the spirit of a crusade and got ready an army of 100,000 to 150,000 men. The two hosts met at the Battle of Kulikovo (1380) in which the Tartars suffered a crushing defeat. This battle was not immediately decisive, for the Tartars were still strong and came back a few years later with a new army. For all that it marks a dividing line in Russian history: up to that date the Russians were on the defensive against the assaults of Asia, but thereafter they were to take the offensive, which eventually carried them right into Asia. In particular, as far as the Mongols were concerned, this change was due to the reversal of the position of the two sides. They conquered Russia because they were united under a strong leader while the Russians were divided. Now the Russians were united under a strong dynasty while the Golden Horde was weakened by dissension. The picture would not be complete without this aspect.

Like the ancient Houng Niou and like all the vast empires set up by Asiatic nomads, the Golden Horde, by now virtually independent from the other remnants of Chengiz's empire, could not survive disintegration from interior discord. And at the time when Moscow's menace was becoming formidable, a new world conqueror attacked the Golden Horde from the rear, Tamerlane.

Once more in Central Asia, where Mohammed of Khoresm and Chengiz Khan had ruled, a great empire had arisen on the ruins of the weak remnants of the Mongol realm. Timur the Lame, or as he is known to Europe, Tamerlane, was not of royal blood, though the son of a chieftain of the Taragai clan of Tartars which had embraced Islam. A Napoleonic career brought him from the position of Ming Bashi (Colonel commanding a force of 1,000 men) in the army of the ruler of Samarkand, through all sorts of vicissitudes to the rôle of deliverer of Samarkand from an invasion of Jat Tartars from the north. The Great Kurultai, called to establish the question of who was going to be the ruler of Samarkand, elected Timur, breaking the rule that the throne could be occupied only by a descendant of Chengiz Khan.

Thus at the age of thirty-four he became the lord of a country stretching 500 miles around Samarkand. Samarkand itself, as Ibn Batuta, the Arab traveller, says, "is one of the greatest, fairest and most magnificent cities in the world." Not far from it were Bokhara with its great academies and libraries, centers of Muslim learning, and Herat with 250,000 inhabitants, several hundred colleges and 10,000 shops. The Kingdom of Tamerlane was thus a center of wealth and culture.

Hither came Prince Toktamysh, a refugee from the quarrels of the Golden Horde. Hearing of Mamai's defeat at Kulikovo, Timur had the idea of making Toktamysh ruler of the Golden Horde. His nominee would thus expand his realm indefinitely to the north. Also, like Napoleon, he was worried about not being of royal blood, and hence he would profit by having a royal prince under his orders. But Toktamysh, once successful in gaining the Golden Horde, turned against Tamerlane just at the moment when the latter was engaged in conquering Persia. In a remarkable march of eighteen weeks covering some 2,000 miles, Tamerlane moved north into Siberia and entered Russia south of the Urals. Here in the vast plains he inflicted a disastrous defeat on Toktamysh (1392). The remnants of the forces of the Golden Horde fell back on the lower Volga, where, it is said, more than 100,000 perished.

Three years later Toktamysh, having reorganized the Golden Horde, tried again. Tamerlane marched a second time into Russia, destroyed Sarai, stormed Astrakhan, and ravaged the country between the Volga, the Don, and the Dnieper. He then marched on to Moscow. Grand Prince Vassili hastily assembled an army and took up a position on the Oka River, covering Moscow. Here the two armies faced each other for a while, then Timur suddenly turned back, possibly frightened by the approach of winter. He went south, sacking Genoese trading posts on the Black Sea, and thus back through the Caucasus to Samarkand. This was the last great invasion of Russia from Asia. Tamerlane now turned to conquer Bagdad and Delhi, setting up his famous pyramids of skulls along the way. There remained only China, and he would have equalled Chengiz Khan's achievements. He set out on an expedition to conquer the Chinese but died on the way and his empire, following the general law, fell apart.

The Golden Horde was now moribund. Moscow, on the other hand, was consistently and methodically growing stronger. A century after the Battle of Kulikovo, John III, who took the title of Czar, was to have no difficulty in definitely throwing off the Tartar yoke (1480). At about the same time a German knight, Poppel, travelling in Eastern Europe, reported to the Emperor Frederick III that beyond Poland and Lithuania, which was commonly known as Rus, there was another great, powerful, and independent country bearing that name. Struck by such astonishing information, the Holy Roman Emperor sent Poppel to Moscow, begging the hand of the daughter of John III for one of his nephews and offering to confer on the Czar the title of King of the Holy Roman Empire. John replied with a great deal of dignity:

"Touching what thou hast said unto us concerning the Kingship, we by the Grace of God have been Emperors of our land from the beginning and from our earliest forefathers and do hold our commission from God himself even as they. Therefore we pray God that He may grant unto us and unto our children to be Emperors of our land forever, even as we are now, and that we may never need to be commissioned unto the same as we have not now." [2]

Moscow was becoming conscious of an imperial destiny.

[2] Kluchevsky, ibidem, Vol. II, p. 24.

CHAPTER I

THE CONQUEST OF SIBERIA

THE overthrow of the Mongol domination coincided with and was the result of the emergence of the Czardom of Muscovy as a powerful empire which had reunited the Russian nation and was taking its rightful place in the world. As it coincided also with the fall of the Byzantine Empire, Russia now took the position so long held by the Eastern Roman Empire, that of a balancing force between East and West. The marriage of John III of Moscow with Zoe Paleologue, heiress to the throne of Constantinople, the subsequent adoption of the title of Czar (a contraction of the word Cæsar) and of the double-headed eagle of Byzantium as crest, were indications that Russia set herself the mission of perpetuating, up to the confines of Asia, the imperial idea of Rome and the *pax romana*, acquired through Byzantium together with the religious tradition of Constantine the Great.

This great rhythmic movement in history, the Roman influence first expanding into Asia, then counterbalanced by the subsequent Asiatic invasions into Europe, was now once more marked by the recurrent wave of white expansion eastward. On the other hand, just as Russia was holding out against the Mongols on

33

one flank of Europe while Spain was doing the same against the Moors on the other flank, so now at the time when Spain and Portugal were discovering a vast new world to the west, Russia was doing the same in the East. The balance of power between Russia and Asia having turned definitely in favour of Russia, her advance into Asia was to be remarkably rapid and in a century she was to sweep across to the Pacific.

After the overthrow of the Golden Horde, there remained three moribund Mongol states, the Khanates of Crimea, Kazan and Astrakhan. The first of these, becoming a vassal of the Turkish Empire, escaped Russian domination until the 18th century, but the other two were immediately attacked by John the Terrible shortly after his accession. In 1552 he led an expedition against Kazan. To this war he gave the character of a religious crusade, and though the Crimean Tartars showed their solidarity with their co-religionists on the Volga by invading Muscovy, John was not deterred from his task. After besieging Kazan and making a passage through its mighty defences by the explosion of a mine, he stormed the city and captured it. Astrakhan followed in 1556, and by these two victories Russia at one stroke reached the Ural Mountains and the Caspian Sea. The way into the heart of Asia was now open.

The Crimean Tartars continued to give trouble. In their peninsula, separated from the mainland by a narrow neck of land, the Perekop, they not only had a hiding-place but also a convenient base for the Turks to land. According to Kluchevsky, more than 120,000

Tartars participated in the attacks upon Moscow in 1571 and 1572. Minor raids on the border occurred once or twice yearly, for the purpose of capturing slaves. The usual tactics were to creep up to the Russian border secretly, avoiding roads and taking care not to light fires which might be discovered by the Russian watches. Then profiting by the population being scattered in the fields during harvest time, they threw out detachments in all directions to capture as many boys and girls as possible. These were taken to Kaffa, the great slave exporting port in Crimea, and from there were dispatched on Turkish ships to the Levant, to Africa, and also to Europe. Western Europeans were not particularly reluctant to purchase Christian slaves. It was however discovered that Russians had an uncanny skill in escaping, so that, compared to Polish and Lithuanian slaves, their price was lower. "Leading his living wares into the square in strings whereof every ten files were chained together at the neck, the slave merchant was accustomed to bawl that 'These my slaves are of the freshest, the most simple and the least cunning and have been brought hither from the Kingdom (i.e. Poland) and not from Muscovy.' " [3]

Notwithstanding the conquest of the Tartar states along the Volga, it became obvious that the Moscow government was still faced with the all-important task of making its frontiers safe from the disastrous incursions of nomads. This was particularly urgent along the southern frontier facing Crimea, but it was also necessary along the eastern border beyond the Volga.

[3] Kluchevsky, ibidem, Vol. II, p. 114.

Only continuous expansion and the establishment of chains of fortified posts would establish security, by placing the central provinces of the empire further from the borders.

Thus expansion and colonization ran hand-in-hand in this quest for peace, and the Government soon discovered what use could be made of the Cossack communities which were springing up in the frontier regions. The great steppe was not solely the abode of the hostile nomads but also, lured by a promise of freedom and adventure, a motley crowd of Russian freebooters. These were either peasants escaping taxes and military service, or criminals escaping justice, or even young men of rich families in search of excitement. At the time of John's expeditions against the Volga Khanates, bands of these adventurers, profiting by the weakening of the Tartar rule on the steppe, pushed far ahead of the Russian settlement and were to be found along the course of the Upper Don in the very heart of no-man's land. A little later, on the Dnieper, a peculiar free military republic of Cossacks sprang up and prospered by participating in the wars fought between Russia, Poland and the Tartars. Being very restless, the Cossacks formed a doubtful asset to the side they were supporting; however, they carried out looting raids against the infidel, i.e. the Turks and the Tartars, sometimes even menacing Constantinople in their light crafts. A vague feeling of Russian nationalism and communion in the Orthodox faith made them less of a menace to the Russian Government than to the Poles whom they hated, and hence the attempt to enlist them for frontier service was more successful on the part of the Moscow Czars than on the part of the King of Poland. Gradually as the power of the government grew, so the hold on the Cossacks tightened. Finally they were organized into special "hosts"—both a military and administrative term—and they systematically settled along the border to form military settlements of colonists, agriculturalists who at a moment's notice might be turned into a cavalry force.

As Russia expanded in the East, new hosts were established along the shifting border. This policy was carried out right up to the 20th century. The names of the various hosts tell the tale of the Russian expansion: Don, Kuban, Terek, Astrakhan, Ural, Orenburg, Siberian, Semiriechensk (Turkestan), Transbaikal, Amur, Ussuri. But even up to the Great War they possessed a certain degree of autonomy and were bound to respond to the call to arms with their own horses and equipment. Though a regrettable tendency gradually developed to use them for police purposes, in times of political disturbances, the service they rendered to the Russian cause in Asia is inestimable. Though at first they were still adventurous freebooters acting on their own and at times in open conflict with the central authorities, they were the leading figures in the conquest of Siberia.

Thus we see that once Russia was started on her expansion towards Asia, the forces driving her made this movement irresistible. These were, first, the quest for security against the Tartars; then, the growing consciousness of an imperial destiny as a result of her adoption of the Byzantine political ideals, and finally, the adventurous quest of the Cossacks. To these must also be added the enterprise and vision of certain merchant families who carried on the great Novgorodian tradition of commercial exploration. Under the pressure of these forces the Russians crossed the Urals only thirty years after the fall of Kazan.

It was the explorations of the Novgorodian adventurers which made Siberia known to Russia. An expedition sent out by that trading republic in 1364 reached as far as the Ob. The inhabitants of the country west of the Urals, known to the Novgorodians as Iougra, were subjected to a regular tribute in furs, silver and metals from the Ural mines. With the conquest of Novgorod by Moscow, the expansion eastward was carried on by the Grand Princes of Moscow in their customary methodical way, moulded by a ruthless military tradition which contrasted with the essentially commercial aspirations of Novgorod. In 1483, eleven years after the conquest of Perm, a Muscovite force under Prince Kurbsky crossed the Urals and followed the affluents of the Irtysh as far as the basin of the Ob. The Siberian Prince Latyk submitted and journeyed to Moscow to offer tribute. Numerous other princes also submitted upon learning of the capture of Kazan by the Russians; the most prominent of these was Prince Yadiger who ruled territories near the present city of Tobolsk. But the payment of tribute in marten skins was often not forthcoming; Russian envoys sent to collect it were killed and John the Terrible found it difficult, absorbed as he was in wars along the western borders of Russia, to assert his authority in these distant and little known regions. This task fell to private enterprise.

In 1558 Gregory Stroganov, a scion of a rich and powerful merchant family which had been prominent in the development of the Novgorodian Far East, applied for a concession of 106 versts along the banks of the Kama River. This concession was granted on the usual terms: exemption from taxes for twenty years and full right to colonize this territory, to build salt works, to break the soil for agriculture and to take all necessary measures for protection against attacks of natives, including the building of small forts, the establishment of an arsenal and the enlistment of a small armed force. In return, the Government reserved the ownership of any mines which might be discovered. Consequently Stroganov built his fort and later was allowed to build a second fort some twenty miles away. By further grants the concession was enormously enlarged and it became increasingly difficult to defend it against the constant attacks of hostile nomads. The Czar advised Stroganov to enroll a sufficient number of volunteers from Cossacks and the intelligence that there were adventurous and well-paid jobs to be found there reached as far as the Don. The call became particularly urgent when Prince Yadiger was dethroned in Siberia and Khan Kuchum, of Khirgiz Kaissak origin, attempted to build up a powerful state by bringing the various Bashkir and Ostiak tribes under his sway.

Alarmed at the increasing menace of the Stroganov concession, Kuchum sent his son Mahmetkul to attack the Russian settlements. Hence an open state of war existed along the border and led John to give further rights to the nephews of Gregory Stroganov who had inherited his domains after his death. The concession was extended across the Urals to the banks of the Tobol and the number of armed forces increased. Responding to the offer of the Stroganovs, a body of 640 Cossacks headed by two outlaws, Yermak and Ivan Koltzo, made their way up north. This was a dangerous expedient for most of these Cossacks had black court records, Koltzo having even been sentenced to death for robbery. But the Stroganovs were in such a predicament that they enlisted them immediately, little suspecting that one of these robbers, Yermak, had in him the stuff of a great empire builder.

Yermak Timofeevich is one of the most picturesque and powerful conquistadores in history and his achievement is on a par with that of Pizarro and Cortez. He was the grandson of a carter from Suzdal, driven by poverty to seek his fortune in the great forests of Murom, at that time infested with brigands. Here he made a profitable living by offering to transport these brigands to and from their robberies in his cart. He was finally arrested and convicted. Escaping from prison he fled down the Volga to Nizhni Novgorod, where he died. His grandson Vassili Timofeevich Olenin showed from early days remarkable qualities of intelligence and physical strength. Running away from home in search of adventure he became a Volga boatman, acquiring the nickname of Yermak (millstone) which he immortalized. He then joined the Cossacks of the Don, became an ataman or leader, and brought his gang to the Volga where he headed a large band of robbers and pirates. His daring made him known and he had to escape government forces which were sent to capture him, and so made his way up the Kama seeking refuge with the Stroganovs.

On September 1, 1581, an expedition under the command of Yermak set out against Kuchum. Yermak's band was strengthened by Stroganov's garrisons, bringing the total of the expeditionary force up to 840 men. Scarcely had Yermak left, when Perm was raided by the Tartars and the local Voevoda applied to the Stroganovs for help. But Yermak was already beyond reach and Stroganov had to refuse, thus incurring the disfavour of the Czar. In true Cossack fashion Yermak proceeded up the rivers in boats, dragging them across the Urals to the basin of the Ob and met the first attacks of the enemy on the Tura. The expedition had been carefully prepared by the Stroganovs. Yermak was accompanied by a staff of interpreters and by three priests for possible missionary work. He was well stocked with provisions and above all well equipped with modern firearms and cannon. These accounted for the terror he inspired in the natives. Kuchum received intelligence that the invader commanded thunder and lightning which pierced the strongest coats of mail. Hence to protect his capital, Sibir, he mobilized a force about thirty times as great as Yermak's band. A desperate engagement took place, and notwithstanding severe losses, Yermak succeeded in putting the

⁴ Governor.

enemy to flight, though the Tartars continued to harass him by a shower of arrows from the banks, as he proceeded in boats. Finally on October 23rd the decisive battle took place at the gates of Sibir, the Russians attacking the enemy intrenched behind felled trees. The Tartars were overpowering the Cossacks by their numbers, when a timely shot wounded Mahmetkul, thus leaving the Tartars leaderless. Blind Kuchum fled south in despair and his capital was occupied by Yermak three days later. Under Russian occupation the name of the city, Sibir, was given to the country around it, which became known as Siberia (in Russian Sibir). Mahmetkul, however, recovered from his wounds and was still to be reckoned with. He attempted a new attack on the Russians in December but was defeated. In April of the following year, a detachment of ten Cossacks succeeded in overtaking him by surprise, scattering his forces and capturing him. This brought all further resistance to an end. Most of the neighbouring tribes submitted voluntarily and the winter of 1582 Yermak spent in organizing the newly acquired territories.

Now Yermak decided it was time to inform the Stroganovs of the results of the expedition. He also wrote directly to the Czar demanding pardon for his misdeeds, and sent to Moscow Ivan Koltzo, his lieutenant, who showed not a little courage in going there with a death sentence for robbery hanging over his head. The Czar, however, was so pleased at Yermak's achievement that not only did he cancel all sentences against him and his men but in sign of special favour gave a costly fur from his own shoulders, two richly adorned suits of armour, a goblet and a considerable sum of money. At the same time two voevodas, Glukhov and Prince Bolkhovskoy, were sent with a force of 500 men to take official possession of Yermak's conquests. But Yermak's difficulties were by no means over. Kuchum in the south was stirring up the fierce nomads against the Russians and one by one Yermak's trusted fellow atamans were killed in various encounters. Then came Yermak's turn.

During his two years' rule in Siberia he had been preoccupied in establishing commercial relations with inner Asia, reaching as far as Bokhara. In this undertaking the former bandit showed the vision of an empire builder, and when he learned that a party of traders had been held up by the Kalmycks in Southern Siberia, he immediately realized the importance of keeping this trade route clear. Hence with a small detachment of fifty Cossacks he marched south to rescue the party. Not finding the traders he settled down for the night on the banks of the Irtysh, August 5, 1584. The enemy, egged on by old Kuchum, had set a trap and had been watching Yermak's movements carefully. The night was stormy and when the nomads surrounded the Russian camp and fell upon the sleeping Cossacks, only two escaped death, one being Yermak and the other a Cossack who brought the tidings of what had happened. Yermak fought for his life and attempted to swim the stormy Irtysh. According to the legend he was drowned by the weight of the armour given to him by John the Terrible. In the meanwhile

the party of 500 men sent out by the Czar's order met
with all kinds of misfortune. One of the voevodas
and a number of men died from disease and privation.
The news of Yermak's death disheartened the remaining members of his expedition and they started to retreat, abandoning Sibir which was immediately reoccupied by Kuchum. On their way back however they met
a detachment of 100 men who had made their way
from Moscow and this brought sufficient courage to
make them advance once more. Without Yermak's
leadership they found Sibir too strongly defended and
so the Russians built a city about ten miles away and
named it Tobolsk (1587). Kuchum, seeing the futility
of resisting much longer, offered submission to the Czar,
but eventually ran away south once more. According
to Chinese sources who call him Kozum Khan, he came
to the Kalmycks near the Lake Dzaisang in 1598 but
the latter drove him away to the Khirgiz who murdered him. Following hard upon the heels of Kuchum,
the Russians now came into contact with the vast new
nomadic empire of the Jungarian Kalmycks which had
come into existence along the Ili River and the Ulias-
sutai and Tarbagatai regions, extending practically into
Mongolia. Here in 1616 a Cossack ataman appeared
on a self-styled mission from the Czar to the court of
the Altyn Khan (The Golden Khan), the ruler of this
new state. At his encampment north of Kobdo the Russian met the envoy of the Chinese Emperor and secured from the Altyn Khan the promise to arrange for
a Russian mission to go through to China. A little later
it was through the agency of the Altyn Khan that the

first consignment of tea, later to become a national
beverage, was obtained by Russia.

In the meanwhile, Russian expansion in Siberia was
being pursued methodically. By 1620 the Yenissei was
reached and the city of Yenisseisk grew up as a center
of the fur trade, attracting the natives for barter. Here
contact was first established with the Buriats, an independent warlike race, the northernmost section of
Chengiz Khan's Mongols. They barred further advance, hence the Russians turned northeast and some
ten years later the Lena was discovered and contact
established with another race, the Yakuts. The fortified post (ostrog) of Yakutsk was founded in 1632 in
an arctic swamp with a dreadful climate. But abundant
furs of high quality attracted swarms of adventurers.
The latter scattered over an enormous area of wilder-
ness covering thousands of square miles. Thus they became isolated and exposed to attacks of savage natives
who subjected to torture those who fell into their
hands. After the founding of Yakutsk it was discovered that the line of communication with the rear was
exposed to constant attacks by the Buriats. Hence a
Cossack ataman, Vassili Vlassiev was sent with a force
of 130 men in 1641 to conquer the Buriats. A long and
ferocious war followed. On one occasion 500 Buriats
were exterminated to a man. Finally the Buriats were
defeated, Lake Baikal was reached and Irkutsk founded
in 1651. From these new centers, Yakutsk and Irkutsk,
exploring parties radiated in all directions. In 1636
Buja with ten men pushed up the Lena and thence east
to the Yana and Indighirka, discovering silver mines.

In 1645 the Kolyma and the Arctic Ocean were reached. In 1647 an ostrog was established at Okhotsk by a party of 54 Cossacks who had routed 1,000 Tunguses and reached the Pacific Ocean. The following year a Cossack, Dejnev, with twenty-five men made a most remarkable voyage from the mouth of the Kolyma River on the Arctic Ocean, around the Behring Straits, eighty years before the official expedition of Behring. Losing two boats in a storm, he reached Anadyr, where he established the ostrog of Anadyrsk, the farthest away from Moscow (some 7,000 miles) on Russian territory.

Okhotsk was burnt by the natives in 1654 but was immediately rebuilt and thus the foothold on the shores of the Pacific was secured. Finally in 1697, a party headed by Atlasov made a long journey on foot and with reindeer from Yakutsk to Anadyrsk, and discovered Kamchatka. At the same time further explorations proceeded across the Behring Straits into Alaska on the one hand and southward from Yakutsk towards the Amur and Manchuria on the other hand. The important events resulting from these new explorations will be discussed in the following chapter. A striking feature of this whole conquest was that it was carried out by an extraordinarily small number of men. But the problem was not so much to conquer as to hold what had been conquered, in view of the tremendous numerical advantage of the natives, not all of whom were peaceful. This was solved by building ostrogs, somewhat similar to the blockhouses built for defence against the American Indians in the frontier days. These fortified posts formed a protective chain all along the border of the Russian expansion.

A typical instance of such an ostrog was Tara, dating from the earlier period of Russian conquest, i.e., 1594. First there was an inner enclosure of wooden walls and defence towers forming a square 98 yards on each side, inside of which was the church, the residence of the voevoda, the powder magazine and the storehouses. A second enclosure 1,400 feet square encircled the first one and between the two walls were located the log houses of the inhabitants. The garrison of the ostrog amounted to sixty Cossacks whose duty was also to police the whole Barabinski plain, some 250 to 400 miles long. The result was that much reliance was put on the moral effect of firearms, hence these ostrogs were well provided with artillery. But occasionally the nomads would succeed in raiding an ostrog, and Tobolsk itself, the headquarters of the Russian settlement, was sacked sixty years after its foundation and had to be rebuilt. With relative security thus obtained, Moscow started developing its new territories. As early as 1586, peasants were sent from Russia for colonization and provided with horses, cows and ploughs. In 1630 another party of 100 men and 150 women was recorded as arriving at Tobolsk, having been sent by the Government. But apart from this, a regular stream of private emigration started attracting runaway serfs, adventurers, Cossacks, merchants, etc. Interesting measures were taken to insure means of communication with Siberia. In 1601 a regular post service with horses was opened at Tiumen, roads made and post stations built.

By 1710 there were 7,000 couriers in this service, mile-posts had been set up and distances measured as far as Yakutsk. By a law passed two years later the roads had to be twenty-one feet wide. An ordinary letter tariff in 1682 was thirty kopecks (fifteen cents) to Krasno-yarsk and forty kopecks (twenty cents) to Nerchinsk, over 6,000 miles away. The rates compare most favour-ably with those of England and France even a century later.[5]

The population increased very rapidly as a result of the influx from Russia. By 1662 it was estimated at 70,000; fifty years later in 1710 it had risen to 250,000. The administration of this vast new empire became more and more complex. Whereas up to 1599 it was under the jurisdiction of the Ambassadors' Prikaz, or the Foreign Department, from that date on it was given to the Kazan Prikaz dealing with the eastern territo-ries. In 1637 a special Siberian Prikaz was formed. Tobolsk became the headquarters of the administration in Siberia and the voevoda of that city was made gov-ernor of the whole of Siberia. Provincial voevodas in distant cities such as Yakutsk or Irkutsk had to refer all matters to him, while he had to ask instructions from Moscow on questions of outstanding importance. With a deputy voevoda under him and an elaborate staff of clerks he had control over the whole admin-istration. Later, as a result of numerous depredations by officials and a great deal of graft, a special treasury

---

[5] The author is indebted for most of these facts to the interesting work of Vladimir, Russia on the Pacific and the Siberian Railway. See also Waliszewski, Ivan the Terrible, and Golder, Russian Expansion on the Pacific 1641-1850.

and customs official was added. In legal matters the voevoda judged all civil and criminal cases except cases involving capital punishment which had to be referred to Moscow. Very few capital punishments were actually carried out, even in such obvious and grave offences as the killing of a superior officer; the criminals were usually given the option of going to explore new lands and collect tribute. Not a few of these made names in history, the most conspicuous example being Atlasov, the discoverer of Kamchatka. The main task of the administration was collecting furs as tribute from the natives. A mixed commission of traders and officials was set up to determine the value of the furs according to the market price in Siberia. The furs were then sent to Moscow accompanied by affidavits and a part was set aside for trade with the eastern countries. As for the natives, they were forbidden to sell furs to anyone but Russians and they suffered from exactions of officials. But if they became Christians they could themselves enter government service. Similarly, marriage with native women was allowed if the latter were baptized; religion and not race was the main issue.

CHAPTER II

EARLY RELATIONS WITH ASIATIC COUNTRIES

WITH the 17th century opens the period when Russia established regular diplomatic and commercial relations with most of the important Asiatic nations. After several centuries of seclusion there awakened in Russia a desire to take part in the affairs of the outside world. In addition to relations with neighbours such as Poland, Sweden, Denmark, the Holy Roman Empire, with which fairly regular relations had existed all through the preceding century, and England due to the accident of Chancellor and Willoughby's voyage, we now find Russian embassies in most European countries including France and Spain. In Asia, Russia's new interests were indicated by the conclusion of a treaty with China, commercial relations with Persia and Central Asia, and an unsuccessful attempt to get into touch with India. The increasingly important rôle Russia was to play in the future as a world power may be traced back to this particular period.

It is important to understand why what may be termed Russian imperialism began to develop at this time. The last decades of the 16th century following the conquest of Siberia, saw Russia plunged into a

period of revolutions and anarchy known as the Time
of Troubles. This was due on one hand to the extinc-
tion of the house of Rurik after the death of Fedor, the
son of John the Terrible, and on the other hand to the
after-effects of John's too violent reformatory measures. In an attempt to break the power of the formerly
independent princes of the other branches of the house
of Rurik and thus secure a moral unity for the country
only recently reunited by Moscow, he pursued a policy
of terror against the aristocracy, which achieved its aim,
but broke the long-established economic fabric of the
country. After twenty years of civil war and foreign
intervention, a new Russia emerged with the advent of
the Romanov dynasty in 1613. The power of the
princes and the aristocracy was gone and a new social
class had taken its place; this was a class of service
men, sometimes self-made, sometimes descendants of
the former aristocracy, which accepted the principle of
service as the sole basis for its rights. This new and
mixed class had decidedly capitalistic leanings and was
interested in commercial expansion. But up to the middle of the century Russia was too absorbed in healing
her wounds after the Time of Troubles to think of
foreign affairs, except for wars to regain the territories
she had lost to Poland in the turmoil. The situation
changed with the advent of Czar Alexis, the second
Romanov. Now pacified and prosperous, Russia was
conscious of a growing strength and began thinking in
terms of foreign markets and economic expansion.

If we turn to China during the same period, we find
her in circumstances somewhat similar to Russia's. The

illustrious Ming dynasty under which China had
reached such heights of power, prosperity and culture,
had fallen, and a period of civil wars during the reign
of the last emperor continued for fourteen years (1630-
1644). Peace was restored by the advent of a new
strong dynasty, the Manchu or Ching dynasty. Like
the first Romanov, Michael, the first Manchu emperor,
Shun Chih, was a mere child in the hands of an able
regent who consolidated the position of the dynasty.
But his successor, K'ang Hsi (1662-1723), was one of
the greatest rulers that the Middle Kingdom had ever
seen. Professor Soothill of Oxford says of him:

"Humane in his government, his tolerance of all religions
is shown in his graciousness to the Jesuits. . . . Under K'ang
Hsi the foundation was laid of the dynasty's wealth of
literary achievement. The Imperial Dictionary containing
44,439 characters with sounds, meanings, and illustrative
phrases historically arranged is still the national standard. En-
cyclopedias, including the great Tu Shu Chih Ch'eng in 1,628
volumes and many other books were printed by a specially
prepared fount of 250,000 movable copper type. . . . Peace
stimulated the fundamental industry of agriculture everywhere, other industries and trade followed and the population
greatly increased. Public works of utility were undertaken
and probably the roads, canals and sanitation equalled those
of Europe at that time as did also the laws, administration,
education, industry and art. . . . K'ang Hsi died leaving the
greatest contemporary empire in the world, in the combination
of extent, ordered government and culture." [6]

It is important to realize the respective positions of
these two empires in order to understand later develop-

[6] Soothill, A History of China, pp. 56-57.

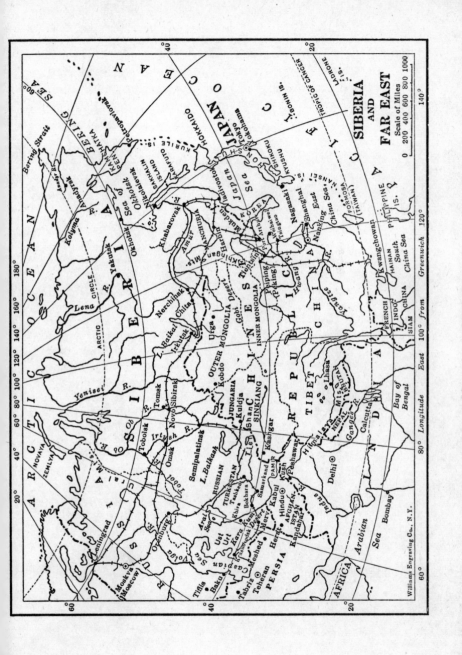

SIBERIA
AND
FAR EAST

Scale of Miles
0 200 400 600 800 1000

ments. Trade started between them spontaneously when the Russian conquest of Siberia made the two nations near neighbours. The exchange of goods indicated the relative stages of economic development. China, being more advanced, sent textiles, silks, gold and silver, and in return received hides, furs and foodstuffs. But at this time there was still no direct contact between the two empires and this trade was carried on by intermediaries. Political issues inevitably arose as a result of the existence of a belt of buffer states which from west to east, were Jungaria, Mongolia and Manchuria. Jungaria or the Kalmyck power of the Altyn Khan had risen to considerable power. Composed of nomadic tribes of Kalmycks and some Khirgiz, this Kalmyck state had no fixed frontiers; they shifted according to the possibilities of loot offered by neighbours. Occupying the northernmost corner of present Chinese Turkestan and extending roughly from the Tian Shan Mountains to the range of the Altai, Jungaria was so wedged between Siberia and China as to be a dangerous and highly unwelcome neighbour for both. Mongolia was a weak theocratic state under a priest-ruler, the Khutukhta, and was divided as to-day into two parts: Inner Mongolia named Chakhar, or the southeastern section of the country close to China and gravitating toward her, and Outer Mongolia or Khalkha, along the borders of Siberia and gravitating toward Russia. The situation was delicate as both parts urged their respective powerful neighbour to protect them from the infringements of the other neighbour. Russian and Chinese influences were thus clearly divided into spheres.

Finally, Manchuria, by giving a powerful dynasty to China in 1644 naturally occupied a special position in the eyes of the Chinese people. Considerable ill feeling had existed between Russia and China when about 1680 the Jungarian Kalmycks had invaded their weak Mongolian neighbour and the Chinese accused the Russians of supporting the Kalmycks, but the decisive clash between the two empires actually occurred in Manchuria. The events which took place along the Amur are highly interesting in that they reveal the character of the two nations.

Curiously enough they were responsible for the establishment of diplomatic relations when all previous peaceful attempts had failed. Indeed in 1654 a Russian ambassador, Baikov, was sent to China, but he refused to submit to the Kotow, or the bow of servile allegiance to the Chinese emperor which was considered a part of the court etiquette for the admittance of any foreign ambassador. From the Chinese standpoint all foreigners were barbarians and the only possible attitude towards them was the acceptance of their tribute and submission. The subsequent Russian embassies in 1657, 1670 and 1675 failed for the same reason. Not all European nations were so particular on this point; the Dutch were willing to undergo this humiliation for the sake of gaining commercial advantages.

When the Cossacks, roving beyond the Lena, reported to the authorities that a great river flowed east across wonderfully fertile country, rich also in silver mines, the Moscow Government ordered this region to be explored. Hence the voevoda of Yakutsk organized an expedition of 132 men in charge of his secretary, Poyarkov, whom he selected because he was the best educated and most literary man available. The expedition started on June 15, 1643, went down the Lena and its tributaries, at one place going through forty-two rapids and losing a boat. After wintering on the way they sailed down the Amur the following year. Reaching the Sungari, Poyarkov detached twenty-five men to explore this tributary. The entire party with the exception of two men was murdered at a day's journey from the main party. The latter reached the mouth of the Amur where they wintered, suffering terrible privations from the cold and lack of food. The following spring, in their small craft they ventured into the open sea which is notably rough in this region, and following the coast northwards, reached Okhotsk and returned to Yakutsk in July, 1646.[7] Eighty members or two-thirds of the expedition perished on the way, but the survivors covered more than 4,000 miles on this remarkable voyage. Poyarkov brought back with him 480 sables and declared that the conquest of the Amur would not be difficult. He also wrote a valuable description of his journey.

Thus the field was opened for private enterprise. Following his footsteps came an adventurer, Khabarov, a remarkable character who may be considered the Yermak of the Far East. He was a peasant from Veliki Ustug in North Russia who went to seek his fortune in Siberia and made a success of various ventures in real estate, transportation and salt boiling. Acquiring great

[7] Golder gives the date of June 12, 1646.

wealth in these various enterprises in the Lena region along the fringe of the Russian expansion, he was tempted by Poyarkov's discoveries to go further afield. Hence he asked for permission from the voevoda of Yakutsk to equip at his own expense an expedition to seek a short cut to the Amur. This permission was granted to him in 1650 but he was cautioned not to use firearms without extreme necessity and not to commit violence. Khabarov took with him at first seventy men and wrote an interesting account of his journey: "In the rapids the rigging was broken, the rudder smashed, the men bruised but by the help of God and Imperial good luck all ended happily." [8] He got to the Amur but meeting with the resistance of warlike natives, returned to Yakutsk for an additional force and obtained 150 volunteers, twenty regulars and three guns. He joined his party with these reinforcements and proceeded further. But now he was coming to walled cities and the Manchu tribe of the Dauria, well equipped and organized under Prince Lafkai. He gave battle to the latter at the town of Albazin and routed him completely. Capturing Albazin, he made it his base and left fifty men as garrison. In the meanwhile the news of his doings had reached Moscow and reinforcements amounting to some 130 men were dispatched to him with ammunition and, characteristically enough, paper for him to write his experiences. Also, the voevoda of Yakutsk was instructed to send an embassy to the Chinese Viceroy of Manchuria, Shamsha Khan, asking him for gold and silver: "For our Lord the Czar

[8] Vladimir, Russia on the Pacific and the Siberian Railway, p. 111.

Alexis Mikhailovich is powerful and great and terrible, but gracious and just and not bloodthirsty." [9] The embassy, however, was massacred by the Daurians. The following year Khabarov went down the Amur conquering cities on his way, and it is said, committing acts of cruelty. This is most probable, for conquistadores have always been tough adventurers, and this small party of men, lost in the midst of warlike populations a thousandfold more numerous than they, were gambling with their lives and would be apt to commit excesses out of sheer fright. This is the story of all colonial conquests, particularly in the 16th and 17th centuries, and it is difficult to understand why some writers lay such stress on this particular aspect of Khabarov's career. This being taken for granted, we will not spend more time on this unpleasant aspect of the conquest.

By now the Chinese Government, informed of Khabarov's advance, had sent a regular force against him, and when he reached the Ussuri river he found a string of Chinese boats with soldiers, stretched across the river blocking his way. He fired a volley, and profiting by the confusion, forced his way through. On another occasion he ran into a Chinese detachment of 2,000 men with eight guns. Though by now he had little more than a hundred men remaining, he succeeded in defeating this force completely. But trouble was ahead for him, due to his men deserting to become roving brigands. Intrigues against him in Yakutsk also resulted in his being arrested and sent to Moscow for

[9] Vladimir, ibidem, p. 115.

trial. The charges were proven false, he was acquitted, made a Son of a Boyar, which was a minor title of nobility, and appointed chief of the Lena district, a position he held until his death. His work of conquest was carried on by a Cossack chief, Stepanov, who in 1654 went up the Sungari and met a large Chinese army in boats. He drove the Chinese ashore out of the boats and boldly attacked the enemy's trenches. Not being able to take them, he shut himself up in a camp and with some 500 Cossacks faced a new force of 10,000 Chinese which had come up and which after a while retreated. Running out of provisions, he decided to advance and penetrated, plundering, right into the heart of Manchuria, as far as Ningut. Retiring to the Amur for the winter, he repeated these expeditions several times. Finally in 1658, the Chinese collecting a large army and concealing a fleet of forty-seven vessels among the islands, set a trap for him. Stepanov fell into it and was killed, together with 270 Cossacks. The remainder of his force, some 200 Cossacks, succeeded in escaping and brought the tidings of his death. The same year the Chinese besieged and captured Albazin from the Russians, thus clearing the whole Amur region from the invader. But the Russians came back, and Albazin, which had been burned, was rebuilt sometime around 1674, a slow infiltration of isolated Russian settlers taking the place of the former conquests. One by one all the ostrogs on the Amur were rebuilt and by 1681 the Russians had once more penetrated into Manchuria even further than Stepanov had gone. Exasperated, the Emperor K'ang Hsi sent an ultima-

tum to the Russian commander, Tolbuzin, at Albazin,
ordering him to evacuate the Amur. No reply being
given, the Chinese besieged Albazin with a force said
to be 15,000 strong, with 150 field guns and a number
of siege guns.[10] Tolbuzin with 450 men and three guns
held out, repulsing assaults until he ran out of ammunition. He capitulated on honourable terms, the Chinese allowing him to retire with arms. They burnt the
city and left, and then the Russians came back once
more. Profiting by his experience, Tolbuzin stood siege
from an army very much more numerous, and when
he was killed in action his successor, Beiton, actually
succeeded in driving the Chinese away. It was under
these circumstances that direct negotiations started
between Russia and China.

The Chinese announced to Spafari, the ambassador
who had gone to China in 1675, that they wanted to
settle the frontier question. Hence a special Russian
ambassador, Golovin, was now appointed with full
powers, and a truce in the fighting was arranged during the negotiations. Golovin's embassy left Moscow
in January 1686 with an escort of 500 men to which
1,400 soldiers were added in Siberia, and met the Chinese envoys at Nerchinsk where the conference took
place. The Chinese came with an imposing escort of
10,000 men, and this fact undoubtedly influenced the
negotiations. After much wrangling, a treaty was
signed on August 27, 1689, and was the first treaty

[10] Golder doubts these figures. His calculations based on the number of Chinese soldiers quartered *after* the siege at Aihun are, however, hardly convincing. A part of the force may have been quartered
elsewhere.

with a European power ever signed by China. Because of the presence of Jesuits as interpreters in the Chinese delegation, the treaty was drawn up in Latin. The frontier, according to its clauses, was fixed along the river Gorbitza, the mountains north of the Amur, up to the river Uda and along the Argun. All ostrogs on the Amur including Albazin were to be destroyed and no Russian colonists permitted to settle on Manchurian territory beyond the river. Those already established had to leave or become Chinese citizens. Furthermore, China was to be given a free hand in the neighbouring buffer states of Jungaria and Mongolia. In return, Article IV opened China to Russian trade by stating that the subjects of both empires could travel freely in the other country to buy and sell whatever was required for the development of trade between the two countries. Further, the treaty speaks of eternal friendship and peace between the contracting parties, and these words proved to be a reality. Peaceful and amicable relations were established between Russia and China for over two centuries, and this attitude towards her neighbour became a dogma of Russian foreign policy, notwithstanding the fact that the long common frontier required constant exercise of restraint and good will. It is curious to notice in this treaty that the name of the Chinese emperor comes first, followed by the title of the czar, thus revealing the standing of both countries at the time. Two weeks after the signing of the treaty, Peter the Great came to the throne and proceeded to make of Russia a great European power. Thereafter the order of the naming of the countries in all future diplomatic documents has been reversed.

The second field in which the new-born Russian economic imperialism was beginning to assert itself in Asia at this time was Persia, Central Asia and India. Causes were at work here similar to those already examined, and here also Russia came into contact with great Asiatic powers, with advanced civilizations of their own. Relations with Persia grew steadily in importance from the 15th century on.

Like Russia, Persia had felt the effects of the great Mongol invasions and the rule of Tamerlane, but by the 16th century she had reëmerged under a powerful national dynasty, the House of Safavi. The beginning of the 17th century found her under the rule of one of Asia's greatest monarchs, Abbas the Great, who died in 1629 after a glorious reign of forty-two years. Under him the Persians defeated the Turks and expanded their empire from the Caspian Sea to Bagdad, and from Kurdistan to Mosul. Abbas was also a great administrator, improving communications and embellishing his capital, Isfahan. His stone pavements and caravanserais for travellers are still in existence. He cultivated foreign relations and encouraged Europeans to come and settle in his realm. It is said that he loaned 7,000 roubles (about 50,000 dollars at present value) in 1617 to the young Czar Mikhail, who upon the accession of the Romanov dynasty in 1613, found the treasury sorely depleted as a result of the Time of Troubles. Later, a great Russian embassy was sent by Czar Alexis to Persia. It was a vast affair with envoys, officials and a retinue of 800 men. Some trouble arose over customs duties and the Shah refused to see this embassy, thus creating considerable ill feeling between the two countries. About the same time, the Duke of Holstein was negotiating with the Czar and the Shah for the exportation from Persia through Russia, of raw silks for his factories, but it was found that the cost of the freight and custom duties would be too high. However, commerce between Russia and Persia seemed to be well established by this time. Russia exported to Persia textiles, copper and furs, particularly sables, and received in return Persian silks, free of duty. This trade was so flourishing that by 1670 there was a colony of Persian merchants in Moscow. At this time also, Russia tried to organize a regular shipping service down the Volga, putting into commission an ill-fated vessel, the Orel (Eagle), which became the prey of the famous Cossack rebel and pirate, Stenka Razine. This vessel had been put together in 1669 on the Oka and launched at Astrakhan at a cost of 9,000 roubles, approximately 60,000 dollars in modern currency.

Relations with Central Asia, important as a gateway to the heart of Asia, dated from an earlier period, though it was only now they came into prominence. After the fall of Kazan and Astrakhan, and the consequent extension of Muscovy to the shores of the Caspian Sea, the Central Asian states which had arisen from the ashes of Tamerlane's empire got to know Russians at first hand. Embassies appeared at the court of John the Terrible from Bokhara and Samarkand, asking for a "free road to guests," i.e., merchants. The czars not only granted this request but encouraged Russian merchants to go to Central Asia so as to avoid

commissions and middlemen's fees on the trade with
the East. The journey across sandy deserts infested
with brigandish and ferocious nomads was, however,
difficult and perilous. In 1589 an ambassador of the
Ameer of Bokhara, Abdullah Khan, appeared at the
court of Czar Fedor, but because the letter of introduction did not bear the correct title of the Czar, he
was not received. This is a curious instance of the extreme sensitiveness on matters of etiquette in Muscovy.
In a similar way a Russian ambassador, Khoklov, sent
to Bokhara in 1620, was instructed not to accept any
invitation to dinner without being sure that he would
be placed higher than any other ambassador who might
be present. No presents were to be given as the price
of admission into the country. The real motives for
this embassy seem to have been a desire to obtain more
information about Inner Asia, to develop trade possibilities by equality of treatment and privileges for Russian merchants with those granted in Moscow, and to
obtain the release of those unfortunate travellers who
had been made slaves by the nomads. This latter question was raised by all subsequent Russian governments
for more than two centuries to come.

By the middle of the 17th century an embassy was
established at Bokhara and this led to interesting developments further afield. In 1644 the secretary to the
Russian envoy succeeded in reaching Balkh. This once
famous city was then the capital of an independent
state in Northern Afghanistan, whereas the territories
beyond the Hindu Kush with Kabul, the present capital of Afghanistan, formed an integral part of the

Indian Empire. The Russian diplomat, Medvediev, reported:

"The Czar of Balkh, Soupcon Kuli Khan wants to be friendly with the Great Emperor, Czar and Grand Prince Alexis Mikhailovich, autocrat of Great, Little and White Russia. Soupcon Kuli Khan says that if the Great Czar desires to send envoys or travellers to Balkh, India or any other state, he will accord them protection and let them through his domains. The Indian road passes through Balkh and goes through inhabited lands. There are no brigands, no harm can occur and there are no duties levied." [11]

This report roused keen interest in Moscow. Like the rest of Europe, Russia was full of tales about the riches and marvels of India. The same lure of the fabulous East which inspired the great discoveries of the Renaissance was now casting its spell over Muscovy, but it had had to travel laboriously through the deserts of Central Asia and hence reached Moscow much later. Moscow was still in the stage of 14th century Europe, reading avidly the descriptions of Marco Polo's travels. But it also had first-hand knowledge of India dating from the 15th century, when a Russian merchant, Athanasi Nikitin had visited the country with a companion on a journey which lasted four years. He left a curious account of his travels, reflecting an indignant disappointment in his commercial expectations:

"Brethren, Russian Christians, if any of you want to go to the Indian land leave your faith behind and say Mohammed

[11] Raskolnikov, Russia and Afghanistan, article in the New East (Novy Vostok) Moscow, Vol. IV, p. 14.

and then you can go. . . . The infidel dogs have lied to me, for there is nothing to be found in India for us; pepper and colors, these are cheap but bringing them by sea costs taxes and there are many pirates on the sea." [12]

The result of this awakening of interest in India was that Czar Alexis in 1648 equipped a great embassy to India with a personal letter to the Mogul Emperor and costly presents, mostly sables. But the embassy was delayed by the wars between Persia and India and was able to proceed only in 1675, in the reign of Aurangzeb, the last great emperor of the magnificent Mogul dynasty, when it was still at the very height of its splendour. The great Mogul, proud of the high degree of civilization of India and its resplendent wealth and culture, was not a little embarrassed by the arrival of an embassy from an unknown country somewhere in the bleak north. The Russian envoys were halted at Kabul by the Indian frontier authorities, who reported to Delhi. After a long delay, the reply came from Delhi and it was negative. The reasons given were most curious: there never had been an embassy from Muscovy because of the distance separating the two countries; there never had been any quarrels to settle and there were none then; the Great Czar's intention was evidently to get money from India, for it was impossible to find any other reasons for sending ambassadors; moreover the Russian faith was different, and Muslims could not be friends with Christians. The letter was returned and all the insistence of the Russians led to nothing. Finally the Indian authorities

[12] Raskolnikov, ibidem, p. 13.

suggested that should the Russians desire to stay they could do so by entering Indian service at a salary. When the envoys refused indignantly, the presents were confiscated and appraised by local merchants. Not only was a low price put on them, the furs being declared of poor quality, but they were not returned, the Russians receiving their value in cash, after deduction of a special customs duty. This was too much. The offended ambassadors left forthwith and returned to Moscow in January, 1677. This failure dampened the hope to get into touch with India, but the interest remained and from time to time was revived.

Before closing this period, mention must be made of an event in itself of little importance but which, by its ominous associations with the past, helps to show how far Russia had travelled on the road of increasing power. In 1636, just at the time when contacts were being established with the Jungarian Kalmycks, there occurred on a diminutive scale what might be termed the last Mongolian invasion of Russia. The Kalmyck tribe of Torgouts started moving westward from its original abode on the Upper Irtysh, conquered the Turkomans in the great desert along the border of Central Asia, crossed the Yaik and settled on the Lower Volga around Astrakhan. This horde had 50,000 kibitkas (tents) representing some 30,000 warriors, swollen by a crowd of Turkomans and Khirgiz which followed the horde in its wanderings. The Russian Government was puzzled. The wounds inflicted by the Time of Troubles had not yet been healed; moreover Russia had just been engaged in a death struggle with

Poland and Sweden for the recovery of lost territories on its western border; more wars were expected and the treasury was empty. Short of a military operation on a large scale, nothing would dislodge the newcomers. So the Government decided to acknowledge the accomplished fact and to content itself with erecting a line of forts for defence and observation of the nomads. It is curious to note that the former great invasions were hardly more numerous, but now when Russia blocked their path, the nomads, lacking aggressive leadership, settled down peacefully.

CHAPTER III

PETER THE GREAT

At the close of the 17th century a new era opened in Russian history. Only two centuries had passed since growing Muscovy felt itself sufficiently strong to challenge the Tartar domination; not only had Russia pushed the Asiatic hordes back beyond the borders of the great Eurasian plain but she had become the sole and undisputed ruler of this vast expanse. Russia swept across Northern Asia to the Pacific Ocean. Her political influence and rising economic imperialism, furthermore, was felt in the heart of Asia—in China, in Persia, in Central Asia and up to the very doors of India. It was this rapid growth of power, coinciding with the reëstablishment of commercial, diplomatic and cultural relations with Western Europe, which made it necessary for her to overhaul and modernize the whole machinery of state and culture.

This work was carried out by the reforms of Peter the Great. Under his rule Russia emerged as a modern state and took her place among the great European powers. With his dynamic energy Peter remodelled everything: administration, finances, army, navy, industry, mining, commerce, church, schools and social customs. But in all this he acted without a preconceived plan and, save for the dominating desire of bringing his people up to the standards of the West, under the spur of immediate necessity. A possibility of free intercourse with Europe was the first need; hence a twenty-year struggle with Sweden for the domination of the Baltic Sea.

His thought thus turned entirely to Europe, and with all his time taken up by his European wars and internal reforms, Asiatic policy necessarily had to occupy a secondary place. But with his capacity for galvanizing everything he touched, important developments occurred each time he had the leisure to turn his attention eastward. It is interesting to notice that there were no revolutionary changes in his Asiatic policy. He carried on in the footsteps of his father, Czar Alexis. Thus the continuity of Russia's policy in Asia was in striking contrast to the revolutionary changes she underwent at home and in Europe.

With regard to China, Peter the Great's policy was based on two considerations: friendship on the basis of strict observance of the Treaty of Nerchinsk, and development of commercial relations. For two centuries this was to be the traditional Russian policy towards her great Asiatic neighbour, even when the balance of power in Asia had so altered as to give Russia an overwhelming predominance. At the beginning of the 18th century however, it was China which under the able and energetic rule of K'ang Hsi pursued a policy of aggressive imperialism and colonial expansion, whereas Russia, absorbed in Europe, remained cautiously on the defensive. The Chinese lost no time in taking advantage of the free hand in Jungaria and Mongolia granted to them by the Treaty of Nerchinsk, inflicted a crushing defeat on the Jungarian Kalmycks who had invaded Mongolia, and thus secured the domination of Mongolia also.

But the nomadic Kalmycks reappeared in 1714 and a new war had to be waged. Both Mongolians and Kalmycks clamoured for Russian help against the Chinese, but Russia, careful to remain within the treaty, acted only as mediator, sending a Russian officer with the Kalmyck embassy to Peking the following year. The Russian Archimandrite, Hilarion, also joined this mission, was well received at Peking and was even made Mandarin of the fifth class. Peter's concern about the success of this missionary work dated from 1698, when he wrote: "That affair is all very well, but for God's sake act carefully so as not to antagonize the Chinese and the Jesuits. We should have priests there not so learned as sensible and subtle, lest through over-pride this holy business should go to ruin." From now on the Russian Orthodox mission was to play a conspicuous rôle alongside the Jesuits, and the achievements of this mission in the study of China's culture and science have not yet received the credit they deserve. Russian merchants being, however, still confined to the frontier cities, in 1719 Ismailov, a captain of the Preobrazhensky Guards, was sent on a new mission to Peking with presents, four ivory telescopes made by Peter's own hands. Upon Ismailov's insistence on commercial relations the Chinese replied: "You estimate your merchants very highly. We despise mercantile affairs; only poor people and servants occupy themselves with them." [13]

In the meanwhile, the Mongolians, restless under Chinese domination, started emigrating into Siberia. Since this gave offence to China, and since Russia was uneasy about this penetration of nomads, in 1727 the two empires negotiated a new treaty known as the Treaty of Burinsk, by which the Russians promised to close their borders to nomad immigration and the Chinese allowed in return two hundred Russian merchants to visit Peking every two years. After 1721 also, a permanent Russian diplomatic mission was established in the Chinese capital to which the religious mission was attached. But the Chinese, anxious to get rid of the Jungarian menace once and for all, wanted Russian coöperation, and for this purpose in 1730 an embassy, the first ever sent to Europe, was outfitted to go to Moscow on the official pretext of congratulating Peter II upon his accession to the throne. It was followed by a second embassy in 1733 in the reign of Empress Anne. Since Russia was finding Chinese policy too aggressive and since, moreover, she had good reason not to antagonize the Kalmycks, the embassies returned empty handed. After the unwelcome coming of the Torgout Kalmycks in 1636 to the lower Volga, there was always the danger that any discontent on the part of Jungarian Kalmycks might result in setting ablaze the whole region east of the Volga.

Thus the Russian Government was paying more and more attention to the vast desert region north of

[13] Schuyler, Peter the Great, Vol. II, p. 458.

Turkestan. There were, however, reasons other than the nomads and Chinese colonial policy, why Peter the Great gradually shifted his attention from the Far East to this part of Central Asia, and inaugurated a policy which was to be followed by his successors.

Foremost amongst these reasons was the hope of finding a feasible route for commerce with India; while on his journey through Europe Peter saw with his own eyes what riches the Dutch and the British derived from their Indian trade. Furthermore, in 1696, two more Russian merchants had succeeded in reaching India through Afghanistan, getting as far as Agra and Delhi, and awakening once more the dormant interest in that country. A more immediate reason was the desire to secure Central Asian cotton for the newly created Russian textile industries, and last but not least a very decided if vague rumour of the existence of gold in the region of Yarkend.

An embassy from Khiva had appeared in Moscow in 1703, offering submission to Russia and asking for Russian military aid against some tribes which had become unruly. Later, when Peter received confirmation from Khiva as to the Yarkend gold fields, he decided to take action. He ordered that a small force under Colonel Buchholtz should proceed to Lake Yamish, build a fort there and find a route to Yarkend. Buchholtz built his fort but, being attacked by some ten thousand Kalmycks, had to fall back to the mouth of the Om where he founded the fort of Omsk (1716), later to grow into a great city. The following year Peter ordered a force of five thousand men to proceed to Khiva to give aid to the tottering Khan and also to find out more about the gold fields and to investigate a route to India. As leader of this diplomatic and military expedition he appointed Prince Bekovich Cherkassky, whose real name was Devlet Kisden Mirza, Prince of Kabarda. He selected this Oriental, who had become Christian and entered Russian service under the name of Cherkassky (the Circassian), because he hoped the latter would be more expert in dealing with Oriental people. The choice proved to be unfortunate, for Bekovich let himself be hoodwinked in a most tragic manner. To be sure, in June, 1717, rapidly crossing the great sandy desert, Bekovich broke the resistance of the Khivans in a three-day battle and entered Khiva at the invitation of the Khan. But the wily Khan suggested that on account of the lack of adequate quarters, the Russian force should be broken up into small units, and when Bekovich had scattered his force the Khivans fell upon the isolated detachments of men, murdered the majority and carried away the remainder into slavery. All the officers were killed and Bekovich's head was sent as a present to the Khan of Bokhara while his stuffed body was exposed in the Khan's palace.

This disaster damped Peter's ardour, but he soon began to look in another direction. He thought of a route to India which would avoid the Central Asian desert. Talking to a naval officer, Soinonov, who suggested the roundabout way of going across Siberia to the Pacific and thence along the coast to India, Peter said: "Have you been in the Gulf of Astrabad [on the

Caspian Sea]. Do you know that from Astrabad to Balkh [in Afghanistan] it is only twelve days by camel? In Bokhara lies the center of all eastern commerce and on that road no one can interfere with us." [14] Here we see him thinking in terms of commercial penetration, and now combining his Indian plan with an attempt to capture the Persian trade.

Already in 1716 he had sent an Ambassador, Volynsky, to Persia. He was well received at first, until the news of Bekovich's disaster reached Isfahan, after which the Persians kept him under guard and forced him to leave without concluding his business. He succeeded, however, in negotiating a treaty giving the right to Russian merchants to trade freely all over Persia and to make purchases of silk in such quantities as they desired. After his ill-treatment, it was natural for him to express uncomplimentary opinions, and he did not restrain himself. The Shah, in his view, was the subject of his subjects, and rarely could one find such a fool even among commoners, not to say crowned heads; he never did any business himself but left everything to the Vizir, who was more stupid than an ox.

Volynsky violently advocated war as the only way of obtaining any results in Persia and gave Peter the idea of combining into one the two schemes of economic expansion. Peter decided upon a war with Persia when in 1721 some Caucasian princes on the border had rebelled and asked for Russian assistance against Persia. When in suppressing this rising the Persians looted some Russian shops, killed a few merchants and car-

[14] Raskolnikov, ibidem, p. 20.

ried off goods to the value of half a million roubles, the casus belli was found. Peter had prepared for this war in a leisurely way. He had just finished his great twenty-year struggle against Sweden so that the army was available. Deciding that he required a vacation, he started on a journey to the Persian border whilst his forces were concentrating in the Caucasus. While travelling down the Volga he visited Kazan, the first Russian Czar to do this since John the Terrible. Always with his bursting energy, he went into the minutest details in inspecting the region. He immediately detected a missing ledger in a government office. On another occasion, seeing that a private cloth factory was doing better than the government-owned one, he ordered the latter to be given over to the owner of the private factory. On the Caspian, Peter insisted upon himself finding a safe bay where the boats which had transported the troops could remain during the hostilities and it was while he himself was taking soundings that the above-quoted conversation with Soinonov took place.

When Peter was ready he invaded Persia, and though that country was still a great Asiatic power, she was easily defeated and sued for peace. By the treaty of 1723, Persia ceded Derbent, Baku, and the provinces of Ghilan, Mazanderan and Astrabad to Russia. This nearly led to a war with Turkey, and it is interesting to find that the British envoy at Constantinople was trying to persuade Turkey that a war with Russia would not be dangerous, because a rebellion against Peter would break out in Russia. The Ambassador also got into touch with Orlik, the lieutenant of Peter's notorious enemy, Hetman Mazeppa, at that time in exile in Salonica. The Anglo-Russian rivalry in the East due to the British fear that Russia was becoming too strong, may be traced back to these early intrigues.

These difficulties were finally overcome peaceably, and the treaty was ratified in 1724. Immediately Peter gave instructions to investigate communications with neighbouring countries, to get information about the resources in the conquered region in copper, madder, naphtha and sugar, and to induce Christian Armenians to settle the country. In 1725 Peter died without having carried out his Indian project. After his death Empress Anne decided upon the return of the conquered territories to Persia, and accordingly the Treaty of Resht was signed in 1732 which granted in return important commercial advantages. It had been found that the climate was unsuitable, that Russians were dying from disease, and also that these possessions drained the treasury without giving anything in return. This return of the Caspian provinces took place in the reign of Nadir Shah and it was fortunate for Europe that Russia was powerful at the time.

For once more there arose in Nadir Shah a great conqueror of the type of Chengiz Khan; the son of a carpenter, Nadir Shah had known captivity among the Uzbegs in his youth and later had delivered Persia from the Afghan yoke. His story has many points of similarity with that of Tamerlane. He played havoc with the Turks and Afghans, conquered Erivan and Tiflis, but did not dare to venture further north and

attack Russia. Instead, capturing Herat and Bagdad,
he followed the great tradition and invaded India.
The Mogul Empire never recovered from the terrible
sack of Delhi. He brought back to Teheran the famous
peacock throne and spoils estimated at four hundred
million dollars.[15] Then he marched as far as the Amu
Darya, conquering Khiva and Bokhara. Thus once
more an enormous empire had arisen where Chengiz
Khan and Tamerlane had built theirs, stretching from
China to the Persian Gulf. But the days when the
great conquerors could sweep across Russia into Europe
were definitely over.

Peter's activities in Asia were not limited to conquests and trade alone, but also embraced cultural and
scientific problems. Though the actual work was done
mostly by his immediate successors, it was Peter's galvanizing energy and his spirit which were responsible
for a vast and successful scheme of discoveries and exploration. He was tremendously interested in the geographical research undertaken by the early Cossack adventurers in the Far East, and worked out a systematic
plan of scientific exploration to follow in their footsteps. Ever since Kamchatka was discovered, the local
authorities had been organizing various expeditions in
an attempt to discover the easiest ways of access to this
distant peninsula. Peter had followed their efforts with
interest, though unable to lend a helping hand because
of his wars and vast undertakings in Europe. Now,
in 1724 when there was nothing more serious than the
Persian War to occupy his attention, he worked out

[15] Sir Percy Sykes, Persia, p. 98.

the plans for an expedition to carry out research further afield. With characteristic clarity and terseness he wrote the following instructions to Captain Behring, a naval officer of Danish extraction who was put in charge of this work:

"To build in Kamchatka or in some other place one or two decked boats. To sail on these boats along the shore which runs to the north and which, since its limits are unknown, seems to be a part of the American coast. To determine where it joins with America. To sail to some settlement under European jurisdiction and if a European ship should be met with to learn from her the name of the coast and take it down in writing, make a landing, obtain detailed information, draw a chart and bring it here." [16]

Volunteers were called for amongst naval officers and the expedition under Behring with Chirikov second in command, left St. Petersburg on January 24, 1725, for Yakutsk. Thence they made a terrible march to Okhotsk and to Kamchatka, where they built boats. The expedition proceeded further north by sea, rounding Chukotski Cape in the Behring Sea, and getting as far as 67 degrees latitude north. Losing sight of land Behring turned back and reported that the two continents were not united. In the meantime another Russian explorer, Gvozdev, had actually succeeded in sailing along the American coast in 1732 but had thought it belonged to an island.

After Peter's death the supervising of these explorations was undertaken by the Academy of Sciences in St.

[16] Golder, Russian Expansion on the Pacific, 1641-1850, p. 134 quoted from the Zapiski Voenno Topograficheskago Depo (Bulletin of the Military Topographical Department).

Petersburg, founded in 1726 according to detailed plans left by the Great Czar. The academy censured Behring for his incomplete work and planned to send him on a second expedition of a more ambitious nature. It was decided to attempt to map the whole coast of Siberia along the Arctic Ocean down to Kamchatka in order to determine definitely whether Asia and America joined. At the same time a thorough scientific exploration of the Siberian hinterland was to be undertaken by specialists in various branches under the direction of the academy. Great care was given to the organization of the exploration, and as Professor Golder puts it, "taking it all in all it was one of the most elaborate, thorough and expensive expeditions ever sent out by any government at any time." The Senate gave official approval to this scheme "for the benefit of Her Imperial Majesty [Empress Anne] and to the glory of the Russian Empire," [17] and in 1733 Behring set out once more from St. Petersburg. The difficulty of transporting the costly and cumbersome instruments across Siberia was so great that the two boats of the expedition, the St. Peter and the St. Paul, built in Okhotsk, were able to put to sea only in 1740.

According to the plans of the Academy of Sciences these two vessels under Behring and Chirikov respectively were to proceed north, following the itinerary of the previous journey. A third expedition under Spanberg was to follow the coast south and try to reach Japan. At the same time the vast northern coastline of Siberia along the Arctic Ocean, stretching from the

[17] Golder, ibidem, p. 170.

White Sea to the Behring Straits, was divided into five sectors, and over each of these an expedition started out with the task of following the coast until it met with the neighbouring expedition.

It is interesting to see how closely this program was followed. The St. Peter and St. Paul sailed together and reached the Bay of Avacha in Kamchatka. Here the important naval base of Petropavlovsk was founded in honor of the two patron apostles. Leaving Kamchatka the two vessels were driven apart by a storm and lost sight of each other for the remainder of the journey. Chirikov on the St. Paul had to winter in the Aleutian Islands. Lack of drinking water brought on disease from which two of his officers and a part of his crew died. Pushing on however, he reached Attu and Atka, followed and explored the coast of Alaska for a considerable distance, and returned to Avacha Bay. This journey laid the foundations for the important fur trade in these regions and the development in later years of the Russo-American Company. Behring on the St. Peter also reached Alaska and made a landing at Kayak Island. On his way back he also sighted the Aleutian Islands but presently he fell ill with scurvy. The St. Peter was driven to an uninhabited island where Behring and a number of his crew died in December 1741.

Spanberg had less difficulty. As far back as 1700 Atlasov, the discoverer of Kamchatka, came across a shipwrecked Japanese by the name of Debne. When Peter the Great found this out he ordered that the man should be brought to him immediately. On Janu-

ary 20, 1702, Debne was presented to the Czar, and
Peter had him give all the information he could about
Japan. Debne was taught Russian and was commissioned to teach Japanese. In 1710 Debne was baptized
under the name of Gabriel. This would appear to be
the first contact in history between Russia and Japan.
Spanberg had therefore first-hand knowledge about
Japan. He left Okhotsk in June, 1738, and cruised
about the Kuril Islands, bestowing names on twenty-
nine of these, then after wintering in Kamchatka, proceeded south with four boats in May of the following
year. In June he sighted Japan and following the
coast for two days, anchored in a bay. He remained
there several days but was afraid to land, though the
Japanese came up to his boats and exchanged goods
with him. It will be remembered that a century earlier
the Japanese had closed their doors to Europeans and
had expelled missionaries and merchants, the English
in 1623, the Spanish in 1624, and the Portuguese in
1638. The Chinese and a few Dutch merchants alone
were allowed to stay. This made Spanberg's visit all
the more interesting. When he returned to Okhotsk
and reported his journey, he was ordered back to Japan
and sailed on his second journey in 1742. This time
his son, who had studied Japanese in St. Petersburg
under Debne, accompanied him as interpreter, but the
boats were by now in such a bad condition that Spanberg failed to reach Japan.

We must now turn to the work done in the Arctic.
The five sectors into which the long coast line of Siberia
was divided were as follows: 1. from Archangel to the

mouth of the Ob; 2. from the Ob to the Yenissei river; 3. from the Yenissei to Cape Taimur; 4. from the mouth of the Lena westward to Cape Taimur; 5. from the Lena eastward around the Behring Straits to the Gulf of Anadyr. The first expedition under Lieutenants Muraviev and Pavlov met with complete success and reached the Ob on schedule time, investigating scientifically the route covered. The second expedition also succeeded in charting its sector and putting up lighthouses. The third was blocked in ice. The record of the last two was tragic. The fourth expedition lost its boat in the ice and proceeded further on foot. Many died on the way, but one Lieutenant Cheliuskin carried on and reached Cape Taimur. In December, 1741, he was instructed to go further and after great hardships succeeded in reaching Cape Cheliuskin, the northernmost point of the Asiatic continent, 77 degrees latitude north, in May of the following year. The fifth expedition had similar experiences. They were also blocked in the ice and compelled to continue with dog sleds. Many of the members died from cold and scurvy, but the party succeeded in charting its sector. Thus the program of the grand total of all of these explorations which became known as the Great Northern Expedition was carried out in its entirety, all goals reached and all scientific questions raised were investigated.

This success was due to the ruthless efficiency and the military manner in which this undertaking was directed by the Admiralty Board in St. Petersburg in conjunction with the Academy of Sciences. Though a

time limit of two years was set for the completion of
the work on the various sectors, the leaders were instructed to carry on, whatever the costs and the time
required might be. Those who fell on the way were
to be replaced by others. Approximately two-thirds of
the members died while on duty and those who survived had their health so impaired that they did not
live long. Chirikov for instance, died shortly after his
return home. But the work of tremendous importance
for science in general and for Russia's position in Asia,
was completed. The driving spirit of Peter the Great,
who tolerated no slackness, was still operative a quarter
of a century after his death.

CHAPTER IV

CATHERINE THE SECOND

THIRTY years separated the death of Peter the Great and the accession of Catherine the Great. Thus at both ends of the 18th century arose a dominating figure in Russian history, and Catherine took up the thread of Russia's progress where Peter stopped. She acknowledged herself his pupil, and her ambition was to complete his life work. The intermediate period was a troubled and dark time in which a rapid succession of mostly unworthy rulers followed each other as a result of palace revolutions. But the driving power of Peter the Great was still there, and the country kept on moving by sheer inertia. Then Catherine came to give a new impetus just at the time when the tempo of the motion was beginning to slow down. This posthumous action of the will of the Czar Reformer, of which we have seen a conspicuous example in the Great Northern Expedition, was due not only to the powerful impression left on the national psychology by his indomitable will and hard work, but also to the fact that the younger generation of statesmen reared in his stern school was now coming to maturity and, notwithstanding the obstruction coming from incompetent and at times vicious rulers, was carrying on the work of the nation.

The nomads of the Central Asian plains continued to hold the watchful attention of the Government and to require careful handling. Along the southern border of Siberia, between the Urals and the Altai Mountains, there was constant unrest and the possibility of brigandish incursions which made imperative the establishment of a definite frontier defended by fortified posts. Furthermore, since the great Siberian postal highway passed close to the desert in this particular sector, it was constantly exposed to the menace of nomadic attacks, and the Government viewed with concern this danger to its communications with Eastern Siberia. On the other hand, in 1723, the Jungarian Kalmycks, pressed by the Chinese, had started moving west. As they had always kept close communication with the tribe which had settled on the Volga in 1636, it was imperative that they should not be antagonized, lest an attempt be made to create a new nomadic empire stretching from the Irtysh to the Volga, an attempt which might set the whole of Western Siberia and Southeastern Russia aflame. The problem was tackled by a remarkable statesman, a disciple of Peter, Ivan Kirilov. His plan was to create a chain of Russian fortified cities along the border of the nomadic region, starting with a base at the mouth of the river Or, from which a gradual expansion would be carried towards the sea of Aral and ultimately Bokhara and Samarkand. Kirilov thus revived his deceased master's idea, and obtaining the permission of the Empress Anne, he took command of an expedition to the river Or. Overcoming the violent resistance of the Bashkirs, he

founded a city named Orenburg, later rechristened
Orsk. Kirilov died in 1737, but his successor Neplu-
iev, also of the school of Peter, built a new city, which
was again named Orenburg, and established a fortified
line from this point to the Caspian Sea.

In 1734, before Kirilov's expedition, the Khirgiz,
pressed in their turn by the moving Kalmycks, had
offered submission to the Russian Government. They
had been divided into three hordes bitterly hostile to
Russia. Great value was attached to this submission,
Peter having been credited with saying: "This Horde,
though a nomadic and light thinking people, is yet the
key and the gate to all the lands and countries of
Asia," [18] thus mapping out the general direction of
Russian advance into the heart of Asia. But the joy in
St. Petersburg proved to be premature. Not only did
these nomads remain brigandish and unruly, but they
secretly offered submission to the Chinese Government
as well, thus bringing highly unwelcome Chinese interference into these regions.

For these reasons it was decided to supplement the
Orenburg-Caspian fortified line, by a line of forts running from Orenburg to the Upper Irtysh. This line
was built in 1752, thereby fencing off completely the
land of the nomads. But as at the same time a slow
concentration of troops was taking place in Siberia, it
was obvious that these measures were not solely directed against the nomads, but also partly against the

[18] Grigorief, The Russian Policy Regarding Central Asia, appended
to Schuyler's Turkistan, Vol. II, p. 403.

Chinese, whose aggressive policy was worrying St. Petersburg more and more.

The Chinese, who were watching Russian activities very carefully, decided to strike boldly before Russia had time to complete her preparations. Consequently in 1757 when the Mongolians had risen rather timidly and asked for Russian assistance, which they did not receive owing to Russia's desire to keep within the Treaty of Nerchinsk, the Chinese dealt them a crushing blow. This was followed by equally swift action against the Jungarian Kalmycks, and both these countries were definitely brought under Chinese domination. The frontier between China and Russia thus became contiguous. The Chinese Government immediately started colonizing these newly acquired territories, particularly Jungaria. Immigrants were brought from Manchuria and distant Chinese provinces, forts and cities were built, among others Kulja. As for the Kalmycks, those who escaped the massacre sought refuge in Siberia, where they were allowed to scatter about the plains.

In 1791 the Chinese suddenly invaded Russian territory, penetrating two hundred miles beyond the fortified line, in an attempt to drive these Kalmycks back. But now under Catherine, Russia was very strong and was not going to tolerate this. Apologies were peremptorily demanded, and the Chinese yielded. The balance of power in Asia had by now completely passed over to Russia. It is, however, curious to note that within this period of a century since the Treaty of Nerchinsk was signed, it was the Chinese who displayed aggressive imperialism, the Russians remaining on the defensive and strictly within the clauses of the treaties.

The skillful Chinese propaganda even went further than the Khirgiz who had sworn allegiance to China as well as to Russia, and reached as far as the lower Volga, being responsible for a particularly tragic episode which occurred in 1771. A steady flow of Chinese emissaries were working among the Torgout Kalmycks who, it will be remembered, settled on the lower Volga in 1636. These latter, moreover, remained in close contact of a religious nature with Tibetan and Mongolian lamas. From both these sources came a continual urge to return to their original home, Jungaria. With a sudden reawakening of the nomadic instinct, the Torgouts decided to heed this call and to leave. One hundred and seventy thousand Kalmycks left the steppes of the Volga just as suddenly as they had come. During their march in winter across the Khirgiz steppe, they experienced terrible hardships and in addition were subjected to continuous attacks of the Khirgiz, with the result that some one hundred thousand perished on the way. The remaining seventy thousand finally succeeded in reaching China, where they were well received and granted land and pastures in Jungaria. In 1805, however, thirty years later they again became restless and wanted to return to the Volga, but this time both the Russian and Chinese Governments saw to it that they should remain where they were.

Catherine II started a policy of winning over the

nomads on the border by caring for their welfare. But at the time the Government had rather hazy notions about the various races inhabiting the steppes, and the results were curious. Imagining, for instance, that in dealing with the Khirgiz they were dealing with Tartars, the authorities corresponded with the Khirgiz leaders in the Tartar tongue, from which the Khirgiz language differed considerably. In 1785 Catherine issued a charter of religious toleration, and measures were taken to educate the Khirgiz, schools being opened for them and special books published in the Tartar tongue. On the assumption that the Khirgiz were Muslims, special Muslim mullahs were appointed from Kazan to teach in their schools. Furthermore, mosques were built with religious schools attached and with caravanserais for pilgrims. Actually the Khirgiz were not Muslims but pagan Shamanists. Consequently, we have the curious sight of Christian Russia on this erroneous assumption, spending vast amounts of money on Muslim religious propaganda. This missionary work succeeded beyond expectation, for the majority of Khirgiz did embrace the Muslim faith, to the Government's discomfiture, for it only increased the already considerable and dangerous Muslim minority in Asiatic Russia.

But it must be said that Catherine's humane policy did succeed in giving the nomads certain elements of civilization. Khirgiz students were allotted grants from the Government for living expenses while they were at school; parents were encouraged by gifts and the granting of certain advantages, to send their children to school. Furthermore, a fairly large judicial autonomy was given to the nomads by setting up special "boundary courts" composed of Russians and Khirgiz for settling disputes between the two races, while courts composed solely of Khirgiz dealt with their own affairs. Further, they were taught the use of bread, of houses especially built for them and of sheds for their cattle.

Most of these reforms, however, aiming at making them sedentary, failed because of the obstinate desire on the part of the Khirgiz to remain nomads. They found it more lucrative to wander about the great desert robbing and marauding the passing trade caravans. Thus they remained a great nuisance for Russia, right up to the time of the conquest of Turkestan. While the Khirgiz plied the trade route from Orenburg to Bokhara, the still more brigandish and wild Turkomans roamed about the routes leading from the Caspian Sea to Khiva and Bokhara. Thus both routes were virtually closed to normal trade, the travellers being almost certain to be captured by the nomads and reduced to slavery.

Beyond this belt of nomads, however, Russian influence was beginning to penetrate into Central Asia, rendering their position more precarious. At the instigation of Catherine, a college for Muslims was built at Bokhara and she herself donated the money. In 1792 when the Khan of Khiva went blind, a Russian oculist was sent to him at his request. The same year two officials were sent from Siberia to report on the conditions in Central Asia and particularly on Eastern Turkestan and the Tashkent region. From Semipalatinsk in Siberia, an active trade and barter with natives was carried on, for it was easier to penetrate into Central Asia from this side. Thus gradually conditions were shaping themselves until the time should be ripe for the inevitable advance of the Russians in this direction.

For the time being, however, Catherine had closer at hand a more urgent task which dominated her foreign policy and caused most of her wars. Although Peter had secured the coast of the Baltic Sea for Russia, Catherine completed what he had started but left unfinished in another direction, namely, the conquest of the coast of the Black Sea, thus securing an additional outlet and destroying the nomadic menace from the steppe zone. The task had become urgent but necessitated a long struggle with Turkey.

The Crimean Tartars had been continuing their raids into Russia with alarming persistency, feeling all the more fearless now that they were backed by the Turkish Empire, then at the height of its power. Immediately after Peter the Great's unsuccessful expedition to the Pruth, the Tartars raided the Government of Voronezh, burning many villages and carrying off some fifteen thousand men into slavery. They pushed as far as the very outskirts of Kharkov and Izum, and also made an attempt to go east and secure Astrakhan. Peter had repeatedly asked the Turkish Government to put a stop to the activities of their Tartar vassals, but to no avail. He had started arranging for an expedition against Crimea when his death put an end to the preparations.

During the reign of Empress Anne, Turkey was engaged in a death struggle with the great Persian conqueror Nadir Shah, and so ordered the Khan of Crimea to attack Dagestan in the Caucasus. Carrying out these orders, the Khan had to march his forces across Russian territory, scattering on the way a feeble Russian detachment on the Terek under Prince Hesse Homburg. The Empress Anne ordered Field Marshal Münnich to punish the insolent Khan. While General Lacy attacked Azov, Münnich marched on Crimea. He then crossed the steppe and attacked the whole Tartar Horde at Perekop, the narrow stretch of land connecting Crimea with the mainland. Taking the fortifications there by storm, Münnich reached the capital of the Khan, Bakhchisarai, but owing to lack of provisions could not hold it indefinitely. Consequently he devastated the country around the city, blew up the fortifications on Perekop and returned to the Ukraine.

This led to a war with Turkey. Lacy in his turn routed the combined Turkish and Tartar forces at Perekop by fording the so-called Putrid Sea, a long stretch of muddy water. After a Russian victory at Khotin in 1739 and the capture of Ochakov, the Austrians having in the meantime entered the war against the Turks and having been badly beaten, peace was signed with French mediation. Russia got territory between the Bug and the Donetz, whereas the Turks dismantled Azov, but received back Ochakov and Khotin. Russian merchants were allowed to cross the Black Sea on Turkish vessels, and Russia promised to leave Crimea alone. Russia proceeded immediately to colonize the newly acquired territory by settling there one hundred and fifty thousand Serbs who had emigrated from the Balkans.

Such was the position when Catherine came to the throne. Turkey was becoming more and more anxious over the increasing power of Russia. Consequently, when Catherine put her candidate, Stanislas Poniatowski, on the Polish throne, they took a hand in Polish affairs and declared war on Russia. The interest they had in reducing Russian influence in Poland was obvious, considering how exposed were their possessions north of the Black Sea. The Sultan therefore prepared an army of three hundred thousand men to drive Stanislas out of Poland, while Catherine sent one of her most remarkable generals, Rumiantsev, to stop this advance.

By the spring of 1770, two hundred and fifty thousand Turks were concentrated between the Bug and the Dniester, waiting for the Khan of Crimea to join them with his Tartars. Rumiantsev with only seventeen thousand men and those weakened by disease, met the main Turkish force one hundred and fifty thousand strong at Kagul. Behind him were eighty thousand Tartars coming up by forced marches. His position was very grave and he decided that the only way out was to attack the Turkish army before it·had completed its junction with the Tartars. His attack threw the Turks into panic, but realizing his numerical inferiority they rallied, and some of the Russian regiments began to waver. But the day was won by a bayonet charge led by Rumiantsev himself. The Turkish camp was captured and the Turks fled in disorder. The victory came just in time, for the Tartars had fallen on the Russian rear. Realizing now the Turkish defeat, they retreated back into Crimea.

The Russian fleet having gone meanwhile in two squadrons around Europe and united off the coast of Greece, met the Turkish fleet in the Gulf of Smyrna. The latter, twice as strong as the Russian fleet, took up a position in a crescent formation in the Bay of Chesme, under the protection of coast batteries. The violence of the battle which took place may be judged from the fact that the commander of the First Russian Squadron, Spiridov, after attacking three Turkish boats, grappled the vessel of the Turkish admiral and both boats blew up together. The battle ended in the complete destruction of the Turkish fleet, of which more than a hundred vessels were sunk.

Turkey sued for peace, and by the celebrated Treaty of Kuchuk Kainardji (1774), Crimea was declared independent, Russia was given outlets to the sea at Azov, Kerch, Yenikale and Kinburn, and Russian vessels were allowed to pass through the Dardanelles. Also the territories of Kuban and the Terek, the northern approach of the Caucasus, became Russian, and following her traditional colonizing policy, the Russian Government immediately organized new Cossack hosts in these regions, bearing their names.

This treaty was a move preliminary to the annexation of Crimea, which was immediately made a Russian protectorate. In 1783 Catherine's remarkable favorite, Potemkin, who was appointed governor-general of these newly acquired territories, flatly invited the Khan of Crimea to resign, offering a pension of two hundred thousand roubles. The Khan betook himself to Moldavia, where the Turks had him murdered, and Russia annexed Crimea. A second war with Turkey followed, equally disastrous for Turkey, and the final result, by the treaty of 1791, was that the whole of the northern coast of the Black Sea became Russian.

In this way the last vestige of the Tartar Invasion was destroyed. The remarkable transformation of this barren steppe, so long the home of nomads, into a flourishing agricultural and industrial region is a tale of successful colonization only surpassed in the American West. The great port of Odessa, founded in 1794, with a population of half a million inhabitants before the Great War, became the chief seaport of Russia, through which passed 14 per cent of the entire Russian trade, with an annual turnover slightly exceeding that of San Francisco. Second in importance, the Bay of Novorossiisk, three miles wide, on the Kuban coast, was transformed into an artificial harbour exporting wheat and oil to the value of some twenty million dollars a year. In Crimea, near the ancient Greek colony of Chersonesus and on one of the finest bays in the world, there arose the city of Sebastopol, which became a great fortress and a naval base for the Black Sea Fleet. Rostov (on the Don) became an industrial city of prominence, and the basins of the Don and Donetz before the War produced 61 per cent of the pig iron, 48.7 per cent of the steel and worked iron and 70 per cent of the coal of all Russia. Crimea, on the other hand, owing to its temperate and sunny climate, became the Russian Riviera, with its mountainous coast dotted with winter resorts.

Thus we have seen not only that the whole steppe zone was restored to Russia for the first time since Kiev days, but that by the acquisition of the Kuban and the Terek regions she was rapidly moving towards the Caucasus, the great mountain range which separated her from Asia on the southeastern border. The last years of the reign of Catherine the Great and the subsequent reign of Paul I marked a further remarkable advance in this direction by the annexation of Georgia.

This ancient kingdom, nestled in the shadow of the towering Caucasian Mountains, was in a particularly disadvantageous position with regard to invasions from Asia. And yet it had succeeded in preserving its culture and its Christianity, which according to tradition was introduced by a Christian slave, Nina, in the reign of Mirian (A.D. 265-342). Tiflis, its capital, was founded as early as 379 A.D., but the truly brilliant period in the development of poetry and the arts was in the reign of Queen Tamar in the 12th century.

In the 18th century the Georgians, wedged in between a powerful Turkey and a powerful Persia, found their position so precarious that Vaktang VI applied for help to Peter the Great and was the first Georgian King to visit Russia. Subsequently, the Georgians came under Turkish domination, but the latter were driven out by the Russians. In 1783 King Heraclius II declared himself a vassal of Russia. In 1793, however, the Persian Shah, Aga Mohammed, making a sudden descent upon Tiflis, sacked and burnt it. Russia immediately interfered and this intervention undoubtedly saved the Georgians from complete extermination. The King, Heraclius, escaped but died shortly afterwards. His son George XIII once more officially asked for Russian help, and in 1799 he abdicated in favour of the Emperor Paul I. The manifesto of the incorporation of Georgia into the Russian Empire was issued on September 12, 1801. The Russians rebuilt Tiflis, which became the seat of the Viceroy of the Caucasus, and grew to be a flourishing modern European city. By a peculiar play of fate, a century and a quarter after the last king of small Georgia asked for the protection of mighty Russia, the son of a modest Tiflis shoemaker by the name of Djugashvilli, was to become the all-powerful dictator of Russia under the assumed name of Stalin.

With the death of Catherine II in 1796 and the accession of her son, Paul I, Russian policy lost its reasoned consistency and became erratic. That Emperor, whose insanity has been grossly exaggerated by modern writers, undoubtedly revealed an unbalanced mind in his actions. The dominating impulse in his policy seems to have been a hatred for his mother, who kept him secluded in the little city of Gatchina until her death and tried to arrange that the throne should pass directly to her grandson. This hatred led to an unreasoning reversal of all her policies, and on the other hand his long seclusion developed in Paul a kind of megalomania. The result was that his policies were inspired by moods and subject to violent changes. Though in most cases it is easy to trace a reasonable motive behind his actions, they tended to become more and more erratic and subject to sudden and violent alteration, at times even to complete reversal. Such waywardness was bound to disorganize the country's policy and lead to disaster; hence a plot was arranged and the murder of the Emperor was looked upon as a deliverance. Nowhere did this erratic policy show itself so much as in the East. Having reasonable grievances against the position assumed by England during his struggle against the French revolutionary armies, Paul lent a friendly ear to Napoleon's intrigues and was inspired by the latter to a madcap adventure, which was largely responsible for his untimely death.

Napoleon had dreamed from the days of his youth of an expedition against India, a dream of which his Egyptian expedition was a partial fulfillment. After the failure of this plan he worked out the idea of a joint Franco-Russian expedition to conquer India. According to this plan a combined force of thirty-five thousand Russians and thirty-five thousand French was to land at Astrabad and march on India via Herat and Kandahar. Prior to this in 1791, a French emigrant by the name of St. Jenis had suggested to Catherine a plan for the conquest of India from the British for the purpose of restoring the dynasty of the Great Moguls, but Catherine rejected the idea as fantastic.

Paul, however, who had broken off diplomatic relations with England, took up the project seriously. Napoleon being in the meantime tied up with his wars in Europe, Paul decided to act alone. Consequently, on January 12, 1801, he issued a written order to Orlov, the Hetman of the Don Cossacks, to march with a force of twenty-two thousand Cossacks and twenty-four guns to Orenburg and thence proceed by three roads via Bokhara to the Indus. The purpose of this expedition was to destroy the British factories and establishments in India, to bring the country under Russian control, and to win over the Indian trade.

The letters written by Paul to Orlov on this occasion are illuminating:

"You can select one of the three roads from Orenburg or march with your artillery by all three roads at once, by way of Bokhara and Khiva to the river Indus and the British establishments located beyond it. The military forces to be found there are of the same type as yours; having artillery you possess an advantage. . . . I am sending you all the maps I have in my possession; they only cover as far as Khiva and the Amu river. It will be your business to find out about the peoples living under Indian domination," and later, "I am sending you a new and detailed map of India. Remember that you are to be concerned solely with the British. You are to offer peace to all who are against them and assure them of the friendship of Russia. Proceed from the Indus to the Ganges against the British. On the way secure the domination of Bokhara so that the Chinese should not get hold of it, and in Khiva liberate our prisoners. If you require infantry I will send you some later, but not elsewise can I dispose of any. But it would be better if you were able to do everything alone." [19]

Six weeks later on March 23, 1801, the assassination of Paul put an end to this venture. His successor, Alexander I, recalled the Cossacks as they were on their way to Orenburg.

[19] Raskolnikov, Russia and Afghanistan, The New East, Vol. IV, p. 21.

Looking upon this mad adventure from the angle of
the impression produced in England, we have to realize that the consequences were very grave. We have
already seen the British ambassador in Constantinople
intriguing against Russia, when Peter the Great was
fighting Persia. England was becoming more and more
uneasy over the increasingly important rôle Russia
was playing in the East, because Russia was the only
power in a position to attack India along her land border. This fear was based mainly upon the lack of
knowledge of Russian history and on the fact that the
famous Khyber Pass, the gateway through which all
the invasions of India had passed, from Alexander
the Great and the White Huns, to Tamerlane and
Nadir Shah, faces northwest, consequently the supposed
line of Russian advance. The English, little familiar
with Russia's past, did not realize that Russia in her
eastern expansion swept first across Siberia to the Pacific
along the line of least resistance. The motives which
made her turn to the Near East were reasons of security and of economic necessity which will be examined
in detail in a later chapter.

Thus it was that, notwithstanding an alliance between
Russia and England all through the period of the
Napoleonic Wars, interrupted only occasionally by cold-
ness, the situation was psychologically ripe for the
bitter Anglo-Russian rivalry in Asia which was to en-
danger peace all through the 19th century. Consequently, the expedition of Paul I, which was dismissed
by the public opinion in Russia as the irresponsible act
of an unbalanced autocrat, was considered by the Brit-

ish a substantiation of their fears and a proof of Russia's designs upon India.

Six years later, at the famous meeting at Tilsit between Napoleon and Alexander I, the issue was once more revived by Napoleon. His famous suggestion was to divide the world in two, France to have the West and Russia the East. But this vast scheme could not work as long as there was a third party, Great Britain, in a position to interfere. Hence in 1808 Napoleon, through his ambassador in St. Petersburg, Caulaincourt, proposed once more a joint march upon India, through Persia. But Alexander was far too much of a realist to heed such a fantastic scheme. He was much more concerned with the growing power of Napoleon himself than with the position of England. He foresaw that the alliance with Napoleon was only a short-lived truce between two wars, and that an English alliance would again be valuable for Russia. Furthermore, there was the potent economic argument that England was Russia's best customer for Russian wheat, and that timber and jute also were required for the English navy. On the other hand, Russia required British manufactured goods. Hence Napoleon's offer met with no response.

CHAPTER V

THE NEAR AND MIDDLE EAST UP TO THE END OF THE CRIMEAN WAR

NOTWITHSTANDING the strain produced on the energies and resources of the Russian people by the Napoleonic Wars of 1805-1807 and more particularly by the great invasion of Napoleon in 1812, which nearly broke Russia, it is astonishing to find that the consolidation of her position in the Caucasus and the Near East was proceeding normally and seemingly independently from these great events. The mountain fastnesses of the Caucasus were to remain unconquered for a few decades, but the acquisition of Georgia was an important step towards acquiring a foothold for further expansion in Transcaucasia. The very next year after the incorporation of Georgia, while the Georgian royal family went to live in Russia and General Knoring made a solemn entry into Tiflis, the neighbouring states of Daghestan, Derbent and Baku gave their allegiance to Russia. Russia hardly realized at that time that by the acquisition of Baku she was getting one of the richest oil fields in the world. The command of the Russian army operating in the Caucasus was now entrusted to Prince Tsitsianov, himself of royal Caucasian descent, and the latter initiated a policy of en-

lightenment, by opening in Tiflis a college for superior studies. At the same time by diplomacy and
arms he obtained submission of the rulers of Mingrelia
and Imeretia as well as of the Khan of Shirvan. The
policy of the Russian Government henceforth was to
win over the members of these ruling families as well
as of the other Caucasian princely and noble families,
by offering them the equivalent of their titles in
Russia, and by giving them important military and administrative posts within the Russian Empire. The
result of this policy was to Russianize many of these
families, and in view of the feudal relations existing in
the Caucasus this in its turn led to a sure hold on the
country. In this way all Caucasia but the main mountain range, so difficult of access, was brought under the
control of Russia. Turkey and Persia were watching
this Russian advance with increasing concern, and attempted to induce the Caucasian states to resist. When
this failed, Persia, the most interested party, declared
war on Russia.

Powerful foreign influences backed Persia. In 1806,
the year after the battle of Austerlitz, the French envoy
in Persia, M. Jaubert, on behalf of Napoleon, offered
to restore Persian rule over Georgia and a subsidy to
the Persian Government should the latter join the
French. After long negotiations, the Shah Fath Ali,
though declaring his unwillingness to be friendly with
a nation which had just killed its king, still found the
offer too tempting and accepted it. But in the meanwhile the Treaty of Tilsit had been signed between
France and Russia, so that Persian assistance was no

longer necessary to Napoleon. French influence, however, remained paramount in Teheran and a French military mission reorganized and drilled the Persian army.

This assistance, however, did not bring success to Persian arms when Persia started fighting Russia. At the battle of Arpatch, near Kars (June 30, 1807) a Russian army under Field Marshal Gudovich inflicted a crushing defeat on the Persians, with the result that the latter lost all their faith in the French. The British Resident at Basra was quick to seize this opportunity and offered the Persians an annual subsidy of one hundred and twenty thousand pounds if they would go on fighting Russia. But most tempting for the avaricious Shah was a magnificent diamond, a personal gift from King George III.

The sequel was that a large Persian army under the personal command of Abbas Mirza, the heir to the Persian throne, and under the actual leadership of two British officers, Christie and Lindsay, attacked the Russians in 1812, at a most inopportune moment, as it coincided with the advance of Napoleon's Grand Army on Moscow. The Russians could only oppose insignificant forces, but a detachment of two thousand three hundred men with only six guns was sufficient to rout the entire Persian army at Aslanduz.

Abbas Mirza, losing all courage, asked for peace and by the Treaty of Gulistan (1813) gave up all rights to the territories occupied by Russia in Transcaucasia. But once more the execution of the treaty proved difficult, the Persians attempting to wriggle out of it. But at that time Russia had a remarkable man in charge of her affairs along the Persian border.

Alexis Yermolov had distinguished himself in the war against Napoleon as Chief of Staff of the Second Army. His courage, physical endurance and will power had given rise among the soldiers to all kinds of legends of his being charmed against enemies' bullets and of being able at will to stop his heart beating.[20] He also was a man of high culture who left a magnificent library to the University of Moscow. Faced with an attempt to break the treaty, Yermolov went to Teheran and forthwith presented himself before Abbas Mirza and the Shah. According to Persian court etiquette, all foreign diplomats were expected to take off their shoes and put on red socks as a token of respect for the Shah. The French and British envoys observed this habit punctiliously, but Yermolov caused a scandal by refusing to take off his boots, declaring that he was a descendent of Chengiz Khan (which was not true), and that it was for the Shah to show respect to him. Though he had only a bodyguard of two hundred men with him, Yermolov stated that a huge Russian army was marching on Tabriz, and so succeeded in bluffing the Persians into complete submission.[21] Thus his knowledge of oriental psychology won the day.

Promoted Field Marshal yet with barely enough troops to carry out police duty, he managed to pacify entirely the territories under his command and established a firm hold on them by means of a line of military

[20] Waliszewski, Le Règne d'Alexandre I (1818-1825), p. 256.
[21] Waliszewski, ibidem, p. 257.

posts from which was carried out the conquest of the remaining parts of the Caucasus. But his main achievement was the building of the famous Georgian Military Road, a strategic highway across the main range of the Caucasus, used to supply the Russian armies. The difficulties of engineering encountered during the building of this road may be judged by the fact that five years' work was required to force a passage across the Darial Pass, and that at Krestovaya the road climbs to a height of 7,800 feet. Because of its extraordinary scenic beauty, this highway is now visited by every tourist who goes to the Caucasus.

The collapse of Persian prestige as a result of the Treaty of Gulistan was a bitter humiliation for that country, which still considered itself a great power. Naturally, it was equally distasteful to the British, and the result was that the very next year a new treaty was signed between England and Persia, according to the terms of which Persia promised not to make any treaties or accord any military coöperation to any power hostile to Great Britain. In return for an annual subsidy of one hundred and fifty thousand pounds Persia promised not to allow any foreign forces on her territory and to induce the rulers of Khiva, Bokhara and Samarkand to promise the same. The duel between Russia and England was starting in earnest, with England building up a zone of defence stretching from Teheran into the heart of Central Asia.

The strong and energetic Nicholas I coming to the throne in 1825, Russia made substantial advances in the Near East, and these in turn aggravated the Anglo-

Russian rivalry. Now that all the great European issues resulting from the Napoleonic Wars had been settled, the attention of European diplomats centered on Eastern affairs and hence we enter the bitterest phase of this rivalry.

At the beginning, however, we find Russia and England coöperating in helping the Greeks to win their freedom from Turkey, and a joint Anglo-Franco-Russian Fleet destroying the Turkish naval forces at Navarino (1827). But when, following this action, Russia alone fought Turkey for the sake of Greece, England and Russia came to the parting of the ways. The rapid Russian successes in this war led to the Treaty of Andrianople which gave Russia a predominant position in Turkish affairs.

The war, which was fought both in Europe and Asia, concerns us only in this latter theater of operations, where important developments occurred. The Sultan's plan of campaign had been to remain on the defensive in Europe but to strike a deadly blow in the Caucasus by invading the latter with an army of forty thousand men and by inducing the natives to rise against Russia. The operation seemed all the more feasible since Russia again had a war on hand with Persia, once more attempting to regain her lost territories.

The Persians had been watching for a favourable moment to wipe out the humiliating Treaty of Gulistan. In 1823 the Persians had had a successful war with Turkey, a victory which turned their heads and induced them to try to match their strength once more against Russia. Consequently, profiting by the vagueness of

the new frontier line, traced after the last war with
Russia, they picked a quarrel about the district of
Erivan and the Lake Goktcha.

Suddenly and unexpectedly for the Russians, a Persian army thirty-five thousand strong under Abbas
Mirza and with British staff officers crossed the Russian
frontier, while the mullahs started preaching a Holy
War against the infidels (1826). The heroic defence
of a small fortress, Choucha, which held out for six
weeks, saved the situation for the Russians, enabling
them to muster up whatever forces were available.
Paskievich, Yermolov's deputy, took command of the
situation and revealed extraordinary energy. He had
distinguished himself in the battle of Leipzig in 1813
where he captured twenty-nine cannons from the
French, but it was in this emergency that he was to
make his reputation. He defeated the Persian van-
guard at Elisabethpol, and then with less than ten
thousand men, he met the main Persian army, now
forty-four thousand strong.

At the battle of Ganja, once more the Persians were
completely routed and retreated precipitately behind
the Araxe. England had promised to send help in case
of the invasion of Persian territory and was also giving
a subsidy of five million pounds. Paskievich, however,
did not give time for these engagements to become
effective. He forced his way through the mountain
passes, took the city of Erivan by storm, entered Tabriz
in triumph and menaced Teheran. Persia asked for
peace and by the Treaty of Turkmenchai (1828) ceded
to Russia the provinces of Erivan and Nakhichevan,

paid an indemnity equivalent to $15,000,000 and granted commercial privileges and extraterritoriality to Russian subjects. Upon this treaty were to be modelled all other subsequent treaties between Persia and European powers. This war marked the final collapse of Persia and the beginning of Russian economic and political penetration into that country.

Following on the heels of this invasion came the more serious Turkish attack. This situation too Paskievich met with his customary energy. Faced also with a dangerous insurrection of Muslims who had responded to the Turkish call for a Holy War, Paskievich decided to forestall the Turkish invasion by himself advancing on Kars. He was not deterred by the fact that he had only twelve thousand men. Kars had resisted for four months against Nadir Shah's army of ninety thousand men but now Paskievich took it in four days. In consequence the Turks who were invading Georgia retreated and massed an army of thirty-nine thousand men near Akhaltsik. Paskievich was faced with a new danger, plague which had broken out in his army. However, he crossed mountain ranges in spite of terrible heat, defeated the Turkish army and laid siege to Akhaltsik. This was a mountain fastness, strongly fortified and held by warlike Circassian tribes some fifty thousand strong. The little town was perched on a high rock with precipices all around, and each house was a fort in itself. Here the defeated Turks locked themselves up. Paskievich was running out of supplies, and yet he realized that retreat would mean a disastrous loss of prestige. Consequently he stormed the place, and notwithstanding desperate resistance of a garrison five times superior in force, captured the city. Akhaltsik was now turned into a fortress to defend Georgia against the Turks.

Paskievich followed up this success by pushing as far as the foot of Mount Ararat. Both the British and the French governments urged the disheartened Turks to carry on the war, but in the following year in addition to the decisive victories of the Russian armies in the Balkans, Paskievich invaded Turkey. Crossing snow ranges, he took prisoner the whole Turkish army and captured Erzerum. Turkey sued for peace and by the Treaty of Adrianople already mentioned, Russia acquired ports along the Caucasian coast of the Black Sea (Anapa, Poti) and thus put an end to the slave trade along this coast. A chain of inland forts, moreover, made Georgia safe from invasions.

The war with Turkey once more gave hopes to Persia. The result was a mob attack on the Russian embassy in Teheran in which the Russian envoy, Griboyedov, with a part of his staff was murdered. Griboyedov was one of Russia's greatest writers, the author of an immortal comedy, *The Misfortune of Being Clever*, and this untimely death certainly deprived Russian literature of several masterpieces. An ultimatum was immediately sent from St. Petersburg, giving Persia the choice of an apology or a new war. The Persian Government preferred the former, and dispatched the eldest son of Abbas Mirza to St. Petersburg, where in a formal audience at court, in the presence of the diplomatic corps, he asked Russia to forgive the occurrence.

To such humiliation had fallen the once great Empire of the Shahs.

The importance of these events lies in the plane of Anglo-Russian rivalry. We have seen the hand of England visibly opposing Russia in all of these wars. To England it was obvious that these activities on the part of Russia in the Near East were preparatory moves in the direction of India. Hence she blocked Russia wherever she could, along an imaginary line stretching from Constantinople through Persia to Central Asia and China.

From the Russian point of view, the main line of activity was in the direction of Constantinople and the Dardanelles; Constantinople, because of sentimental motives based on the Byzantine tradition, and the Dardanelles because of the necessity of securing an outlet from the Black Sea to the Mediterranean. Persia and Central Asia were to Russia of secondary importance, but meeting with British resistance in Turkey, Russia increased her pressure further east, to frighten Great Britain and oblige her to release her diplomatic resistance in Turkey.

In this way a vicious circle was created, the British finding confirmation of their suspicions as to Russian activities in the events which occurred, and consequently opposing Russia all the more violently, and the Russians in their turn, infuriated by this opposition where they had historical claims and the British had none, consequently became the more aggressive further east where the British were more sensitive for the security of India. If we wish to understand the events which follow we must bear in mind these observations.

Events following the Treaty of Andrianople, which had given so much power to Russia in Turkey, favoured a further development of Russian influence. Faced with a rising in Egypt and having asked in vain for help from other European powers, Turkey accepted Russian assistance. As a Turkish diplomat put it, "a drowning man will clutch a snake." The appearance of Russian armed forces and a Russian squadron were sufficient to turn back the Egyptians who were menacing Constantinople, and in return for this service Turkey signed the famous Treaty of Unkiar Skelessi (August 8, 1833), according to which the Turks promised to close the Dardanelles to all foreign vessels, except Russian.

To the dismay of England, Turkey was rapidly becoming a Russian protectorate. Shortly after this, events occurred in Persia which from the British point of view were more than alarming. The Persians, not willing to accept their fate, decided to try and compensate for their losses in another direction. Consequently, Persia made a bid to recover Herat and such portions of Afghanistan as had once belonged to her. Abbas Mirza started this campaign by attacking the Turkomans of Merv. He died shortly after this, and the reigning Shah, Fath Ali, also having died, the throne came to Abbas Mirza's son, Mohammed Shah, who was credited with being entirely under Russian influence. The British Government immediately saw in these hostilities which had spread to Central Asia and Afghanistan, an attempt to extend Russian influence as far as Kabul and Kandahar, to the very Khyber Pass, the gateway into India.

In 1837 the Persians besieged Herat, and that city under the command of a British officer held out for a year. The Persians were compelled to raise the siege when Great Britain occupied the Persian island of Kharak and threatened immediate war. This action, it must be pointed out, was a break of The Definite Treaty between England and Persia, for in that treaty it was clearly specified that Great Britain would not interfere in a war between Persia and Afghanistan.[22] This whole episode was a particularly interesting test of Russian designs in the East. Had she had any real intention of attempting to conquer India, as was taken for granted in England, this would have been a favourable chance.

Russian power was now at its zenith. Psychologically, Russia was still exultant from her victory over Napoleon and the subsequent victorious wars we have just discussed. The triumphal entry of her armies into Paris, the submissiveness of the French people, who accepted their new constitution from the hands of the Czar, the rôle played in the subsequent period of congresses—these were facts apt to strike the popular imagination glamorously and to create a mood conducive to imperialistic adventures.

Actually, we find such tendencies developing along the main line of Russian interests, i.e., in Turkey and the Caucasus, but further afield we find Russian policy not only restrained but even timid. With a small Rus-

[22] Sykes, Persia, p. 125.

sian force backing the Persians, Herat would have been
easily captured and made into a base for further Russian advance. But nothing of the sort occurred, and the
Persians were left to their fate. Equally hesitating was
to be Russia's policy in Central Asia and Afghanistan.

True, in 1836, upon demand of the Persian Government which had been unable to protect its Caspian
coast from the ravages of Turkoman pirates, Russia
wiped out the pirates' nest on the island of Ashurada
and converted it into a naval base, but this was only a
police measure which made navigation safe on the Caspian and had scarcely any political importance.

Just at that time, a certain retired lieutenant by the
name of Vitkevich appeared in Kabul and was said to
have had instructions from the Russian Minister in
Persia, Count Simonich. The arrival in Afghanistan of
this unofficial Russian agent was immediately followed
by a British counter move. Alexander Burns was sent
from India to Kabul on a "commercial mission." [23]
Both these agents started to try to win over the Ameer
Dost Mohammed, who shrewdly realized the advantage of playing one great European power against the
other, and so began a campaign of diplomatic black-
mail by threatening to go over to the competitor. At
first Dost Mohammed turned a cold shoulder to Vitkevich, in his immediate concern to get back Peshawar
from the British. Vitkevich, knowing Oriental ways,
waited patiently and contented himself with winning
over the Ameer's entourage. Presently when Burns remained adamant on the question of Peshawar, Dost

[23] Sykes, ibidem, p. 122.

Mohammed turned about, and Vitkevich, who had been waiting for that, promised all kinds of things on behalf of Russia.

The sequel was unexpected; Vitkevich was recalled to St. Petersburg and entirely disavowed by the Russian Government. The Foreign Minister, Count Nesselrode, always violently opposed to any Asiatic entanglements, was said to have stated on this occasion that he knew of no Lieutenant Vitkevich, but had heard of an adventurer by that name who had been intriguing in Kabul without any authority to do so. Vitkevich committed suicide. Burns finished just as tragically; his house was attacked by a mob in Kabul and he himself dragged into the street and murdered. As for the Ameer, he had to pay a heavy price for his pro-Russian policy. The Anglo-Indian Government decided to get rid of him in favour of Shuja ul Mulk, and the First Afghan War was the result. The British army reached Kabul, and Dost Mohammed surrendered his throne in favour of his son. But the British force was driven out of Kabul in midwinter. In a dreadful retreat across the mountains it was cut to pieces, and Dost Mohammed got back his throne.

A word must also be said of the events which were taking place in the Caucasus all through this period. Here the Russians were methodically carrying out the conquest of the main range, where wild and warlike mountaineers, particularly the Circassians, were offering a stubborn resistance. The Russians had the advantage of dealing with many races, some Muslim, some Christian, hostile to each other; nevertheless the difficulties for the Russian soldiers to overcome, unfamiliar as they were with mountain warfare, were formidable. The central chain of the Caucasus has forty peaks of over thirteen thousand feet and the highest of these, Mount Elbruz, towers as high as 18,465 feet. Here the mountaineers had converted every "Aul" (village) nestling high upon a precipice, into a fortress, and they fought with an indomitable spirit, applying their favourite method of hiding behind the rocks and then suddenly falling upon the advancing Russian columns.

Things became particularly difficult when these mountaineers found a leader of great organizing ability and military genius, who gallantly held out for some twenty years. This was a Lesghien mullah, Shamyl, who, with Ghazi Mullah declared a holy war. Ghazi Mullah was eventually killed, but Shamyl spread the rumour that he was protected by Heaven from the enemies' bullets, and he knew how to inspire his followers with fanatical courage. He succeeded in uniting the various tribes and establishing an organized government by dividing the Caucasus into twenty provinces. By 1841 he had his own arsenals and foundry, and moreover was receiving assistance in munitions and money from the British Government.

In 1836 the Russians captured a British vessel, the Vixen, off the coast of the Black Sea, which was landing ammunitions for the rebels, an incident which obviously did not improve the already strained relations with Great Britain. After having crushed a rising in Daghestan in 1831-1832, the Russians for seven years carried on the subjugation of the Abkhasians and the western Circassians along the Black Sea coast. In 1842 Shamyl succeeded in badly defeating a Russian force under General Grabbe, who had attempted to storm his fastness. A new governor-general, Vorontsov, was appointed and proceeded methodically to encircle the whole region and gradually to press harder upon the mountaineers by tightening the net of military posts around them. In 1845 Dargo, the fastness where Grabbe had been defeated, was captured.

In this connection it is interesting to note that one of the rules of Russian strategy in warfare against Asiatic peoples consisted in never letting a defeat remain unavenged. Over and over again we shall see this policy carried out in various parts of Asia, and it undoubtedly accounts for a large part of the success of the Russian expansion in Asia. This policy was based on the correct understanding of Asiatic psychology, and it was this that accounted for the tremendous prestige the "White Czar" enjoyed in Asia in the 19th century. Conversely, when crumbling Czarism found it impossible to enforce this rule in its struggle against Japan, in 1904-1905, it suffered a loss of prestige which proved fatal.

Now the days of Shamyl were numbered, though he held out for fourteen years longer. Finally, after three years of extremely strenuous fighting, Shamyl was driven by Prince Bariatinsky onto the inaccessible plateau of Gunib, where he surrendered on September 6, 1859. This gallant leader who had excited the admiration of the whole of Europe was given a pension by the Russian Government and passed his last days residing in honourable captivity in Kaluga, St. Petersburg and

Kiev. He died in 1871 at Mecca, during a pilgrimage, and his son entered the Russian Army. Following the conquest, several thousand Circassians migrated to Turkey, where they are still residing.

The conquest of the Caucasus stirred the imagination of the Russian people on account of the splendour of the scenery and the chivalry and Oriental picturesqueness of its inhabitants. It so happened that the two greatest poets of Russia, Pushkin and Lermontov, both participated in this conquest. Hence Russian literature and later Russian music were strongly impressed by it; the colourful Oriental strain found in modern symphonic music, particularly in Rimsky-Korsakov, Borodin and Balakirev, must be traced to this origin.

To these widespread activities of Russia in the East must be added important developments in the Far East and the beginning of a serious attempt to subdue the brigandish nomads in northern Turkestan, which will be dealt with in detail in subsequent chapters. The reaction that all these activities were producing in London may be judged by Palmerston's letters. From being a friend of Russia as a result of the influence exerted over him by the beautiful Princess Lieven, wife of the Russian ambassador in London, he now gradually became a bitter foe. In 1838, writing about the Egyptian crisis he says:

"The object now to be attained is to stop Mehemet Ali, and Mehemet Ali is weak and England, France, Austria and Russia are outwardly at least and professedly agreed to stop him. If we let him go on we shall have to stop Russia and Russia is strong and Austria might not help us against her," and again, "in such conflict the Turkish troops would probably be defeated, that then the Russians would fly to the aid of the Sultan and a Russian garrison would occupy Constantinople and the Dardanelles and once in possession of these points the Russians would never quit them." In connection with the events in Persia and Afghanistan he writes, "The success of the Shah in Afghanistan would be full of danger and embarrassment to us in India . . . the proceedings of Russia in Afghanistan are certainly as direct an approach to British India as it is *at present* in her power to make. She has opened the first Parallels and it would not be wise in us to delay the defensive measures till she has reached the glacis." [24]

Thus the energetic Russian advance in Asia was storing up a cumulative explosive atmosphere in Europe where the balance of power was working for an alignment of European powers against Russia. This process was also strengthened by the extraordinary diplomatic predominance exerted in European affairs by Russia during this period, and as Nicholas I came out as the champion of the ideals of the Holy Alliance and of Metternich in a time when public opinion was increasingly democratic and nationalistic, a moral divorce between Russia and the more liberal European powers such as France and England was to add to the danger of an imminent clash. The sending of a Russian army into Hungary in 1848, to break the Hungarian rising and to restore the authority of the Habsburgs, produced a tremendous impression all over Europe, and Russia was nicknamed "the European policeman." Thus fear, jealousy and clashing political ideals all worked to increase the tension in Western Europe.

[24] Guedalla, Palmerston, pp. 219, 220.

No wonder that an insignificant incident in the East produced a war against Russia, in which the European powers joined or assumed a position of hostile neutrality towards Russia. The peculiar feature of the Crimean War which broke out in 1853 was that it was fought over an issue which ought to have met with the greatest sympathy in Europe. Nobody denied the fact that the Christian populations were undergoing a dreadful persecution at the hands of the Turks, and as to the question of protecting the rights of the Orthodox Christians in the Holy Land held by Muslims, which was the actual cause of the war, it was an issue which could only be beneficial to Christian Europe. The truth was that, as we have seen, there were other and more important causes which completely overshadowed the original conflict, and which were the real issues at stake. Lord Aberdeen wrote to Palmerston:

"If the war should continue and the Turkish armies meet with disaster we may expect to see the Christian population of the [Turkish] Empire rise against their oppressors, and in such a case it could hardly be proposed to employ the British force in the Levant to assist in compelling their return under a Mohammedan yoke." [25]

This letter reveals the nobility of Lord Aberdeen's character, but also his complete misjudgment of the complex game played upon the diplomatic chessboard of that time. Palmerston was more outspoken:

"My beau-ideal of the war," he writes, "which is about to begin with Russia is as follows: Aland and Finland restored

[25] Morfill, History of Russia, quoted from Sir Arthur Gordon's Life, p. 235.

to Sweden, some of the German provinces of Russia on the Baltic ceded to Prussia. . . . The Crimea, Circassia either independent or connected with the Sultan as suzerain." [26]

To what extent public opinion in England was befogged by war propaganda may be seen from the fact that the actual reason for bringing England into the war was the outburst of public indignation following the destruction of the Turkish fleet by the Russian fleet at the battle of Sinope. The British Admiral Sir Arthur Gordon said later in a quieter mood:

"Looked at in the light of after years there was nothing in the battle of Sinope to justify the outcry of horror which it called forth. Russia and Turkey were at war, declared not by Russia but by Turkey. When nations are at war an attack of the fleet of one belligerent by another is to be expected. Nor does the number of ships sunk or the completeness of victory affect the legitimate character of the action. The English public had taken the Turks into friendship and now saw its friends worsted. It dubbed the battle a massacre and called for vengeance." [27]

It is not within the scope of this work to study the Crimean War in detail. It was a European war fought on European issues, though started in the East. Of all the allied powers, England alone was interested in the Oriental stake at issue. Napoleon III had involved France for reasons of French home policy; Cavour brought Sardinia in to get a "tip" for Italy in the forthcoming peace conference. This war, the first to be lost by Russia in one hundred and fifty years, if we consider the Napoleonic wars as a whole, put an end to

[26] Guedalla, ibidem, p. 391.   [27] Morfill, ibidem, p. 404.

Russia's supremacy in Europe dating from the Congress of Vienna. But we shall see that as an after-effect, it actually brought a further large expansion in Asia with the annexation of Central Asia and the Amur district in the Far East.

The war rapidly spread to Asia, though as theatres of operation both the Caucasus and the Pacific coast remained secondary. In the Caucasus, the tremendous hopes the allies had of Shamyl's creating a powerful diversion were not substantiated; the Turks were defeated and Kars once more taken by the Russians. The events in the Far East will be described in the following chapter.

In connection with these operations a word must be said about the revival of the idea of invading India. The theory which dominated the Russian General Staff was that Russia's coast line was open to English naval attack, but that England, being a maritime and an island power, was invulnerable to any Russian aggression save in India, which could be made the object of a land attack through Central Asia. Accordingly three projects for an expedition to India were worked out during the war, by Tchihachev and Duhamel in 1854 and Krulev in 1855. Tchihachev conceived the advance in two stages: first, the conquest of Herat by a force of fifteen thousand men and then the assembling there of a corps of thirty thousand which would march on Lahor via Kandahar. Duhamel, who was Russian Minister in Teheran, suggested the itinerary of the Caspian Sea to Astrabad, thence via Kabul and Jelalabad to Peshawar. The Afghans were to be won over and given sympathetic support, and if possible a rising of the Sikhs in India was to be arranged. The third project also suggested an expeditionary force of thirty thousand men which was to march via Meshed to Kandahar. The actual attack on India was to be accomplished after securing an Afghan alliance and inviting the frontier tribesmen to rise.

Nothing came of these projects, and at the end of the Crimean War they were automatically dropped. Since, however, they once more substantiated the claim that Russia had designs on India, it is necessary to point out that the smallness of the expeditionary force, not exceeding thirty thousand men in any of the projects, in itself precluded any real desire of conquest. Obviously it would have been unreasonable to set out upon the enormous adventure of conquering a subcontinent having a population of three hundred million, at a time when Russia herself was absorbed in a death struggle with England, France, Sardinia and Turkey, and could therefore only devote such insufficient forces to this task. Viewed as a side scheme fitting into the general conduct of the war and to be carried out to divert England, but not for the sake of India, such an operation acquires an element of plausibility and reasonableness.

CHAPTER VI

THE ANNEXATION OF THE AMUR REGION

APPARENTLY during the whole period covering the reign of Catherine the Great, the French Revolution and the Napoleonic Wars, Russia was too absorbed in her European policy to be interested in Far Eastern affairs. But Russia emerged from the Napoleonic Wars as the dominant power on the continent of Europe, a position she was to hold unchallenged, as we have already seen, right up to the Crimean War in 1854-1855. This resulted in a kind of exhilaration from her own power which was translated not only into an expansion in the Near East but also a revived interest in colonial problems covering a field wider than Asia. Hence we now have a new chapter opening in the history of Russian geographical explorations, coinciding with an interest in the economic development of Siberia, an interest which also overflowed into Alaska.

These new tendencies had appeared as early as 1803, when the Czar Alexander I fitted out an expedition around the world under Captain Krusenstern. It is interesting to notice that this voyage was decided upon after the latter had published a paper pointing out the importance for communications between Russia and the Far East of the route around the Cape of Good Hope.

Leaving Cronstadt with two ships in August, 1803, Krusenstern circumnavigated Africa and, passing by Hawaii, reached Kamchatka. He completed the journey around the world in three years, but his explorations centered mainly around Japan, where the expedition made several important geographical discoveries. However, his supposition that the island of Sakhalin was a peninsula was to be important in determining later Russian policy in this region.

In 1815 a second expedition left Russia to explore the American coast north and south of the Behring Straits, and if possible to discover a route connecting with Baffin Bay. This expedition was equipped by Count Rumiantsev at his expense and put in the charge of Kotzebue, who had been a member of Krusenstern's party. On his brig Rurik, Kotzebue set out with a crew of twenty-seven men. Rounding Cape Horn he discovered the Rumiantsev, Rurik and Krusenstern Islands, a group of 399 islands. Reaching the American coast he discovered Kotzebue Sound and Krusenstern Cape. On his return journey he stayed three weeks in Hawaii, making a curious if unsuccessful attempt to convert it into a Russian naval base. After this, he discovered the New Year Islands and returned to Russia in 1818 bringing with him a collection of unknown species.

On his second voyage in 1823 Kotzebue once more visited the Rurik Islands; the inhabitants, remembering him, showed great joy at his arrival, carried him ashore and wanted to make him their king. He reached Kamchatka the following year, made several new discoveries and rectified previously taken bearings. Returning by way of Hawaii, New Caledonia and Marianne's Islands, he reached St. Petersburg in 1826.

From a scientific point of view the voyage of Bellingshausen was more important. He set out with Lieutenant Lazarev in two vessels to supplement the results obtained by Captain Cook in the Antarctic. After discovering the Traverse Islands in 1819, the expedition crossed the Antarctic Circle and went further south than Cook had, reaching seventy degrees latitude south. It followed the edge of the ice pack and succeeded in circumnavigating the Antarctic Ocean, notwithstanding terrific gales which drove them north. The Island of Peter I and Alexander I Land, the first land to be discovered near the South Pole, were sighted by Bellingshausen. After thus completing the task assigned and putting into Rio de Janeiro, the Vostok and the Mirni, the two vessels of the expedition, finally reached Cronstadt in 1821. To quote the *Encyclopædia Britannica:*

"The voyage was a worthy pendant to that of Cook; it was carried out with a faithful devotion to instructions and consummate seamanship and as a result it left only half the periphery of the Antarctic Circle within which land could possibly project beyond the frigid zone."

Simultaneously with these geographic explorations, the new interest shown in Russia's Asiatic possessions led to the appointment of the greatest statesman Russia had at the time, Speransky, as governor of Siberia with a mission to study the conditions of that domain extensively and to draw up any scheme of reforms deemed advisable. Full dictatorial powers were granted to him in this respect. After a sojourn of two years, Speransky brought back to Russia with him ten projects of reforms comprising more than three thousand articles, supported by a mass of statistical and documentary data. A special committee created to study this material completed its work in August, 1821, and as a result, Siberia was divided into two governor-generalships, Western Siberia and Eastern Siberia. With practically viceregal powers granted to them, in the course of time these governor-generals came to be the foci of Russian expansion and relations in countries along their border, the administration of Western Siberia controlling Russian affairs in Central and Inner Asia, and that of Eastern Siberia dealing with the Far East and the Pacific region, including Russia's overflow into North America.

Though Russian activities in Alaska are properly speaking outside the field of this study, they are so closely connected with Russia's Far Eastern policy that a word must be said about them. As far back as 1781 a Siberian fur merchant from Irkutsk by the name of Shelekhov formed with partners a company for the exploitation of Alaska and the Kuril Islands. Six years later a new life was given to the venture by the appointment of an energetic director, Alexander Baranov, and in 1799 the company merged with a rival company founded in Irkutsk, taking the name of the Russo-American Company. Its object was the discovery and colonization of new territory in Arctic America, the extending of Christianity amongst the natives and trade relations with the Far East. A very detailed charter was granted to the Company by the Emperor Paul I, giving among other privileges, the right of drawing upon Russian military and naval forces for protection in case of emergency. In 1800 the Company's headquarters were transferred from Siberia to St. Petersburg and its share capital increased from seven hundred thousand roubles to over two million five hundred thousand roubles. This rapid growth was due to the activities of a new member of the board, Nicholas Rezanov, former procurator-general of the First Department of the Senate, an able and ambitious man with wide and influential connections in St. Petersburg. However, there being scarcely one hundred and fifty Russian settlers in Alaska the Company's work there was difficult. The first settlement at Sitka was destroyed by the natives in 1801, all Russians being murdered, but the town was rebuilt and reoccupied three years later. Rezanov pushed work ahead there: a school and a children's poor house were established for the natives; a fairly large library, a physical laboratory and observatory were built.

An acute difficulty was the question of supplies to be brought the whole way from Siberia, through one of the stormiest and foggiest seas in the world. Hence Rezanov was induced to search for a possible source of supplies down the coast of America and it was this that started him on the famous voyage which brought him to San Francisco. Here he fell in love and became engaged to Doña Concepcion Arguello, daughter of the

Spanish Commandant. But the local Spanish authorities not having the authority to grant him supplies from California, he worked out a scheme of going to Madrid to get the necessary permission from the Spanish Government. He therefore left San Francisco on a long journey through Siberia to Europe, and it is said that his fiancée waited in vain for his return as he was killed by a fall from his horse.

Baranov carried on the work and in his turn went to California, where in November, 1811, Fort Ross was established on the Russian River north of San Francisco. The Spaniards in California welcomed the Russian settlers and gave them all necessary implements. By 1819 the chain of Russian settlements on the American coast had grown to nineteen, producing a net income of six million roubles. But the difficulty of the situation lay in Madrid. During the Napoleonic period Spain under French domination had no time to think of her distant colonies, but after regaining her independence she became extremely sensitive in regard to this Russian intrusion in California. It was also discovered that it was practically as difficult to supply Sitka from California as it was from Siberia.

The main object of the Russians had always been the fur and seal trade in Alaska. The Russian Government had never endorsed this venture of the Russo-American Company, and finally by a charter and an Ukaze of September 16, 1821, it limited Russian expansion to the 51st degree latitude north, but at the same time reserved to the exclusive use of Russians the fishing, hunting and trading rights in the Pacific north of that

latitude on the American coast and north of 45 degrees
51 minutes on the Siberian side. This transforming the
northern Pacific into a Russian lake provoked serious
diplomatic incidents with the United States of America
and was no negligible influence in the formulation of
the Monroe Doctrine. It also added fuel to the already strained relations with Great Britain, extending
the acute rivalry in the Near East to these latitudes.
After long and difficult negotiations, by the agreement
with the United States in 1824, and with England in
1825, it was agreed that the citizens of each country
should not penetrate into the establishments of the
other party without express permission of the authorities, and that the freedom of the seas was to be guaranteed all over the Pacific Ocean. The geographic limit
of Russian activities was set at 50 degrees 40 minutes
latitude north.

In this same year (1825) events in Russia had a
curiously beneficial repercussion on Siberian and Russian problems in the Far East. Profiting by the inter-
regnum between the death of Alexander I and the accession of Nicholas I, a revolutionary movement known
as the Decembrist Rising made an attempt to impose
upon Russia a parliamentary régime or a republic. The
movement was sponsored by enthusiastic young officers
who were members of a secret society of the Carbonari
type. It failed completely, meeting with no response
among the masses, and the result was the exile to Siberia
of a number of scions of the most aristocratic families
of Russia, who had been involved in the revolution.
These were all highly cultured, enthusiastic young

men, and finding themselves obliged to remain in
Siberia for over twenty years until they were pardoned,
they applied their noble ideals and enthusiasm to the
study of Siberian conditions and problems. After their
pardon some settled for good in Siberia, while others
by correspondence or upon their return to Russia
brought Siberian affairs to the attention of influential
circles in St. Petersburg.

These circumstances and the flourishing condition of
the seal and whaling industry in the Okhotsk and
Behring Seas were the contributory causes for a rising
interest in Far Eastern issues at that time. Kamchatka
and Alaska came to the foreground of public attention,
and the difficult question of securing rapid and convenient communication with these distant lands became
the subject of wide discussion. An attempt to build a
land route through a thousand miles of arctic swamp
and great mountain ridges to Kamchatka, from there to
connect by sea with Alaska, had to be abandoned owing
to insurmountable natural obstacles. A sea route was
the only alternative, but Russia had at the time only
one sea port on the Pacific coast, Okhotsk, and this port
was located in the arctic region on the sea of the same
name, frozen every year up to the month of June and
notorious for a practically constant fog. Besides, the city
was situated on a shallow river, made difficult for navigation by dangerous sand bars blocking its mouth.

Consequently, once more there arose the question of
the Amur River. Should that river prove to be navigable for seagoing vessels and come into Russian possession as an outlet to the sea from Siberia, all difficul-

ties would be solved. But it will be remembered that Krusenstern reported that the Island of Sakhalin was a peninsula which would block this outlet from the south.

The issue became suddenly of vital and immediate importance with the breaking out of the so-called Opium War in 1841-1842 between Great Britain and China. The war resulted in the opening of five Chinese ports to British trade. This appearance of England as an important factor in China worried the Russian Government as much as the simultaneous Russian advance in Central Asia was a source of concern for England. The two great countries were clashing in a dangerous rivalry in this part of Asia as well as in Central Asia. Much has been said of Russian ambitions in India as a result of Russia's advance towards Afghanistan, but equally justifiable was Russia's fear at seeing England advance in China towards the vitally important Russian Pacific coast. The taking of Hong Kong by Great Britain, her securing a predominating influence in the valley of the Yang Tse Kiang were interpreted as forecasting a similar move by the British to gain control of the mouth of the Amur and thus make the Russian position on the Pacific untenable. There was as much justification in this fear but no more as in England's concern for the security of India.

Nicholas I was not a man to shirk taking a decisive action in such circumstances. He decided that it was necessary first of all to have a strong, energetic man on the spot to look after Russia's Far Eastern interests. With customary swiftness he made his choice, which fell on the Governor of Tula, Muraviev, who though only thirty-eight years of age was appointed Governor-General of Eastern Siberia. This appointment took place at a meeting which the Emperor had with the young governor at 7.00 o'clock in the morning on September 6, 1847, at a small railway station in the neighbourhood of Tula. Owing to the distance separating St. Petersburg from Eastern Siberia the new Governor-General received practically unlimited viceregal powers. The nomination, passing as it did over the heads of so many older officials, caused consternation and much gossip in St. Petersburg, but Nicholas proved to have had an unerring eye. In Muraviev he had found a man with first-class administrative abilities and untiring energies, fired with all the enthusiasm of an empire builder. The territory which he was to govern stretched from the Yenissei to the Behring Straits. Its enormous size was jokingly stressed by the Emperor in a farewell audience when he remarked to Muraviev, "If any power seizes Kamchatka, you in Irkutsk will only find out about it six months later."

Reaching his headquarters, Irkutsk, in 1848, Muraviev at once found his attention focused on the Amur question. He appointed a special commission for this purpose. Explorations were to be carried out by sea. At Muraviev's suggestion a young naval officer, Nevelskoi, was appointed as head of the expedition, which was to proceed in a ship especially constructed for the purpose. He had come to know Nevelskoi while still in St. Petersburg and had had many talks with him upon this subject. The Naval Ministry in St. Petersburg had suggested the possibility of building a naval base at Konstantinovsk on the Bay of Tugur, north of the mouth of the Amur; consequently Muraviev instructed Nevelskoi to explore down the coast from this bay to the Amur. In the meanwhile he himself started on a tour of inspection of his vast domains, and after a journey of two and a half months reached Kamchatka via Okhotsk. The only Russian settlement there was Petropavlovsk, founded by the Behring expedition on the Bay of Avacha. He found the bay one of the most beautiful and spacious in the world, ranking with those of Rio de Janeiro, San Francisco and Sydney. In his enthusiasm he decided he had found the Pacific base for the Russian fleet and consequently in 1850 he had the Russian naval base officially transferred from Okhotsk to Petropavlovsk. Though there was a decided gain in this change, it was soon discovered that the Bay of Avacha was unsuitable, because it was too far away and was located too far north, the climate being inclement. This move, however, resulted in Petropavlovsk being carefully fortified, and this action was to prove very valuable during the Crimean War, which was only four years in the future.

In the meanwhile Nevelskoi carrying out his instructions, had made an important discovery: Sakhalin was not a peninsula but an island and the Gulf of Tartary was connected with the Amur by straits which made the river accessible from the south as well. The Amur, furthermore, proved easily navigable for seagoing vessels. But Muraviev was now beginning to find strenuous opposition in St. Petersburg to his schemes, particularly on the part of the Minister of Foreign Affairs,

Count Nesselrode, who in view of the strained situation in Europe leading up to the Crimean War, was energetically opposing any entanglements in the Far East.

Muraviev, therefore, decided to go himself to St. Petersburg to discuss the matters, and while he was there there came a bombshell. The impetuous Nevelskoi, having received instructions to found a Russian settlement at Petrovskoie in the Bay of Happiness, not far from the estuary of the Amur, went beyond the orders given to him. On his own initiative, finding the Bay of Happiness ice bound, he sailed up the Amur in a sloop with six sailors and one gun and established a post some twenty miles from the estuary. Here he landed on August 6, 1850, hoisted the Russian flag, and gave his post the name of Nikolaevsk in honor of the Emperor. The native Giliaks who had flocked to see him land were ordered to swear allegiance to the Russian crown, which they did without protest. Leaving five men to garrison this post, he returned to report the matter.

This incident, which was the beginning of the Russian occupation of the Amur, produced a tremendous outcry in St. Petersburg. Count Nesselrode in particular spoke of the "extreme danger" of this action and the imminent danger of a war with China at a most inopportune moment. Influential circles demanded the immediate abandonment of Nikolaevsk and the court martialing of Nevelskoi for disobedience. Nevelskoi, who was thus menaced with degradation to the rank of sailor in case of court martial, found a staunch defender in Muraviev, who won over the Emperor to his views. Nicholas I pardoned Nevelskoi and on this occasion uttered a famous sentence which produced a great sensation at the time in Europe: "Where the Russian flag has once been hoisted it must not be lowered."

The compromise solution adopted was to give Nikolaevsk over to the Russo-American Company so as to make it belong to private interests, but as the charter of the Company made it possible to ask for naval protection, a Russian cruiser was dispatched to stand by the post and guard it. We shall see a similar method of camouflaging occupation adopted in regard to the Chinese Eastern Railway in Manchuria half a century later.

Muraviev was concerned with having adequate military forces to cope with the problems arising from this expansion. He consequently converted the peasants in the Nerchinsk district into Cossacks, and created the Transbaikal Cossack Host. The peasants greeted this measure with joy, for it relieved them from serfdom, and the Government pursued its policy of stringing military-agricultural Cossack settlements along the expanding border.

In the meanwhile Nevelskoi, now an admiral, converted Nikolaevsk into a city and pursued the exploration of the Amur region. In February, 1852, he sent his lieutenant Boshniak in a sleigh across the narrow frozen channel separating Sakhalin from the mainland, and the latter, notwithstanding great sufferings from cold and lack of food which caused ulcers and killed his dogs, succeeded in getting back to Nikolaevsk after having crossed the whole island. Nevelskoi followed in September of the following year on his vessel, the Nikolai, and anchoring before the largest native settlement on the island, Tamar Aniva, took possession of it and renamed it Muravievsk.

This action was the logical outcome of the occupation of the Amur, Sakhalin blocking its estuary from the ocean, but the consequences were important. Sakhalin was populated by the Aino, the aboriginal and wild natives who also made their home in the northern islands of Japan. The Japanese had long had commercial relations with the Aino of Sakhalin, and they were greatly aroused by Russia's penetration there. They tried strenuously to oppose Nevelskoi's occupation by stirring up the Aino against him, but met with no success, and not feeling strong enough to oppose Russia openly, withdrew sulkily, holding this grudge for the future. Thus occurred the first serious clash of interests between Russia and Japan. Nevelskoi immediately issued an official statement in which he said rather inconclusively: "In accordance with the Treaty of Nerchinsk concluded between Russia and China, the island of Sakhalin, being a prolongation of the basin of the Amur, incontestably belongs to Russia." [28]

Nevelskoi followed up this expedition with further explorations along the coast of the mainland southward and discovered several magnificent bays. Here he heard from the natives of another bay further south, where Vladivostok was later to arise. Along with these

[28] Cheradame, Le Monde et la Guerre Russo-Japonaise, p. 65.

explorations, Nevelskoi, with his customary enterprise and initiative, established Russian posts at strategic places in these bays, and thus occupied virtually the whole coast to the Korean frontier. He did it first and then asked permission to do so.

Muraviev once more supported Nevelskoi, and after long deliberation Nicholas I sanctioned these occupations, giving instructions to start immediately upon diplomatic negotiations with China to this effect. The remarkable feature of this annexation of an enormous territory was the small number of men employed. Nevelskoi had only the crew of his ship at his disposal, hence he garrisoned the posts of Mariinsk with eight men, Alexandrovsk (De Castries Bay) with three and later seven men, Konstantinovsk (Imperatorski Bay) with eight men and Ilinsk with six men.[29]

Another peculiar feature of the situation was that the nation which ought to have shown the most concern with this Russian advance, China, appeared to be not in the least disturbed, and this indifference goes far to show the peculiar mentality of old China. No shadow was cast on Russo-Chinese relations, which remained as friendly as before. The Chinese looked upon the whole situation as just one more frontier incident, but not of sufficient importance to provoke a serious quarrel. It must be noted, however, that the Chinese had a very vague suzerainty over these regions, which for them represented the northern limit of the known world, and it also must be pointed out that the Treaty of Nerchinsk was concerned solely with the upper course of the

[29] Vladimir, Russia on the Pacific and the Siberian Railway, p. 195.

Amur, so small value did the contracting parties attach at that time to the little known region around its estuary.

If, however, diplomatic negotiations with China were sufficient to settle the question of the transfer of this territory to Russia, the latter's newly acquired position on the Pacific was to be almost immediately challenged by the other European powers as a result of the Crimean War. Though the main fighting took place in Crimea, war was carried into the Pacific as well, and Russia owed much to Muraviev's foresight in increasing the Russian defence on the Pacific. Muraviev had rapidly prepared Eastern Siberia for the struggle, and now owing to the difficulty of communications by sea with St. Petersburg as a result of the war, the Emperor had granted him the right of conducting all diplomatic negotiations in the Far East directly and independently of the Russian Foreign Office (January 11, 1854).

Thus receiving full sovereign powers, Muraviev lost no time in informing the Chinese of this change and over-riding Chinese objections he started a steamship service on the Amur for the purpose of connecting it with Kamchatka, then menaced by a naval attack. A flotilla was especially constructed for the purpose, and in May, 1854, a force of eight hundred men with artillery went down the river under the command of the Governor-General in person. For the first time since the days of Poyarkov and Khabarov, the Amur was travelled by Russians in its entire length, and in passing before a particularly beautiful and convenient spot, Muraviev decided to found a city, which he named in honour of Khabarov. Thus arose Khabarovsk, one of the most important cities in Eastern Siberia.

The expected attack on Kamchatka materialized shortly; an allied Anglo-French squadron appeared before Petropavlovsk. Two attacks were beaten off and a landing party seven hundred to one thousand strong had to retreat back to their boats after losing its colours and three hundred killed and wounded, whereas the Russian losses amounted to thirty-one killed and sixty-five wounded. This Russsian victory was highly useful to Muraviev. Not only did the enemy abandon any further attempts on Kamchatka, but the news of it spread over the Far East and resulted in an increase of Russian prestige which was useful in the pending negotiations with China.

To make the newly acquired seacoast safe from allied attacks, Muraviev decided to colonize it, and hence a new expedition went down the Amur, this time bearing eight thousand settlers and three hundred cattle. During this voyage Muraviev met the Chinese plenipotentiaries. Russia made a formal demand for all territories where Russian settlements and posts had sprung up. The Chinese showed themselves obdurate concerning their sovereignty on the left bank of the Amur. Thus no conclusion was reached and the negotiations dragged on indefinitely.

Immediately after the Crimean War China found herself at war with England and France. The war led to the signing of the Treaty of Tientsin which gave the British further important privileges in China: eleven new ports were opened to European trade, legations and consulates were established at Peking and other cities, foreigners were permitted to travel in China, extraterritoriality and mixed courts were introduced. Thus China came out of the struggle deeply humiliated.

This war gave Russia a chance to conclude the pending negotiations. A Russian observer, Admiral Prince Putiatin, had been closely following the events in China. Muraviev now suggested a conference at Aigun, May, 1858, and stressing the danger of the Amur becoming British, produced a draft treaty. According to this treaty, the left bank of the Amur from the Argun River to the sea was to go to Russia, and China was to keep the right bank down to the Ussuri River, beyond which the territory between the latter and the sea was to be ruled jointly by both Empires until further notice. The river was to be open only for Russian and Chinese navigation, and the inhabitants on both banks were to have free access across the border, and not suffer from vexations in carrying on business and commerce. After much wrangling and a menacing attitude assumed by Muraviev, the Chinese plenipotentiaries signed the treaty on May 16, 1858.

Immediately following this Muraviev started investigating the Ussuri region and he discovered: first, that the formation of the ice on the lower Amur was such that unless he held both banks he would have no control over navigation, since the ships had to pass through Chinese waters; second, that the bay near the Korean frontier about which Boshniak had learned from the natives was the most suitable for a large port. Hence he had this bay, which was given the name of Peter the

Great, occupied on July 20th, 1860, by a party of forty men who founded the city of Vladivostok immediately. Russian imperialism showed itself in the peculiarly ambitious name of the city (Rule of the East), and in rather romantic reminiscences of the imperial city of Constantinople to be found in the names given to the various parts of the bay, such as "Eastern Bosporus" and "Golden Horn."

In the meanwhile, China had not reached the end of her troubles. The disastrous foreign war was followed by a violent explosion of popular indignation, which became known as the Taiping Rebellion, and this led to the occupation of Peking in 1860 by an Anglo-French force. The Court ran away, and the Forbidden City suffered badly from looting. In these tragic circumstances the Russian Minister in Peking, Count Ignatiev, offered his services as an intermediary and succeeded in getting the allies to evacuate Peking under not-too-unfavourable conditions.

In return for this service the Chinese Government willingly negotiated the Treaty of Peking (November 2, 1860), which gave to Russia the whole region of the Ussuri down to the sea. The frontier, which is the one still existing to-day, followed the Shilka, Argun, Amur and Ussuri rivers to the Lake Henkai, thence the Belenho River to the ocean. Other clauses of this important treaty established the frontier of Sinkiang (Chinese Turkestan) in the west and gave Russian merchants the right to proceed via Kiakhta to Peking, including the permission to establish wholesale depots in Urga and Kalgan. A consulate was established at Urga in

Mongolia. Kashgar in Chinese Turkestan was opened to Russian commerce but at the risk of the Russians and with the restriction that not more than two hundred Russian merchants could congregate in any one single place.

Thus by one stroke, Russia acquired valuable trading rights in China proper and a rich fertile region with a magnificent bay. Vladivostok grew rapidly and in 1872 the naval base on the Pacific was transferred there from Nikolaevsk, to which it had been transferred from Petropavlovsk. Strenuous efforts were made to colonize the hinterland, the Ussuri region. At first the country was infested with brigands but colonists were brought from Russia around Asia by boat pending the establishment of railway connections, and once more a Cossack host was created, the Ussuri Host, the last of the belt of Cossack hosts following the Russian advance in Asia.

This tremendous expansion in the Far East was watched with growing concern by Japan, still too weak to have a voice in the settlement. We have seen that the occupation of Sakhalin by Nevelskoi produced a great deal of ill feeling among the Japanese. In 1862 the Shogun sent a mission in the name of the Mikado with a proposal to delimit spheres of interest on the island by cutting the island into two along the 51st degree latitude north. After long and fruitless negotiations, a condominium was established according to the precedent of the Ussuri territory, with the inevitable result of producing friction and increasing ill feeling.

Further negotiations were carried on in 1867. The Russians now proposed the exchange of Sakhalin for the Kuril Islands, and however unprofitable such an exchange was, the Mikado in 1875 ordered Admiral Enotomo to settle the issue definitely by accepting the offer and giving up all rights to Sakhalin. Little did Russia realize at the time how antagonized Japan was, and that here was growing a rival who was to jeopardize her whole position in the Far East.

CHAPTER VII

THE CONQUEST OF CENTRAL ASIA

In the preceding chapter we have seen that it was the Crimean War which really gave the impulse for the acquisition by Russia of a vast new empire on the Pacific coast. Similarly the conquest of Central Asia may be traced to the after-effect of the same war. Consequently though upon entering the war England hoped that by defeating Russia she would succeed in checking Russia's expansion in Asia, it may be said that not only did she not achieve this purpose but actually was faced with the opposite result. There was nothing surprising in this: it becomes a law in Russian history that every time Russia finds herself checked in Europe she intensifies her drive in Asia.

Though the Russian Chancellor, Prince Gorchakov, made the famous statement that Russia was not sulky, she was only biding her time ("La Russie ne boude pas; elle se receuille"), actually Russia was very bitter against the humiliating clauses of the Peace of Paris, particularly the one most favourable to England, implying the demilitarization of the Black Sea. This clause cancelled the results obtained since the reign of Catherine II, and Russian diplomacy was to work henceforth for its nullification. As at this time Bismarck was building his united German Empire which was a counterpoise to the influence of France, England and Austria, the obvious channel for obtaining this annulment was friendship with Prussia and support of Bismarck's aims. And in fact, Gorchakov won the cancellation of the Treaty of Paris after the Franco-Prussian War of 1870.

Now Bismarck's idea was to get Russia absorbed with Asia, where she would not be a menace to Europe and where she had, as he said, a great civilizing mission. A curious parallelism has been noticed by the Soviet historian Pokrovsky between the Convention of Alvensleben, which consecrated the Russo-Prussian friendship, and Russian activities in Central Asia, which were resumed immediately after the signing of this convention. "In the summer of 1866 Austria was beaten by Prussia and the western ally of Prussia became a great power, and in August of the same year Tashkent was annexed to Russia. In some mystical way the Prussian victories in Bohemia gave a new push to the Russian penetration in Asia, then already in the valley of the Amu Darya which up to this time had been beyond the sphere of Russian influence." [30] How far Pokrovsky's arguments are correct it is difficult to say, but it would appear plausible that the alliance with Bismarck, giving Russia a feeling of security for her western frontiers, enabled her to carry out schemes which had long been delayed by more urgent tasks. It will be remembered that the idea of conquering

[30] Pokrovsky, A History of Russia, Vol. IV, p. 330.

Turkestan and putting an end to the nomadic nuisance
had already germinated in the reign of Peter the Great
and much ground-work had been done. Now the moment appeared as most suitable for the fruition of the
whole scheme.

To get a clear understanding of the events which developed in Turkestan, it is necessary to visualize the
geography of that region. Bordering on Siberia two
vast deserts, sandy or saline, stretch themselves on both
sides of the Sea of Aral. Their size may be judged by
the fact that it takes two days for an express train to
cross them. Further south begin the more fertile
regions of Turkestan, where life depends on the water
available from the mountains and where the great cities
and civilizations of the Middle Ages flourished. This
region is clearly marked out between the Caspian Sea
to the west and a semicircle of towering mountains to
the south and the east, the Hindu Kush, the Pamir and
the Tian Shan ranges. From these mountains two
splendid rivers, the Amu Darya and the Syr Darya run
parallel, and fall into the Aral Sea, watering the whole
region, the Amu Darya being some three thousand
miles long. But as a means of communication they are
useless because they are not connected with the outside
world and lose themselves in the center of the great
desert region. In the desert, life means a desperate
struggle for water; consequently this is the abode of
the nomad. More or less sedentary conditions prevail
only in the rare oases, such as Khiva. In the fertile
region within the basin of the rivers, the oases become
larger and much closer together.

With a primitive system of irrigation known as "aryks," the whole region was transformed into a flourishing garden, and here was the heart of Tamerlane's Empire with the great cities of Samarkand and Bokhara. On the ruins of this empire there arose, as we have already seen, a few native states, of which the most prominent were Khiva and Bokhara. The other states to be mentioned were the Khanate of Khokand with the important cities of Tashkent, Khokand and Tchimkent, and the Khanate of Samarkand subjected to Bokhara.

From the standpoint of economic development, the most important of these states at the time of the Russian conquest was Bokhara. In 1872 the Russian financial agent there wrote: "Bokhara is the chief point of the Central Asian trade. . . . Being an important depot for Russian and Anglo-Indian wares, Bokhara carries on an immense and active trade with all the remaining Muslim countries receiving from them their local productions and supplying them in return. The bazaar is overflowing with all sorts of goods from distant India and still more distant Moscow. . . . Bokhara is literally filled from top to bottom with Russian cotton goods and there seems to be at least six times as much of them as of English goods." [81]

If therefore Turkestan was an important market for Russian goods, it could in return supply its main article of export, cotton, for the growing Russian textile industry, which otherwise would have to import it at a much higher price from America. These economic reasons

[81] Schuyler, Turkistan, Vol. II, pp. 95, 96.

in themselves were sufficient to warrant Russian penetration.

But closely connected with these economic factors were considerations of a military order. We have seen that no regular trade could be carried on unless the attacks of brigandish nomads upon the caravans passing through the desert were stopped. All attempts in this direction had failed dismally, and it was clear that only a large-scale military operation could be successful. From the military angle, therefore, the regions which required the closest attention were the great desert around the Aral Sea where dwelt the Khirgiz and the Turkomans, with Khiva as base, and a second desert along the South Caspian coast and the frontier of Persia, inhabited by particularly fierce and warlike Turkomans who had Geok Tepe as their stronghold. The sedentary population of the fertile regions, a jumble of races, Uzbecks, Sarts, Tadjicks, Dungans (Chinese Muslims), and Bokharian Jews would easily accept Russian domination, once the desert was conquered.

There was further a strategic consideration of a more remote nature, in the fact that the Siberian frontier was entirely open towards Turkestan. The natural frontier of the Russian Empire here was the great semicircle of mountains, which protected this region on the east from China and on the south from Afghanistan and India. Also it was important to hold the great Gateway of the Nations, the valley of the Ili, through which, it will be remembered, the great Asiatic invasions had poured into Russia. Thus in view of the tremendous international repercussions which the advance of Russia in Central Asia produced, it is necessary to realize that whatever the ultimate aims of this conquest may have been, there were, from the Russian standpoint, *in Turkestan itself* without looking further, plenty of reasons warranting this action.

On the other hand, though geographically an extension of the Siberian plain, Turkestan with its extremes of cold in winter and tropical heat in summer, with different vegetable and animal life, would always remain a region where the Russian settler would find totally unfamiliar conditions. Hence it was to remain for Russia only a colony for exploitation and not for colonization; the Russians came to develop its riches but not to populate it. To some extent it may be considered Russia's overseas colony, the great sandy waste of the desert assuming the rôle of the sea.

Since the middle of the 18th century no more active steps had been undertaken to penetrate into Central Asia, with the exception of the Indian expedition of Paul I. In 1824 an attempt was made to protect the caravans from the marauding attacks of the Khivans by a military convoy, but the small escort could not do much; the first caravan to cross the desert was attacked, the escort destroyed, the goods taken and the merchants sold into slavery. The idea was therefore abandoned and replaced by the idea of sending once more a regular military expedition to Khiva, following the footsteps of Bekovich.

In the meanwhile Russian colonization was slowly infringing upon the edge of the desert, and in this way the base for such an operation was moved nearer to

Khiva. In 1810 the district of Iletsk in the Ural steppe was opened for Russian colonization, and from the opposite side, Russian Cossack villages appeared south of the Irtysh, and in 1824 a new administrative district was formed north of the desert along the Chinese border. In 1834 a particularly important foothold was acquired on the Turkestan coast of the Caspian Sea, approximately opposite the mouth of the Volga. Here on the Mangishlak peninsula, a fort was established named Novo Alexandrovskoye. Thus the attack of the desert could be conducted from three different sides, from the Caspian Sea, from the Urals and from Siberia.

Five years later in 1839 an expedition under General Perovski set out against Khiva. It was composed of five thousand men with twenty-two guns, ten thousand camels and two thousand Khirgiz porters and camel drivers. The dreadful tragedy which followed was caused by an erroneous assumption of the General Staff. Arguing that it would be easier to cross the waterless desert in winter when it was snowbound, than under the tropical summer sun, the expedition was ordered to start its march in the late autumn. But the winter came earlier and was more severe than usual. The result was that the camels ran out of fodder and began dying. Relief transports with food were held up by severe blizzards and were unable to find the column in the vastness of the desert. Left to itself, the expedition turned back when half way, after nine thousand camels had fallen, leaving only one thousand exhausted beasts to carry its baggage. In the meanwhile the men too had run out of provisions, and had to make their way back through terrific snowstorms and blizzards. Only about one thousand bedraggled men succeeded in reaching the Russian base, the rest having died on the way back from starvation and cold. It will be remembered that in these same steppes one hundred thousand Torgout Kalmycks perished during their winter migration from the Volga to China.

The news of the disaster befalling Perovski's expedition spread rapidly throughout Central Asia, and the Russian Government, rightly fearing its loss of prestige, immediately ordered that preparations should be made for a second expedition to start in the spring. But Perovski's attempt proved to have been not entirely fruitless, in that it seriously intimidated the Khan of Khiva, who understood that the Russians would not give up the task after this first failure. Therefore before the second expedition had started, he sent a request for peace, releasing at the same time 418 Russian captives and also issuing an order that any further attacks on Russian merchants would be punishable by death. In the negotiations which followed, the Russian envoy Danilievsky, succeeded (1842) in obtaining from the Khan a formal treaty in which he promised not to attack Russians and to cease taking prisoners into slavery.

But these promises remained unfulfilled, particularly when the Khirgiz along the Siberian border broke into rebellion. Under an energetic leader, Kenissar, they attacked the Russian border forts and caused much trouble to the Russians until Kenissar was killed in an encounter in the Alatau Mountains in 1847. The Khan of Khiva openly sided with the rebels and gave them every help possible. Now the Russian Government decided to change its tactics. Instead of sending across the desert an expedition doomed to failure by the superhuman natural obstacles it had to overcome, it was decided to proceed slowly and methodically, by adopting similar tactics to those used in the Caucasus. Consequently the Governor of Orenburg, Obruchev succeeded in 1846 in establishing a fort on the Syr Darya, near the Aral Sea, where the next year a flotilla of boats was launched in readiness to flank the advancing column. The Khirgiz in the rear gave their submission, permitting the dispatch of an expedition from this new line of forts. The second expedition under Perovski in 1853 succeeded in capturing the strategically important village of Ak Masjid, renamed Perovsk. All further attempts ceased for the time being, for the Crimean War was absorbing the whole attention of the Russian Government.

After this war a new and decisive phase started, and this time the struggle was in another part of Central Asia, namely Khokand. The war was started by the Khan of Khokand, who objected to the neighbouring Khirgiz passing under Russian domination. This little state together with Bokhara had preserved a medieval atmosphere and kept intact the organization and the grades established first by Chengiz Khan and carried on by Tamerlane. The highest military officer was still the Atalyk; the Ming Bashi was commander of one thousand, the Pansat Bashi commander of five hundred, Yuz Bashi commander of one hundred, a system which still attested to the survival of the Tartar organization and the stamp of the Yassak.

But this proved to be a poor arm in modern warfare. Military operations started in 1860 when Colonel Zimmermann dispersed five thousand Khokandians and Colonel Kolpakovski routed fifteen thousand with a detachment of eight hundred men. In 1863 a converging movement was started from Orenburg and Western Siberia. The first column, under Verievkin, took the city of Turkestan which guarded the entry into that region. After Tcherniaev, a name memorable in the conquest, leading the second column from Siberia, took Aulie Ata, the two columns joined and captured the important city of Tchimkent. The newly acquired territory was immediately converted into a Russian administrative unit, the Gubernia, and Tcherniaev was made governor. In 1865 the latter acting on his own initiative conquered the great city of Tashkent with more than one hundred thousand inhabitants. Thus the Khanate of Khokand was stripped of its most valuable possessions.

The capture of Tashkent roused the Ameer of Bokhara who in his turn declared a holy war against the infidel, and hostilities now spread over the greater part of Central Asia. But the Ameer was beaten in his turn and lost his main fortress of Khodjent. In 1866 Turkestan was made a Russian governor-generalship and an extremely able administrator, Kauffman, was appointed Governor-General with such extended powers as to make him virtually independent of the Central Government. Like Muraviev in Eastern Siberia, he was given the right to conduct diplomatic negotiations independently in Central Asia and with the powers along the border. Bokhara not having paid the indemnity imposed after the war of 1866, Kauffman renewed hostilities and captured Samarkand. The moral impression of this conquest was tremendous throughout the East, owing to the association of that city with the memory of Tamerlane. By the Treaty of 1868 all these acquisitions were confirmed and both Bokhara and Khokand came under a Russian protectorate.

But Khokand's days were numbered. The new Khan of Khokand, a Russian nominee by the name of Kudaiar, made himself so hated by his tyranny and exactions that a revolt broke out against him in 1875, his own sons joining with the people to overthrow him. Kudaiar took his wives and treasure and escaped to Orenburg where he settled for the remainder of his days. Khokand was then annexed to the governor-generalship of Turkestan under the name of the province of Ferghana, which became the most flourishing and luxuriant part of Russia's new possessions. A modern Russian city grew up beside the native city of Khokand and developed rapidly.

Bokhara remained semi-independent as a vassal state, and Khiva was as defiant as ever in its desert fastness. As long as Khiva remained independent and menacing communications from Russia to Turkestan, Russia's hold on Central Asia was precarious. The Khivans carried out attacks on Russian convoys, totally undisturbed by the events in Turkestan. The double failure of Bekovich and Perovski made them feel secure, and therefore it became urgent to wipe out these memories.

But the task remained a formidable one, notwithstanding the adoption of the method of gradual approach. Khiva in the midst of its sandy desert was five hundred miles away from the Caspian coast, six hundred miles from Tashkent and nine hundred and thirty miles from Orenburg, which necessarily would form the base for any large-scale operation. The advanced Russian posts in the desert could only serve as jumping-off-places for the final attack, but not as an actual base camp. It was this distance from its supplies and reserves which in the face of climatic and natural difficulties made the task so formidable for any attacking force, taxing human endurance to the utmost.

The importance attached to the expedition against Khiva may be judged by the fact that the plan of campaign was worked out in St. Petersburg at a Crown Council, presided over by the Emperor himself. An attack on Khiva converging from all three bases was decided upon. The main column under General Kauffman was to advance from Tashkent; General Verievkin was to march from Orenburg to Fort No. 1 on the Syr Darya, wait there for the approach of General Kauffman and then to follow up the Amu Darya to make a junction with him. Boats of the Aral flotilla were to try and force the sandy estuary of the Amu in conjunction with Verievkin's advance. Finally, a third column under Colonel Markozov was to cross the desert eastwards starting from the newly founded Russian city on the Caspian coast, Krasnovodsk. Profiting by the lesson learned in the previous failures, much attention was given to a careful organization of supplies. By the spring of 1873 everything was ready, and Kauffman started out in a snowstorm on March 28th. Like Perovski, he lost a part of his camels and consequently had to leave half of his supplies on the way. Then in the beginning of May it became intensely hot, and the expedition met with violent sandstorms. The column stopped in the desert and erected a fort, waiting for an additional batch of eight hundred camels.

Upon their arrival the advance was resumed and then the real hardships began. The column ran into one hundred and twenty miles of deep shifting sands and the supply of water having come to an end, the camels began to die and the men, weakened by the intense heat, had to face constant attacks of the tribesmen. Kauffman fell back to the nearest well but its muddy contents was not sufficient for six thousand men. The danger of a part of the expedition dying from thirst was obviated by a native guide discovering a second well some thirty miles away, to which a part of the force was dispatched. The expedition crossed the sands in eleven days and reached the Amu Darya, but had lost eight thousand eight hundred camels out of a total of ten thousand.

By the first week of June, Kauffman had defeated a force of four thousand Khivans and taken the city of Hazarasp, forty-five miles from Khiva. In the meanwhile the Krasnovodsk column under Markozov (two thousand men) failed to reach the appointed rendezvous. On May 1st this force had had to make its way over a waterless sandy stretch fifty miles in length. At ten o'clock in the morning the thermometer showed one hundred and forty-nine degrees Fahrenheit and at midday it burst, ceasing to register.[32] Enormous casualties by sunstroke were suffered and when finally the stretch was crossed, a new waterless desert of unknown dimensions was lying ahead. The column fell back on Krasnovodsk, arriving there in a pitiful condition not only from the hardships endured but also from the constant attacks of the Turkomans during its retreat.

The Orenburg detachment of General Verievkin accomplished its program according to schedule and on June 7th was within three miles of Khiva and had received intelligence of the approach of Kauffman. Two days later the junction was made and Khiva was stormed immediately. The city fell and General Kauffman entered, ordering the immediate release of all slaves, of which there were some thirty thousand.

A treaty was signed with the Khan, giving to the Russians all territories on the right bank of the Amu Darya and the exclusive right of navigation on the river. The territories remaining under the Khan's rule were made into a Russian protectorate, and were opened to Russian commerce, Russians having the right to establish ports and factories. A contribution of two million two hundred thousand roubles was levied and all sorts of additional clauses made Russia's hold on Khiva secure; for example, no foreigners were to be

[32] Schuyler, ibidem, Vol. II, p. 345.

admitted without a Russian passport. Then after a while, the Khan himself decided to follow the example of his colleague of Khokand. He accepted a Russian pension, was made Lieutenant-General of the Orenburg Cossack Host, and retained his throne only nominally.

Russia's rapid advance all over Central Asia was being carefully and anxiously watched in England, and the repercussion of events in London was becoming dangerous. The excitement prevailing may be seen by the number of books and pamphlets published with such alarmist titles as "Russia's March towards India," etc. Sir Henry Rawlinson worked out a theory that Russia was approaching India like an army investing a fortress; she had laid the first parallel along the Orenburg-Irtysh line, the next one from Krasnovodsk to Tashkent, and was preparing to establish a third preliminary to the assault along a line running from Herat to Kabul. Needless to say that such clocklike efficiency on the part of the Russians, if it had been the case, would have given Russia the possibility of conquering not only India but the whole world. The Russian bogy later gave place to the fear of Germany and the Germans were also credited with carrying out machinations with scientific efficiency.

But the result of this agitation was that the British Government took official action and Lord Clarendon in 1869 asked the Russian Ambassador, Baron Brunow, in view of the rising fever of the public opinion in England, what this advance in Central Asia meant. Prince Gorchakov replied that Afghanistan would remain beyond the sphere of Russian influence on the condition that it remained independent and that Great Britain would not interfere in its affairs. This was followed by a series of conferences in St. Petersburg with a representative of the Anglo-Indian Government, Mr. Forsyth, for the purpose of establishing a line of delimitation between the Russian sphere of influence and Afghanistan.

The conquest of Khiva produced a new outbreak of excitement in London. The British Government made an unsuccessful effort to win over Afghanistan to an alliance and at the same time occupied Beluchistan. Following this in 1876, Disraeli had Queen Victoria crowned Empress of India. The general idea dominating British policy was on one hand to strengthen the prestige of Great Britain in India by increasing the glamour of the crown, and on the other hand to establish a girdle of semi-independent states as a padding along the "scientific frontier" which would keep Russian influence away from immediate contacts with India proper. Beluchistan, Afghanistan and Kashgar in Chinese Turkestan were to fulfill this function, whereas Bokhara, Khokand and Khiva were to be in the same relation towards Russia.

But the acute question about the actual boundary line between these two spheres of influence along the border of Afghanistan and along what territories might be considered a part of Afghanistan still remained unsettled. The disputed territories were Afghan Turkestan and the Great Turkoman desert stretching from the Caspian Sea along the Persian and present Afghan border to the Amu Darya, and at that time not yet conquered by Russia.

The English proposal was to consider as Afghan territory, first, Badakshan and Vakhan, second, Afghan Turkestan, and third, the undefined territory bordering independent Turkoman tribes and stretching from Andkhui to the Persian frontier. Gorchakov yielded on the first point, slyly saying:

"We are more inclined to this act of courtesy as the English Government engages to use all its influence with Shir Ali [the Ameer of Afghanistan] in order to induce him to maintain a peaceful attitude, as well as to insist on giving up all measures of aggression or further conquest. This influence is based not only on the material and moral ascendency of England but also on the subsidies for which Shir Ali is indebted to her." [33]

England was thus to take the responsibility for the actions of the Ameer and to guarantee his favourable attitude towards Russia. Gladstone saw the danger and repudiated this responsibility by saying in Parliament that he could give only friendly advice to the Ameer. This allowed Russia to say in her turn that she could not be bound by obligations, and so things remained where they were. A contemporary American writer says: "The attitude of England towards Russia with regard to Central Asia can hardly be called a dignified one. There are constant questions, protests, demands for explanation and even threats, at least in the newspapers and in Parliament, but nothing is ever done." [34]

[33] Schuyler, ibidem, Vol. II, p. 268.
[34] *Ibid.*, p. 269.

But it was this mood in England which made public opinion back Disraeli's policy of supporting Turkey against Russia in the war of 1877-1878, in which Russia was pursuing the mission of liberating the Christian populations from the Muslim yoke. Gladstone, who had invoked the solidarity of Christian nations in the face of Turkish atrocities, found himself unsupported, and Disraeli scored his triumph at the Congress of Berlin by humiliating victorious Russia.

These events, though they belong to European history, had important repercussions in the East and particularly in Central Asia. Although the conquest of the remaining part of Turkestan had been abandoned for the time being on account of the war in the Balkans, once more expeditions against India were planned by the Russian General Staff. When the British fleet entered the Dardanelles and was within sight of the Russian army standing before the gates of Constantinople, the long heralded war between England and Russia appeared to be on the point of breaking out, and actual movements of troops were carried on in Turkestan preparatory to a march on India.

This was to be effected by three columns. General Grotenhelm (right wing) was to march from Petro Alexandrovsk to Tchardjui, General Kauffman (main force) was to proceed via Bokhara and Samarkand to Kabul and the Khyber Pass, and General Abramov (left wing for the purpose of demonstration) was to go from Samarkand across the difficult Alai mountain passes on Chitral and into the valley of Kashmir. The total force was once more to amount to thirty thousand men.

At the same time a diplomatic campaign was being carried out in Afghanistan, and just as the Berlin Congress was opening, a Russian mission under General Stolietov arrived at Kabul and was received by the Ameer with royal honours. Three days after the arrival of the Russians, a British mission headed by Neville Chamberlain was announced. The Ameer asked Stolietov's advice and the latter suggested that the mission should not be received. But when the Congress of Berlin settled the issues at stake, the movements of troops in Turkestan were countermanded and Stolietov was secretly recalled. He left Kabul on August 24, 1878, leaving subordinates behind to wind up the affair.

Lord Lytton reported shortly afterwards, that all these conciliatory measures could not erase the fact that the Russians had been well received in Kabul and had succeeded in impressing the Afghans with Russia's power and instilling in their minds a hatred for Great Britain. The result was the declaration of the Second Afghan War by England on Afghanistan, and Field Marshal Roberts, in his book, *Forty-one Years in India*, pointed out how remarkably similar were the causes leading up to the two Afghan wars, namely, the presence of a Russian mission in Kabul.

The Ameer, who was clamouring for support from Russia, received the following letter from General Kauffman, written in January, 1879:

"Your Highness requests me to send troops. Probably you had not yet received the information that His Majesty the Emperor, desirous to help Your Highness has succeeded in negotiations with Great Britain in obtaining that the British

Government formally promised to our Ambassador in London that the independence of Afghanistan will be respected." [35]

Peace was signed between Great Britain and Afghanistan on May 15, 1879, and though Afghanistan remained technically independent, the Indian Government acquired virtual control over the country. After another renewal of hostilities the final treaty provided for a British protectorate; Afghanistan was to have no dealings with any foreign power outside of Great Britain, and the latter promised protection in case of attack by any power (meaning Russia). The Ameer was also to receive a subsidy from the British Treasury.

In this way the two great Empires of Russia and Great Britain, by expanding in opposite directions were coming dangerously close to each other. There still remained a gap, the uncharted region of the Turkoman tribes along the Afghan border. This region was populated by the Tekke Turkomans, the fiercest and most warlike nomads, bitterly opposed to the Russians. Their capital was Merv, once a very great city, one of the four imperial cities of Tamerlane, but at this time containing only some three thousand inhabitants. Its importance lay in the fact that it was located only two hundred and fifty miles away from Herat on the direct road to India, so that naturally the occupation of this city was looked upon with great concern by England. More important from the military point of view was the formidable stronghold of Gheok Tepe. These Turkomans roamed freely about their desert, at times

[35] Raskolnikov, Russia and Afghanistan, The New East, Vol. IV, p. 38.

menacing the Russian ports along the Caspian includ-ing Krasnovodsk, or entering into Bokhara. Unless they were subdued, the conquest of Turkestan was not completed, but by the very geographical position of this region every move Russia made there was fraught with the most serious international complications.

The first expedition against the Tekke Turkomans was organized in 1875 as a preliminary reconnoitering move. Colonel Ivanov with a force of one thousand five hundred men started from Krasnovodsk and struck terror in the nearest tribe by capturing its camp and ravaging the country. In the same year a second expe-dition under General Lomakin pushed further, and reached the river Atrek. This was the border of the Tekke country, and except for the difficulty of crossing patches of waterless desert in June, the expedition met with no other hindrance. In England, however, it was interpreted as a move in the direction of Merv and pro-duced tremendous excitement, Sir Henry Rawlinson even advocating war with Russia.

But the tension was relieved by the news that Gen-eral Lomakin had subsequently sustained a serious reverse. After returning from the expedition men-tioned, he had collected three thousand camels at wells some thirty miles from Krasnovodsk, preparatory for a new expedition. A detachment of two thousand men were camping nearby. The Turkomans had followed these preparations carefully, and on the night of April 15, 1879, they suddenly fell upon the Russian camp, and succeeded in driving away the camels in the sub-sequent confusion.

The Russian Headquarters ordered the immediate recapturing of the camels. Lomakin pursued the robbers and eventually overtook them. The Russian troops were suffering badly from the heat, the bad water and continual sandstorms which were affecting the men's eyes. However, they beat back the enemy, who was offering resistance by his favourite method of making the camels kneel and firing from behind them. The Russians, pursuing from oasis to oasis, went dangerously far away from their base and soon found the enemy well intrenched in sand dunes. When they started an attack, they found all the surrounding dunes covered with Turkoman horsemen. The little force, outnumbered, lost five hundred dead in a hurried retreat.

As usual the news of this disaster spread all over Central Asia, and it was necessary to take rapid measures to check the loss of prestige. A new expedition was immediately ordered, and this time the command was given to General Skobelev. Only thirty-five years of age, Skobelev had already acquired a European reputation and was a picturesque and romantic figure. He first distinguished himself in the campaigns against Khokand and Khiva. On one occasion, dressed as a native, he crossed the desert alone reconnoitering the road for the expeditionary force. Another time with one hundred and fifty Cossacks he attacked a Khokandian camp and put to flight an enemy six thousand strong. But it was in the Russo-Turkish War at the siege of Plevna that he made his name. Appearing in action in a white uniform on a white charger, he became

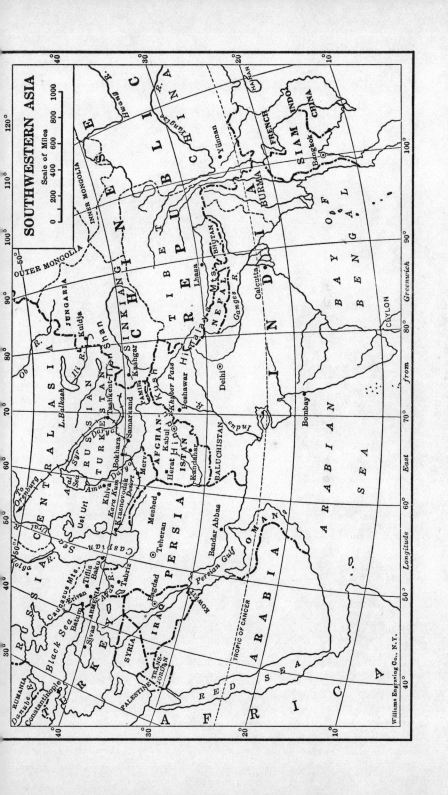

SOUTHWESTERN ASIA

Scale of Miles

0 200 400 600 800 1000

known as the "White General." But with reckless bravery he combined careful organization which made the troops under his command the best equipped and best fed. It was this combination of vigour with careful preparation which was to ensure his success against the Turkomans.

Receiving an order to avenge Lomakin, he said he would advance only when he was ready, and insisted that a railway be constructed from Krasnovodsk or any other point on the coast to the fighting front as it would advance. Then he proceeded to conquer methodically the tribes on the side, so that the Tekke Turkomans would be isolated; he took nearly two years to accomplish these minor operations. Only then did he march into the heart of the Tekke country, menacing their fastness of Gheok Tepe. He had received stringent instructions not to take Merv, for fear that the British might use the fall of that city as a pretext for occupying Herat. He pushed beyond Gheok Tepe, reconnoitering the country towards Merv. Only when he had covered the country with his outposts and secured his communications did he besiege Gheok Tepe.

This city, located in an oasis, had a walled enclosure of one and three-quarters miles in circumference, with walls eighteen feet high and from twenty to thirty feet thick, which were defended by twenty-five thousand Turkomans. After besieging it for twenty-three days he stormed the walls with only six thousand men and took the city, losing only nine hundred and thirty-seven men, whereas the Turkoman losses amounted to eight thousand. The fall of Gheok Tepe led to the submission of all the Tekke tribes.

There remained only Merv. The Russian Government cunningly invited the newly conquered Turkoman chieftains to the coronation of the Czar Alexander III. The gorgeous display of pageantry and splendour in Moscow and the tremendous revelation of military strength so impressed these natives that they came home, declaring that further resistance against Russia was a folly. Consequently in 1883 the Turkomans of Merv sent a delegation to Tcherniaev, who now replaced Kauffman as governor-general, and asked for the appointment of a Russian administrator to settle their quarrels. The time was appropriate because England was involved in Egyptian affairs. Nevertheless the international aspect of the submission of Merv remained dangerous and very nearly led to a European war. Before we discuss this problem it is necessary to examine the building of the Transcaspian Railway, an event of great cultural importance, which was facilitated by the annexation of Merv.

The first rails of this line were laid in October, 1880, at the insistence of General Skobelev to facilitate his operations. Starting from Fort Mikhailovsk [36] on the Caspian coast, a narrow-gauge line was built as far as Kizil Arvat (two hundred and thirty-one kilometers). The traction was not by steam, but by a method probably unique in the world, by camels. After the fall of Gheok Tepe the line was converted into broad gauge and changed to steam traction. It was planned to extend the line into the newly acquired territory, and supervision of the construction was given to General

[36] Ouzun Ada.

Annenkov and a staff of military engineers. General Annenkov followed the progress of the construction by living with his staff in a special two-storeyed carriage containing all the required technical equipment, which was hauled to the sector under construction.

The progress at first was extremely slow, owing to the resistance of the only half-pacified Turkomans, but by 1883 it became possible to advance rapidly. The conversion of the first sector into broad gauge took three years; although the first train reached Merv in 1886, only two years later in 1888 the road had reached Samarkand.[37] The main difficulties of construction apart from the danger of roving Turkomans, were the sandy desert patches and a large bridge to cross the Amu Darya. The railway passes through one of the most terrible desert regions in the world and the shifting sands more than once covered the track and destroyed the work already accomplished. These sand-storms remained a permanent menace until a special shrub "saxaul" was discovered, which when planted in hedges formed an effective barrier against the drifting sand. Last but not least among the difficulties was the heat.

The railway was formally opened on May 27, 1888, the day of the anniversary of the Czar's birthday, but much additional work was completed later. Branches brought it to Tashkent and Andijan, in the proximity of the Chinese border. A branch which excited special animosity on the part of the British was constructed to

[37] Tcharykov in his recollections "Glimpses of High Politics" gives the date as May 27, 1889. The date given in this work is taken out of the periodic press of the time.

run from Merv to the Afghan frontier where a fortified post, Kuchka, was erected. The total length of the line was one thousand and sixty-four miles and the cost was forty-three million roubles, this figure covering only the temporary structures, mostly of wood. Much more money was spent in converting the bridges, stations, etc., into permanent structures of iron, stone and concrete.

With the exception of the Indian system, of only local importance, this was the first great railway built in Asia, and its economic and cultural importance cannot be overestimated. It was a revival of the great Khorassan route, which in the days of Tamerlane was the main commercial line connecting China with Persia and Europe, and which accounted for the extraordinary prosperity of the great cities lying along it in Central Asia. With the construction of this railway not only was China brought nearer to Europe, at least until the building of the more convenient Transsiberian, but the moribund cities of Turkestan obtained a new lease on life. Modern Russian cities grew up at Tashkent, Khokand, Bokhara, Samarkand and Merv, Marghilan and Andijan. The population of Tashkent alone had nearly doubled in the ten years after the completion of the line; it increased from seventy-eight thousand to one hundred and fifty-six thousand by 1897.

An extremely valuable complement to the Transcaspian was the Orenburg-Tashkent Railway (one thousand one hundred and eighty-five miles) completed in 1905 and connecting the Central Asian lines with the All-Russian system. This railway crossed the great desert east of the Aral Sea which, as we have already seen, had been such a formidable obstacle for Russian penetration, and thus made possible an easy journey of some six days from Moscow to the borders of Chinese Turkestan or Afghanistan in a comfortable sleeping car without the inconvenience of crossing the Caspian Sea. Russian merchandise flowed easily into Central Asia in return for the greatly needed cotton goods and strategically speaking these railways gave Russia a definite hold on Turkestan, making possible rapid transportation of troops, a fact which was tested during the earlier period of the Soviet régime.

Mention must also be made in connection with this early period of Russian penetration, of the scientific work of exploration carried on by Russian scientists in unknown parts of Central Asia and within the confines of Mongolia, Tibet and Jungaria. One name is particularly conspicuous, that of Nicholas Prjevalsky, who acquired an international reputation through his work. For a time a teacher of geography in a military school, Prjevalsky started his work of discovery by exploring the unknown highlands of the Ussuri basin in 1867. In 1870-1873 with only three men and on his meager pay of a young officer, he undertook a daring voyage through the Gobi Desert to the Upper Yangtse and thence to the Di Chu River in Tibet. His description of this journey was immediately translated into all European languages, the first English edition dating from 1879. On his second journey through Eastern Turkestan he rediscovered the Lake Lob Nor, unknown to Europeans since it had been mentioned by

Marco Polo in the 13th century. The third journey
(1879-1880) brought him within one hundred and
seventy miles of the forbidden capital of Tibet, Lhasa.

Prjevalsky was the first European to penetrate so
far into that mysterious land. On a later journey he
discovered several new species of animals, such as the
wild camel and the *Equus Prjevalsky*. He died in 1889
during his fifth journey on the shore of the Lake Issyk
Kul. It is interesting to note the rapid transformation
these remote regions have since undergone. To-day in
the lonely spot where he met his death, there has arisen
a health resort for the inhabitants of Turkestan which
has been named in his honour, Prjevalsk.

CHAPTER VIII

THE AFGHAN QUESTION AND THE KULJA INCIDENT

IT is now necessary to see what the reactions were in London to these manifold activities of Russia in a region to whose fate England was so peculiarly sensitive. In the period following the Berlin Congress and covering the conquest of the Tekke Turkomans and the building of the Transcaspian Railway, we have the most bitter phase of the Anglo-Russian rivalry. It will be remembered that the attempts to delimit a frontier between Afghanistan and Russian Turkestan had failed. The Russian Foreign Minister, Giers, gave an illuminating account of the Russian point of view in his instructions to the Russian Ambassador in London, Baron Staal, under the dates of August 6, 1883, and June 8, 1884. Speaking of Russia's position in Turkestan, he wrote:

"This position . . . is purely defensive, considering that we have neither the intention nor any interest in menacing England in India. But it gives us a base for operations which if required can become an offensive one." And again, "England could strike us everywhere with the aid of continental alliances, whereas we can not reach her anywhere. A great nation can not accept such a position. . . . This has led us to build for ourselves in Turkestan and the Turkoman steppe a suffi-

177

ciently strong military position. . . . We are satisfied with this defensive position." [88]

A joint Anglo-Russian frontier commission was to work out a satisfactory frontier, but it became involved from the very start in a maze of futile technicalities, such as the size of the respective escorts, the presence of Afghan experts on the British side, and lastly whether or not the zone of delimitation was to be defined prior to the commission starting its work. All this led to delays and difficulties which, together with the growing excitement of public opinion in England, were reacting dangerously on the situation.

In the meantime, Adjutant-General Prince Dondukov Korsakov, commanding the military district of the Caucasus and consequently the superior military officer in charge of the Turkestan forces, inspected the newly acquired territories around Merv. In his report from Tiflis dated June 15, 1884, he wrote that the only object of Russia in these regions was the pacification of brigandish tribes, and economic development. As for the idea of advancing beyond the Amu Darya he calls it, "fantasies of ill brains . . . which dream of a campaign against India." [39]

The whole position from the Russian angle was clearly defined at an important Crown Meeting which was held in St. Petersburg on Christmas Eve, 1884, where it was decided that the frontier line must be traced at a distance of one hundred and ten kilometers

[88] Baron Meyendorff, Correspondance Diplomatique du Baron de Staal, Vol. I, pp. 18, 26.
[39] Meyendorff, ibidem, Vol. I, p. 121.

from Herat, and therefore include the district of
Pendjdeh and the Pass of Zulficar. The Russian troops
were to occupy and hold this line, but were not to
advance any further.

When the occupation of the Pass of Zulficar became
known, a new wave of excitement broke out in London,
and a discussion ensued to establish whether the point
concerned was in Afghanistan or not. Both sides showed
a lack of knowledge of the geography of the region.
The Russian Ambassador in London wrote that he
could not dispel the firm belief of the English that
Russia was advancing on Herat, and he reported military preparations. On March 15, 1885, Giers wrote to
Staal:

"Please inform His Excellency [Lord Granville] once
more that the Imperial Government has none of the intentions
which are attributed to it. It has no hostile designs of any sort
in regard to any part of Afghanistan and is desirous of main-
taining friendly relations with England, free from any mis-
understanding. It considers that the best way of realizing this
aim is to establish a good frontier between the zones of influence of the two powers." [40]

Following this and inevitable in such a tense situation came a clash between Russian and Afghan forces
at Ak Tepe, known as the incident of Kouchka. Both
sides threw the blame on the other, the English accusing the Russians of aggressive action, and the Russians
saying that British officers had led the attacking Afghan
forces. Gladstone made a speech in Parliament asking
for additional funds and hinted that war was inevitable,

[40] Meyendorff, ibidem, Vol. I, p. 177.

while the Russian Government announced that the port
of Vladivostok had been mined. For several weeks war
appeared unavoidable; then a suggestion of mediation
was made by the King of Denmark coupled with a Russian proposal for a slight modification in the frontier
line, and the dangerous corner was turned. After long
and laborious negotiations, an agreement was signed
on September 10, 1885, giving Russia the desired
frontier line.

A new flareup with England over Central Asia
occurred in 1892, when a further rectification of the
frontier of Turkestan in the Pamirs took place. This
incident was brought on through the occupation of that
distant mountain plateau by Russian forces, and necessitated three years of negotiations before a satisfactory
frontier line could be marked out there. In the Pamirs,
India and Russia virtually met, without even a buffer
zone such as Afghanistan between them; though the
mountain ranges some twenty-five thousand feet high
formed an insurmountable barrier for any large-scale
operation, the Indian Government feared for the safety
of the valley of Kashmir, and so viewed this new Russian advance with misgivings.

In one respect, however, this incident served a useful purpose: it furthered the scientific exploration of
this remote region, hitherto practically unknown.
Skobelev was the first European to penetrate the northeastern part of the range. He was followed by a number of other explorers, such as Gromchevsky and
Yanov, who completed the exploration from the Russian side. On the Indian side Lockhart, Littledale,

Younghusband, Sven Hedin and above all Lord Curzon saw to it that the scientific interest kept pace with
the political motive of trying to stem the Russian
advance.

In 1895 the controversy was settled through the
meeting of a Russian mission under General Shveikov-
sky with the British mission of General Gerard at Lake
Victoria in the Great Pamir. A successful demarcation
of the border from this lake up to the Chinese frontier
was carried out, achieved by the pooling of the results
of Russian and British surveys. In this way practically
the whole region was explored.

This incident is also illuminating from another angle.
It reveals a changing trend in Russian foreign policy.
Giers, the cautious and balanced Russian statesman,
was dying, and Russian foreign policy was in the hands
of subordinates who did not have the power to oppose
the growing influence of military circles. Furthermore
the strong-willed and peacefully minded Emperor
Alexander III had been succeeded by his weak son
Nicholas II. The result was that whereas the Foreign
Office was thinking in terms of international relations,
the War Office was concerned only with the strategic
value of the Pamirs as an advance cover against possible
British aggression in Central Asia. In the name of a
defensive policy, invoked by both Great Britain and
Russia, war clouds once more loomed in Central Asia.
But now we are in the presence of a real military party
in Russia putting obstacles in the path of the smooth
workings of the Foreign Office. In despair, Count Kap-
nist, temporarily in charge of foreign affairs, wrote pri-

vately to Baron Staal, speaking of the aggressive attitude of the War Minister, Vanovsky, "The beast is often as stubborn as an ass." [1]

This situation foreshadowed dangerous developments; Russia from now on was to depart from the methodic cautiousness of her former Asiatic policy, which had been the reason for her success throughout a century.

The repercussion of the Russian conquest of Central Asia was felt beyond the actual territory occupied by the Russian armies. We have already seen how Afghanistan was drawn into the struggle. On the eastern border of the newly acquired Russian territory, the Chinese province of Sinkiang, better known as Chinese Turkestan, was also to be deeply affected. Due attention has not been paid to the happenings in Kulja and Kashgar, the two important centers of this territory, so remote as to be scarcely known to the outside world. And yet here may be traced the initial cause of those events which in the last decade of the 19th century and the first two decades of the 20th century so thoroughly altered the face of the Far East as to unbalance world affairs, namely the attempt to partition China, the Sino-Japanese and Russo-Japanese wars, and the Chinese Revolution.

Though politically a part of China, Sinkiang is in reality an extension of Turkestan with the same ethnographic mixture of Khirgiz, Tartars, Tarantchis, Dungans, Uzbegs, Kara Kalpaks, Torgouts, Kalmycks, etc. The prevailing religion, Mohammedanism, and the

[1] Meyendorff, ibidem, Vol. II, p. 223.

prevailing language, Jagatai Turkish, made it completely distinct from China, from which it was also separated by the great Gobi Desert. The northern half of the province was composed of territories formerly belonging to Jungaria, colonized by the Chinese, it will be remembered, after the destruction of this Kalmyck state in the 18th century.

Here the Chinese founded the city of Kulja as the administrative center, and six forts garrisoned mostly by Manchus. They imported settlers from China and created military colonies populated by warlike Manchu tribes. In doing this they to some extent paralleled the Russian policy of forming Cossack settlements on the border. The Chinese also followed the Russian example in regard to Siberia, by sending their criminals to Kulja. A similar policy was applied in regard to the southern portion of Sinkiang, Kashgar, which after the fall of Jungaria was conquered by a Chinese army from Kulja, which practically exterminated the population by a great massacre.

Notwithstanding these gruesome measures, the hold of the Chinese upon the Ili region (Kulja) and Kashgar remained precarious. Infiltration of the population from Turkestan was continually taking place, and though the Chinese relied upon the mutual hatred of the various races, they could not avoid continual rebellions and unrest. Under these circumstances, this region was naturally particularly sensitive to the happenings in those parts of Central Asia which were to become Russian.

In 1862-1864 a particularly serious revolt amount-

ing to a general insurrection broke out, first led by the
Dungans and later by the Tarantchi. Chinese cities
were destroyed and burnt, and the Chinese or Manchus
massacred. One hundred and thirty thousand perished
in the Urumchi region alone. By capturing the city of
Urumchi, the rebels cut the communications of Sinkiang with China, and set up independent states. In desperate straits, the Chinese Government asked Russian
authorities on the Siberian border for immediate assistance, but the Governor-General of Western Siberia remained strictly neutral. He ordered the closing of the
frontier and the reinforcing of the military posts.

When, however, the neighbouring Russian district
of the Seven Rivers, the Semirechye, was administratively detached from Siberia and came under the jurisdiction of the Governor-General of Turkestan, Kauffman was given the right to conduct his own foreign
policy. The reasons which prompted Kauffman to take
action were the marauding expeditions of insurgents
across the border into Russian Turkestan, and above all
the events in Kashgar. Here a powerful insurgent state
had been set up through the energy of an adventurer,
Yakub Beg, who proclaimed himself Ameer. This title
had been conferred on him by the Sultan of Turkey in
his capacity of Caliph, as a result of the pressure exerted
by the British Ambassador in Constantinople. Kashgar's coming under the influence of Turkey, the heredi-
tary enemy of Russia, meant increase in the difficulties
of the Russian position in Central Asia. British influence being at the time paramount in Constantinople, it
also meant a veiled British protectorate. Indeed,

British and Polish officers appeared at Yakub Beg's court; a modern army of forty thousand men was organized by them and arsenals representing the last word in modern technique were built in Kashgar. Kauffman was alive to the danger of this situation. The Russian position in Central Asia was now menaced not only from the south, from Afghanistan, but from the east as well.

The Russian Government refused to recognize Yakub, and the latter in return closed his country to Russian trade, but in a typically Oriental way he wrote:

"The land of the Great Russian Czar is great and broad and full of all sorts of wise men and artificers, more than there are in the seven great lands. Our land in comparison to yours is a poor ruin. Now after the destruction of the Chinese power, during six years all has been destroyed that was good and that which commerce had created, so that nothing remains of it all. This was the reason why your rich merchants were not allowed here, for they could find here nothing but ruin." [42]

Finally a commercial treaty was signed with Yakub to the great satisfaction of the latter, who saw in it a proof of his recognition.

In the meantime General Kauffman was preparing for eventualities by occupying the Mujart Pass from which the Russians could watch the situation, and by having his military engineers build roads across the mountains leading to Kulja. Thus ready, he waited for developments. Presently a British mission under Mr. Forsyth came to Kashgar, and Yakub, now quite

[42] Schuyler, Turkistan, Vol. II, p. 318.

dizzy with the sense of his importance, wrote, "I have great desire to live in peace with my brother the Emperor of Russia." At the same time he started expanding his power northward with the intention of subjugating the Tarantchi Sultanate of Kulja. This meant the encircling of Turkestan by the British and their penetration as far north as Jungaria, the land located at the junction of Turkestan and Siberia. A flank attack through the valley of the Ili would be as dangerous as the great Mongol invasions of the past, menacing not only Russian Central Asia, but Siberia and European Russia as well.

Now Kauffman, deciding to act without delay, ordered General Kolpakovski to advance and occupy Kulja (1871). At the news of the coming of the Russians, the Tarantchi started a general massacre of the Chinese and Dungans, but this was stopped by General Kolpakovski, who threatened to have the Sultan of Kulja beheaded if he did not put an end to it. An official report to the Chinese Government by a Chinese scholar, Lu Tsu Han, who witnessed these events is worth quoting:

"The balls and bullets of the Russian army flew like a shower, like a flight of grasshoppers. The Turkistanis were defeated and in great confusion returned to the city of Kulja. The Dzian Dzin of the Seven Rivers [General Kolpakovski] quieted in every way those who remained, both Chinese and Manchus, not harming anyone. Not even a single blade of grass nor a single tree nor a fowl nor a dog received any harm or injury, not a hair was touched. . . . Happily heaven did not permit the human race to end. Now the leader of the Great Russian Empire, the Dzian Dzin of the Seven Rivers with his army inspired with humanity and truth quieted everyone. This petty foreign power [sic] saved the nation from water and fire, subdued the whole four countries without the least harm so that children are not frightened and the people submitted not without delight and ecstasy." [48]

In the eyes of this learned mandarin, the human race would have ended with the destruction of Kulja. What a lesson in humility for the students of the great events taking place at that time in Europe and America.

When Kauffman occupied Kulja he was prompted by considerations of interest to Russian Turkestan alone, without taking a broader view of Russia's policy in Asia as a whole. In a report which he sent to St. Petersburg after ordering Kolpakovski's advance into the Ili region, he motivated his action by the well-substantiated arguments of the danger created by Yakub Beg's designs on Kulja and the necessity of keeping British influence out of that region. But the Foreign Office in St. Petersburg, responsible for the general coördination of Russia's policy, was much puzzled. The danger of giving too much independent power to the Russian pro-consuls in the East became apparent when it was realized that twice within a period of little more than a decade, the Russian Government, anxious to keep up the traditionally friendly relations with China, had been faced with the awkward necessity of giving explanations with regard to the spoliation of Chinese territory by subordinate officials, Muraviev in the Far East, and now Kauffman in Central Asia.

Consequently, immediately after the occupation of

[48] Schuyler, ibidem, Vol. II, pp. 187, 188.

Kulja on August 28, 1871, the Russian Legation in Peking was instructed to inform the Chinese Government of the fact, and Mr. Vlangali, the Russian Minister, asked for the appointment of Chinese officials to discuss the retrocession of the city. Marshal Yong was nominated for that purpose, but as things began to drag the Chinese delegation hinted to the Russian representatives that matters ought to be speeded up, by saying that the Russian troops which occupied Kulja must be very tired and that the expense for their upkeep must be considerable. The Russian envoys replied that the matter of expense was of secondary importance, the main consideration being that of restoring order and that it was necessary to secure this first so that the Chinese domination should not be shaken any more after the territory was retroceded.

Seeing that no headway was being made, the Chinese concentrated their attention on Kashgar. Matters were entrusted to the energetic and warlike Chinese Viceroy of Shansi, Tso, who finally reported that he had overcome the resistance of the rebels and had reconquered Kashgar, Yakub Beg being murdered in 1877 and the other rebel chieftain, Po Yen Hon, having taken refuge in Russia. Thus came to an end the independence of Kashgar, which for a moment had played such a conspicuous rôle in the complex game of international rivalries.

In the meantime the Sultan of Kulja gave up his throne and taking all his possessions including six thousand horses, went to live in Vierny, a newly founded Russian city not far from the border of Sinkiang. He confessed after his arrival there that for the first time he had been able to sleep quietly without fear of assassination. But the Russian troops remained in occupation of Kulja.

The Chinese, having regained possession of the southern half of Sinkiang, now concentrated upon getting back the remainder. A Manchu dignitary of very high standing, Chong Ho, former Vice President of the Department of Personnel, was sent on a mission to Russia with the double object of securing the retrocession of Kulja and the extradition of Po Yen Hon. He had an interview with Prince Gorchakov in May, 1879, in which the Russian Chancellor asked for an indemnity of five million roubles as cost of the occupation, and the cession of a strip of territory along the frontier of Sinkiang following the line Ili, Kashgar, Tarbagatai, which would give Russia control of the mountain passes of the Tian Shan and the famous Gateway of the People, the Ili gorge. The Chinese Government stated that these conditions were unacceptable, but Chong Ho had already, on his own initiative, given his assent and on October 2, 1879, had signed the Treaty of Livadia, informing his government that it was too late. When the news of the signing of this treaty reached Peking, the Grand Council was called to examine the situation and declared that the treaty could not be ratified. The Ambassador Chong Ho was judged, deprived of his rank and title, thrown into prison and condemned to death, the execution to take place later.

In the beginning of 1880, a new Chinese embassy under Marquess Y—Yong was sent to Russia to explain why the treaty was not ratified. But the Russian Government took the stand that the cancelling of a signed treaty which had been approved by the Czar was an offence to the latter, and that the imprisonment of the Ambassador who had negotiated it was an insult, and consequently they demanded the pardon of Chong Ho. This led to the first serious quarrel with China since the signing of the Treaty of Nerchinsk in 1689. A struggle took place in China between the military party demanding war on Russia and the great Chinese statesman, Li Hung Chang, and others favouring conciliation.

Finally on June 26, 1880, as a result of the pressure of Anglo-French diplomacy, China agreed to accept Russia's demand concerning Chong Ho and released him, but the question of Kulja remained open, the Chinese demanding the unconditional return of the occupied territory. Both sides prepared for war, Russia mobilizing in Turkestan and along the Manchurian border. She also concentrated at Vladivostok the greatest naval force which up to that time had ever been assembled in Far Eastern waters. It was this that proved to be the decisive argument, and one more Chinese embassy journeyed to St. Petersburg, asking for the revision of the Treaty of Livadia and offering concessions in return.

The final treaty signed in August, 1881, and known as the Treaty of St. Petersburg, provided that Kulja should be returned to China but that the non-Chinese population in that region should be given the choice of remaining or emigrating into Russia. Actually, some forty thousand Dungans and Tarantchi had already migrated, fearing Chinese reprisal. A strip of territory (from the post Boro Kudzor to the river Kargas) was given to Russia for the settlement of these emigrants, but the remaining territories, including the all-important passes in the Tian Shan range, were returned to China. The other clauses of the treaty were: full amnesty to those engaged in the rebellion, an indemnity of nine million roubles paid by China, and the opening of the whole of Chinese Turkestan to Russian trade. Consular posts were to be established at Kobdo (in Mongolia), Kashgar, Turfan and Kin Yu Kwan, and a second entrance for Russian trade through the Great Wall was to be opened at Soochow.

Of particular interest for the understanding of later events is the attitude during this crisis of the other great European powers and in particular Germany. The reports of the French Minister in Peking to his government as quoted by Cheradame in his *Le Monde et la Guerre Russo-Japonaise* (pp. 74-79) are highly illuminating. On June 5, 1880, the French Minister wrote:

"Mr. de Brandt [German Minister in Peking] is credited with having stated that all the Christian powers ought to come to an agreement to crush China simultaneously, so that each one could derive from it what would be suitable for itself." Three weeks later on June 29th: "As I was insisting in my conversation with Mr. de Brandt that Western powers would get little profit from Russian conquests in any one point in Asia, my interlocutor limited himself to observing: 'Well, we will always fish something in the troubled waters.' " Then again on July 16th: "Mr. de Brandt does not hide the intentions of his government, the moment war has broken out, to secure possession of some well chosen position, from which the German navy would be in a position to give useful support to their trade operations or to the action of their diplomacy in Peking." Finally Mr. de Brandt is quoted as saying: "I do not think, personally that the Russians would easily overcome the Chinese. . . . The Chinese are so numerous, they have many arms and munitions and for one thing their field artillery is excellent and they know very well how to make use of it."

We have in these words the core of the attitude of European powers in this period of imperialistic development: the desire to secure territorial gains at the expense of China, restrained only by the belief in Chinese military power. When the weakness of China was to be revealed by her defeat at the hands of Japan, this fear was to vanish, and China was to face disintegration at the hands of greedy colonizing powers. It is curious to observe that it was to be Germany who would start this "grab and take" policy, Russia taking the lead shortly afterward.

CHAPTER IX

PERSIA, ASIA MINOR, TIBET, SIAM, ABYSSINIA

WITH the annexation of the Amur region and of Central Asia, an important phase in Russian history came to an end. The possession of the entire Eurasian plain and of its geographical extensions had been secured, and the natural limits of greater Russia in every direction had been reached. In the face of terrible odds the work of a thousand years had been completed, and the building of the Russian Empire was now an accomplished fact. Necessarily, further Russian activities in Asia now had to alter in character.

There remained the quest for the open sea, and Russia, having sought in vain for the possession of a port free from ice, first in the Baltic and then in the Black Sea, was now turning her attention towards the Pacific Ocean. Vladivostok being icebound during the winter meant that a naval base must be secured either in Korea or in the Gulf of Pechili. An alternative was Bander Abbas on the Persian Gulf, but the difficulties in securing such an outlet in view of its proximity to India and the impracticability of such a distant port were so obvious that this issue was not pressed. To this new aim must be added an evergrowing quest for markets. Russian goods were unable to compete in Europe with those of other European manufacturing powers, but they were conspicuously successful in this competition in Asia; hence Russia concentrated on Asiatic markets.

These two new factors are therefore to dominate Russia's policy from now on, involving an important shift in the moral aspect of Russian imperialism. Whereas the conquest of the Eurasian plain and its extensions had been a task of obvious necessity and had met with the complete moral support of the whole nation, this new policy was serviceable to only a comparatively small group of industrial, commercial and banking interests, while the greater majority of people, living on agriculture, were not interested in this policy and at times deliberately hostile to it. Wheat and agricultural products were exported through the Baltic and Black Sea ports and their destination was Europe; hence the landowning nobility, backed by the voiceless mass of the peasantry, really had no direct interest in this new Asiatic policy. When the latter involved Russia in wars, the Government found itself completely divorced from the great mass of public opinion. This was the first and most important cause for the ultimate failure of the policy.

The second was that by an inevitable effect of inertia Russia could not stop over-expansion, and whereas the nation instinctively felt that there was no more necessity for additional territory or new spheres of interest and that it was time to put a stop to expansion, the Government carried on a feverish policy of imperialism which made Russia's hand apparent not only in Manchuria, Korea and China, but also in Persia, Tibet,

Asia Minor, Siam and even Abyssinia. Her aggressiveness everywhere provoked many hostile forces for her to cope with, and her enemies took immediate advantage of this dissemination of her energies. To understand the cause of this aggressiveness it is necessary to examine the very important developments which occurred in Russia itself throughout the second half of the 19th century.

Russia's exceptionally rapid evolution from an agricultural state based on serfdom to a modern capitalist and industrial system was dominated by two events of paramount importance: the liberation of the serfs in 1861 and the rise of heavy industries about 1885. The setting free of some twenty-three million peasants resulted in the creation of an acute land problem, the rapid rise of democratic elements forming a radical intelligentsia, and the corresponding weakening of the political and economic power of the nobility.

The creation of great industrial concerns in large cities created a demand for labour which was filled by the migration to the cities of some five million peasants, where in unfamiliar conditions, discontented and detached from the wholesome soil, they formed a regular hotbed for revolutionary activities. The importation of foreign socialistic ideas grafted on these receptive stocks created a revolutionary agitation of ever-increasing gravity. At the same time a new middle class composed of industrialists, bankers and merchants, mostly liberal minded and in sympathy with the radical intelligentsia, came more and more to the forefront.

Together with these profound modifications in the

social structure of the country, Russia was undergoing a period of exceptionally rapid economic development, as may be judged by the following data: In the period from 1890 to the Great War the total industrial production increased fourfold, mining also increased fourfold, and the gold stock of the country more than doubled, the total railroad mileage doubled and the population rose from one hundred and twenty-nine million (census of 1897) to roughly one hundred and seventy-five million. In the face of the growing revolutionary menace, particularly in the reign of Alexander III, the Government adopted a stringently reactionary policy coupled with energetic fostering of this economic development. Education was hindered, but technical colleges and schools were opened. Great public works were undertaken, such as the Transsiberian Railway and the construction of the ports of Libau on the Baltic Sea, of Novorossiisk on the Black Sea and the great new harbour of Odessa, to mention only the most important.

These works gave an artificial stimulus to the Russian industry, and when they were completed the search for markets became all the more imperative. Thus the rapid economic development of Russia was the main underlying cause for the new aspects of Russian imperialism in Asia, and perhaps without being fully conscious of it, the Government was coming more and more under the influence of the new capitalist classes interested in economic penetration into these regions of the Asiatic continent where foreign competition was not too severe.

A field in which the Russian economic and political penetration was particularly intensified in the last two decades of the 19th century was Persia. Simultaneously and always as the result of the same rivalry, the British drive in Southern Persia became more noticeable, with the result that the once powerful Empire of the Shahs under the unworthy dynasty of the Kajars was in danger of sharing the fate of Afghanistan and the Central Asian states.

The Russians scored a great success when they were able to induce the Shah Nasr Ed Din to create a Persian Cossack Brigade. In 1878 the Shah undertook a journey to Europe to investigate what could be done in the way of modernizing his country, and especially of creating a modern army. After inspecting the armed forces of various European powers, he selected the Austrian army as a model for the infantry, artillery and engineers, and the Russian Cossack force for his cavalry. Accordingly, he engaged Austrian and Russian military instructors. The Austrians arrived first, so that when the Russian instructor, Lieutenant Colonel Domantovich of the General Staff, reached Teheran, he had the Austrian contract as a model. Having signed this contract, he brought over from Russia a staff of instructors and started his work.

By July, 1879, he had trained the first Cossack force of six hundred men and at the manœuvres which took place his Cossacks defeated the opposing forces, at a cost of several lives to be sure, but to the delight of the Shah. Seeing a photograph of the Russian Cossack Guard Mounted Artillery in evolution, the Shah ex-

pressed a desire to have a similar force. The Emperor
Alexander III made him a present of a battery of four
cannons with complete equipment, and the Shah enjoyed toying with this gift. In the meantime the Austrians had failed in their mission, with the result that
the Cossack brigade expanded into three regiments and
by 1883 had become the sole efficient military force in
the country. Manned by Russian officers it naturally
became a powerful instrument for furthering Russian
influence in Persia.

Parallel with this action by the military circles, Russian economic penetration was being carried out. Russia was approaching Persia with her railways. The two
countries had a common frontier of some two thousand
miles if we count Turkestan, and here the building of
the Transcaspian Railway brought the fertile Persian
province of Khorassan within reach of Russian trade,
as the line ran along practically the whole length of
the Persian frontier. More important, however, was
the construction of the Transcaucasian Railway, which
was extended to Julfa on the Persian border, on the
road to Tabriz, Persia's second city, and Teheran. The
special privileges granted to Russia by the Treaty of
Turkmenchai were now extensively used and made
Russian economic domination in Persia inevitable.

In 1889 a naturalized British subject, Baron de
Reuter, obtained a concession for the Imperial Bank of
Persia, with a capital of one million pounds. This bank
became the State Bank of Persia with the right of issuing notes. This important privilege was paralleled immediately by a concession of banking rights to Russia,

and in 1890 the Russian financier, Poliakov, founded the Discount and Loan Bank of Persia with a capital of twelve million roubles. The shares of this bank were owned by the Russian Ministry of Finance, so that it was a veiled government institution.

With branches all over Persia, the Discount Bank became a powerful instrument for economic penetration. It granted loans to the Persian Government for sixty million roubles, guaranteed by Persian customs revenues; it opened one hundred and twenty million worth of credits to Persian merchants for purchase of Russian goods, as well as credits against land mortgages; and last but not least it granted many loans of a political nature, to win over prominent Persians. Within the scope of the bank also came the financing of all Russian concessions in Northern Persia.

According to a secret agreement, all concessions in Northern Persia were to be given solely to Russians, and in 1891 an important concession gave them the monopoly of all transportation and insurance of goods, for seventy-five years. Later, the postal service was added to this concession. Next, in 1893 followed a concession for the construction of an Enzeli-Teheran-Hamadan highway which was built. A mail service by motor car was subsequently run on this road. The road from Ashara to Ardebil was constructed next. In 1902 the same company acquired the concession for the highway from Julfa to Tabriz and in 1913 this was transformed into a railway concession.

The railway was completed during the World War, being the first one in Persia. Originally this road was planned to be extended into the Transpersian Railway to connect the Russian railroads with Bagdad and India, but this vast scheme was thwarted by political obstacles. The Julfa-Tabriz concession carried with it the right of exploitation of all mines and oil fields along a stretch of territory sixty versts wide on both sides of the track. To this must be added a short narrow-gauge line to the Lake Van, known as the Maku Railway, and shipping on Lake Urmia.

Further, between 1883 and 1902 the Russian Government obtained the right to build and exploited the telegraph lines Meshed-Nasretabad (eight hundred and eighty-four kilometers) and Astrabad-Tchikishliar (fifty kilometers). A remarkably profitable concession was the one granted in 1886 to the Lianosov interests for the fisheries in Persian waters of the Caspian Sea. Other concessions included forests in Northern Persia, the port of Enzeli, the electric power and light of the city of Tabriz. Last and of real political importance was a steamship service subsidized by the Russian Government from Odessa to Bander Abbas on the Persian Gulf, an obvious intrusion into the British sphere of interest. This enumeration together with the fact that between 1901 and 1910 Russian exports to Persia doubled, representing sixty-nine per cent of the total trade of Persia, suffices to show what a hold Russia had on that country.

An issue which was attracting more and more the attention of Russian diplomacy because of the increasing gravity it was assuming in the early nineties, was the Armenian question. It was particularly difficult because Armenia, located between Russia, Asiatic Turkey and Persia, was territorially divided between the three countries and their boundaries converged to a common point on Mount Ararat. There were nine hundred and seventy thousand Armenians in Russia according to the census of 1897, some one hundred and thirty thousand in the neighbouring Persian Armenia and two million in Turkey. The bulk of the Armenian population in the Turkish vilayets of Erzerum, Van, Bitlis, Kharput, Diarbekr and Trebizond formed from fifteen to twenty-five per cent of the population in these districts.

The question had become acute as a result of the persecution suffered by the Turkish Armenians, and was assuming international importance. The task facing the Russian Government was to protect these Armenians from consideration not only of humanity but also of policy, in order to placate her own Armenian population, which was nervously reacting to the sufferings of their brethren across the border. On the other hand, it was imperative to preclude the unwanted intervention of rival powers on behalf of these persecuted populations. The championing of their cause by Great Britain would mean the extension of British influence into that most vulnerable zone along the Caucasian frontier at a time when the rivalry between the two powers was at its most acute stage.

The Armenian question had been inherited by Russia from Persia, when she obtained Transcaucasia by the Treaty of Turkmenchai. The Armenians were left with a large degree of national autonomy and, with their skill for commercial affairs, many of them rose to considerable wealth and prominence in Russian financial circles. After the Russo-Turkish War of 1877-1878, the Russian statesman, Loris Melikov, sponsored a project for the creation of an independent Armenian state, to be formed of the three Armenias and placed under Russian protectorate. The scheme was dropped with the advent of Emperor Alexander III and his policy of Russification of the alien minorities in Russia, resulting in the closing of Armenian schools and an attempt to introduce the Russian language among the Armenians. Still, because the head of the Armenian Church had his seat in Echmiadzin in Russian Armenia, and because he claimed jurisdiction over the whole of Armenia, the Russian Government conserved an interest in the question of the welfare of all the Armenians, and did not discourage the plotting which took place on Russian territory to start a movement amongst the Turkish Armenians.

The refusal on the part of the Turks to introduce any reforms in Armenia led to unrest, and this in its turn resulted in a series of dreadful massacres which under the slogan "Islam or Death" broke out sporadically between 1894 and 1896, organized by the Muslim population with the occasional help of Turkish soldiers. The number of Armenians who perished was estimated at about twenty-five thousand.

These events stirred Europe, and at no time was the ferocious hypocrisy of international relations more apparent. Great Britain showed as much zeal in securing reforms for the Armenians as she had shown in

getting the persecuted Balkan Slavs who had been liberated by Russia back under the Turkish yoke, and
Russia, who had fought a war on account of Bulgarian
massacres, was only lukewarm in supporting the British
action and by a policy of non-interference effectively
blocked Armenian reforms. The reason for this double
attitude was that Armenia was just one more pawn
played in the vastly more important game going on
between England and Russia all over the map of Asia.
The Russian Government now began to fear that Great
Britain was pursuing a policy aiming at the destruction
of Turkey. Furthermore, as Baron Meyendorff says,
the radical character of the Armenian insurrection
movement in Turkey was frightening the Russian
Government.

In regard to the first point, it is clearly confirmed in
a secret message from the Foreign Minister, Prince
Lobanov-Rostovsky, to the Russian Ambassador in
London, dated November 22, 1895:

" . . . according to certain confidential information which
is reaching us," he writes, "one is inclined to believe that Lord
Salisbury is aiming at the final disruption of the Ottoman
Empire. . . . There is more. The British Government is
credited with the idea of establishing a European condominium at Constantinople. . . . One thing is clear to us, that
this idea is directed against the most vital interests of Russia
and that consequently if applied, it would inevitably lead to
a conflagration, the incalculable gravity of which I need not
stress to you." [44]

According to G. P. Gooch, Lord Salisbury had sug-

[44] Baron Meyendorff, Correspondance Diplomatique du Baron de
Staal, Vol. II, p. 193.

gested to Germany the idea of partitioning Turkey.
Consequently, the joint action of England, France and
Russia in the Armenian issue limited itself to investiga-
tions by the consuls on the spot and to platonic suggestions to the Turkish Government which were not
heeded by the latter. But when four years later in
1900 Britain was engaged in the Boer War and consequently out of the picture, and when the Armenian agitation had subsided, Russia easily imposed the desired
reforms upon Turkey.

She also acquired the right of building all railways
in Turkish Armenia. This matter of railways in Asiatic
Turkey was another source of worry for Russian diplomats, and here again the question was less a matter of
the constructing of Russian lines than a matter of not
allowing other powers to build theirs, in certain directions which were deemed menacing to Russia. Already
in 1878 Prince Lobanov, then Ambassador at Constantinople, pointed out the danger of foreign railway
concessions in Asia Minor:

"In the place of a weak and ruined Turkey, we shall have
on our Caucasian frontier a power controlling tremendous
resources," and further, "Not only our Caucasian frontier
will be opened to an attack from a first class power but . . .
the Bosporus or the Dardanelles . . . might become a second
Gibraltar." [45]

In 1891 the question was considered sufficiently urgent
to warrant the formation of a Special Committee for
Railways in Asia Minor, and the Russian Chargé

[45] Popov, The Struggle for Railways in Asia Minor, The New
East, Vol. VII, p. 130.

d'Affaires in Constantinople, Charikov, now reported that the danger had definitely shaped itself, and spoke of the possibility of a British protectorate over Asia Minor or of a combined influence of Western powers, even more difficult to fight.

Indeed, German, British, French, Belgian and even Austrian capitalists were attempting to acquire rights for railways in Asiatic Turkey, and one concession granted to a Belgian company for a line from Sivas to Samsun on the Black Sea near Batum was of a nature to considerably alarm the Russian Government. The latter was carefully watching the future Bagdad Railway, which began as a modest concession granted to Germany for a line from Ismid to Angora, and when the question of its extension was discussed, the Russians insisted that it should be deviated to Konia instead of by Sivas to Erzerum.

In 1899 Russia made a formal if rather vague demand for a concession for a railway in Asia Minor, and the Turkish Ambassador was assured that Russia had less the intention of building one than of not allowing a German company to acquire rights for the line to Samsun on the Black Sea, which the Belgians had in the meantime forfeited. After several months of negotiations, a compromise solution was found, embodied in the secret agreement of March 31, 1900. Should the Turkish Government find it desirable to construct any lines north of the line Angora-Cæsarea-Sivas-Kharput-Diarbekr-Van (in other words in Armenia and the Black Sea region) and be unable to do so itself, concessions would be granted only to Russians, and on terms similar to the concession for the Bagdad Railway. Here a notable success for Russian diplomacy was scored at the expense of Germany and England. In these eventful years Russian diplomacy did not limit its attention to the Near East alone. Its main field of activity at the close of the century was to be in the Far East, but the events taking place there are so important that they will have to be dealt with in a separate chapter.

Mention must now be made of two new countries where contacts were established for the first time, namely, Tibet and Siam. Special attention must be paid to the geographic position of these countries with regard to India. Tibet stretches along the northern border of India and is separated from it by the highest mountain range in the world, the Himalayas, which make any attempt to penetrate into India from there well-nigh impossible. Nevertheless, from the English standpoint Russian influence in Tibet indicated an attempt to go around the defences of the Khyber Pass and the "scientific" Afghan frontier. Similarly, the importance of Siam to Britain lay in the fact that it represented the western approach to India through Burma.

As far as Tibet was concerned, relations were established in an accidental way which excluded the possibility of any long premeditated scheme on the part of Russia, but the move appeared as such in the eyes of foreign observers, and it is that belief which is important. It will be remembered that Tibet was a forbidden country, and that the mere fact that Prjevalsky had succeeded in coming within a distance of one hundred and seventy miles of Lhasa, was in European scientific circles hailed as a marvel. This barren unhospitable plateau with one of the severest climates in the world, and a wild, poverty-stricken population of which Buddhist monks constituted the majority, was hardly important in itself. But the supreme theocratic ruler of the country, the Dalai Lama, wielded an enormous influence over the teeming Buddhist masses of Asia, and this was to be taken into consideration.

Early in the nineties a Siberian-born Buriat, by the name of Dorjiev, succeeded in getting into touch with the Dalai Lama through Mongolian lamas. He revealed to the surprised Dalai Lama that Europe was not as he had thought one single country, but was composed of many states, and that there were two great empires fighting for supremacy in Asia. Fearing the Anglo-Indian Government along his southern border, the Dalai Lama, with Oriental shrewdness, saw the part he could play in this rivalry. He consequently sent Dorjiev at the head of an official Tibetan embassy to St. Petersburg in 1898 and again in 1900. There is no proof that the Russian Government was in any way alive to the importance of this move. The embassy was received in an official audience by the Czar, but returned with no more concrete assurance than that Russia wanted the maintenance of the status quo in Lhasa.

But the Indian Government took note of this, and when in 1904 Russia was engaged in the Russo-Japanese War, it sent the famous military expedition of Colonel Younghusband, who conquered Lhasa for the

first time in history. The Dalai Lama fled to Urga in
Mongolia, where he placed himself under the protection of the Russian Consul General. The parallel between these events and the two Anglo-Afghan wars
is striking.

As in the case of Tibet, it was Siam that first attempted to get into touch with Russia; the Russian
Government showed complete indifference to these advances until certain developments made it apparent
that Siam owing to its geographical position might be
useful both from the political and economic angle. As
far back as 1865, officers of the Russian ships visiting
Singapore reported on possible commercial relations
with Siam, and when a Russian squadron visited Bangkok in 1882, a positive offer was made by the Siamese
Government for the conclusion of a commercial treaty.
No favourable response being given to this request, in
1891 Siam sent an official mission under the King's
brother, Prince Damrong, to St. Petersburg to negotiate a treaty including a clause of the most favoured
nation.

It was discovered, however, upon investigation that
there were only three Russian subjects living in Siam,
the Ministries of Commerce and Navy both stressed
the complete uselessness of the treaty, and the issue
would probably again have been shelved if a political
issue had not been raised by the Russian Consul in
Singapore, who reported that the object pursued by
Siam was "to secure even on paper an additional pro-
tector in case of need." That very same year was concluded the Franco-Russian agreement preliminary to
the Franco-Russian alliance.

Siam, wedged like a buffer state between British India and French Indo-China, was the field of a bitter struggle for influence between France and Great Britain, in all respects similar to that which took place in Afghanistan. As in the case of Afghanistan, difficult negotiations were carried out between the two powers with regard to the delimitation of the frontiers of Siam, and after a war between the latter and France in 1893, a Franco-British convention neutralizing Siam proper was signed in 1896.

This struggle involved Siam in the European rivalries in Asia, and so Russia took an interest in Siam not only as one more move against England but also in relation to her new friendship with France. By supporting the French position in Siam she could count in return upon French support for her Far Eastern policy. Furthermore, with an increase of eight hundred per cent in production of her Baku oil fields between 1882 and 1897, of which eighty-two per cent was exported abroad, Russia was seeking new markets, and Siam appeared as a possible one. It was pointed out that this might be achieved through helping France to win a predominant position in Siam, since American oil, which had control of the Siamese market at that time, was introduced there through English channels. This view was endorsed by the Russian Consul General in New York. Thus both political and economic factors were blended in this scheme.

From now on Russia showed an increasing interest in Siam. In 1891 the future Czar Nicholas II, then heir to the throne, undertook his famous journey to the Far East for the purpose of inaugurating the con-

struction of the Transsiberian Railway at Vladivostok.
On his way, he visited Bangkok and was enthusiastically received. With the advent of this Emperor to
the throne, relations with Siam grew in cordiality, and
in the early months of 1898, the King of Siam, Chula-
longhorn, dispatched Prince Damrong on a mission to
Europe. The latter brought to the Czar a personal
letter in which, in veiled terms, Russia was asked to
assist Siam in the settlement of outstanding questions
with France.

Now the Foreign Office decided it was time to ap-
point a Chargé d'Affaires to Bangkok and the first Russian representative, Olarevsky, a specialist on Siam,
received secret instructions that his mission was essentially that of an observer. "Bangkok is a center of important political interests of several great powers and
their mutual relations on Siamese soil must be taken
into consideration in the general scheme of foreign
policy of the Imperial Government." [46] The Russian
diplomat was received with exceptional signs of honour
by the Siamese Government, and to stress these good
relations many young Siamese princes and nobles were
sent to St. Petersburg to complete their education in
Russian schools. Some of these remained in Russia for
good, entering the Russian service. When the Russian
Revolution came on they shared the fate of the White
Russian émigrés, but did not return to their native
country. This friendship resulted in 1899 in the signing of a treaty patterned on an earlier treaty with Eng-

[46] Popov, History of the Establishment of Relations between Russia
and Siam, The New East, Vol. VI, p. 40.

land, defining ownership of land, customs and trade dues and various trade facilities.

Interest in Siam grew in the latter part of the nineties as a result of the realization that Siam was an important subsidiary field in connection with the vast scheme of expansion being carried out in the Far East. A survey of these secondary theaters of Russian activity would not be complete without the mention of a curious attempt to get a foothold also in Africa, namely, in Abyssinia.

Here other considerations were at work, mainly religious. The Abyssinian Church, dependent on the Patriarch of Alexandria and representing to-day the last stronghold of Monophysitism, was by its historical antecedents closer to the Greek Orthodox Church than to any other Christian Church. Hence it attracted the proselyting attention of the Russian clergy at a time when the Russian Church was more and more assuming a missionary task. But we also find in the Abyssinian policy of Russia in supporting the French stand in the Franco-British conflict over Egypt, the same desire to oppose Great Britain which so nearly led to war between these two nations. The political motives were, therefore, the same as in Siam.

But oddly enough the early Russian activities in Abyssinia produced a violent conflict with France, which for a while endangered the growing friendship between the two countries. 1889, an adventurous Cossack by the name of Achinov, at the head of a party of one hundred and seventy-four people including priests, women and children, landed on the coast of the Indian Ocean in French Somaliland, near the city of Obok, occupying the little fort of Sagallo and hoisting the Russian flag. The Russian Government declared that this was done without its knowledge, and Achinov, calling himself a free Cossack, assumed the responsibility for his act. The French, with their customary love for direct action, did not settle the matter through diplomatic channels. The French Foreign Minister, Goblet, instructed Admiral Orly, commanding the naval forces in the Indian Ocean, to recapture the fort, which the latter did by bombarding it and wounding a number of Russians. The incident produced a tremendous sensation in St. Petersburg and only by direct government action was public opinion quieted; the political issues at stake in the rapprochement with France were too important for it to be endangered by such minor episodes, but nevertheless it did throw a bucket of cold water over the honeymoon of the alliance.

The incident, moreover, brought Abyssinia to the attention of Russia, and as a sequel in 1889-1892, a Russian officer, Lieutenant Mashkov, accompanied by Russian monks, made two journeys to the Court of the Emperor Menelik. The idea of founding the first Russian colony in Africa now took root, and was blended with an earlier suggestion by a Russian monk, Ouspiensky, of bringing the Abyssinian Church under the Russian Church by detaching it from the Patriarchate of Alexandria, supposed to be under British influence. For this purpose the Abyssinian clergy was to be trained in Russia. The Abyssinians responded to these advances, the Abuna or head of the Abyssinian Church declaring that Russia ought to take the Armenian, Cophtic and Abyssinian Christians under her protectorate. This expression was followed in 1895 by an embassy sent by the Emperor Menelik to St. Petersburg for consultation with the Russian Holy Synod.

At the same time the Russian Captain Leontiev and a monk, Father Ephrem, were welcomed in Adis Ababa. He was followed by Colonel Artamonov, who was attached in a commanding capacity to the Abyssinian army. When the famous incident of Fashoda broke out between England and France, Artamonov was found with his Abyssinian forces supporting the French colonel, Marchand. Russian interest in Abyssinia, however, soon waned, as attention became more and more concentrated on Far Eastern issues.

CHAPTER X

FAR EASTERN AFFAIRS AND THE RUSSO-JAPANESE WAR

In the preceding chapter we have seen that as a result of new economic factors in the development of Russia, a widespread impulse was given to the furtherance of Russian imperialistic designs all over Asia and even in Africa. Gradually the Far East came into prominence as the field where the main Russian effort was to crystallize itself, and here it soon became evident that Russia was over-reaching herself. By a movement of inertia, ambitious designs went far beyond the actual needs and the actual strength of the country from both the economic and military standpoints, and were to lead inevitably to disaster. To understand why this occurred, certain political and psychological factors now have to be taken into consideration. However much Russian autocracy may be criticized, one thing must be granted, that all through the 19th century it showed in its foreign policy and more particularly in its Asiatic policy, a remarkable sense of continuity and methodic cautiousness. This was due to the fact that during these ninety years only four Czars had succeeded to the throne and each reigned long enough to carry his plans to fruition. All four, Alexander I,

Nicholas I, Alexander II, and Alexander III were outstanding personalities, each in his own way. Furthermore, the foreign policy of the country was in the
hands of capable men who also held their positions
long enough to ensure continuity. Count Nesselrode
directed Russia's foreign policy from 1812 to 1856;
he was followed by Prince Gorchakov from 1856 to
1882, succeeded in his turn by Mr. de Giers until the
death of the latter in January, 1895. What was more,
each successor had worked with his predecessor in his
earlier career and had been carefully trained by him.
Mr. de Giers was followed by Prince Lobanov-Rostovsky who may be considered the last statesman of
this school. Though his cynical Armenian policy has
rightly been much criticized, he was a man of strong
will and purpose, but his untimely death did not allow
him to develop his policy.

After his death, a period of waywardness and reckless gambling started. The young Emperor Nicholas
II had shown from the very beginning how susceptible
he was to outside influences, and the Court became a
happy hunting ground for all kinds of adventurers
from occultists and cranks, including a Frenchman from
Lyons, a Buriat quack doctor and the notorious Raspu-
tin, to much more dangerous speculators and promoters
such as those who were responsible for the Yalu affair.
The Foreign Office in its turn became a mere reflection
of the moods of the Court and was more intent upon
guessing them correctly than on safeguarding the dignity and safety of the country. With an unofficial
shadow government weighing heavily on the activities

of the responsible statesmen, something disastrous had to happen, and the defeat in the Russo-Japanese War was the inevitable Nemesis of this state of affairs. Furthermore, and because of this, the kind of religious reverence in which the throne had been held by the bulk of the Russian people with the exception of a comparatively small radically minded intelligentsia, was rapidly evaporating and revolution was rising. This in its turn helped to paralyze the Government with fear and tempted it to find a diversion in foreign adventures, the usual and fatal policy of all crumbling governments. These explanations suffice to show under what unfavourable auspices Russia embarked on her Manchurian policy. Underlying it, however, there was a sound idea.

The Crimean War had revealed the acute dangers resulting from the enormous expanse of Russia's dominions in the Far East, and from the lack of adequate communications with the metropolis. The first of these handicaps was obviated by the sale of Alaska to the United States of America and by the concentration of Russia's colonizing efforts on the Ussuri-Amur region, to the detriment of Kamchatka. More serious was the question of communications. Without the foresight and genius of Muraviev, the whole Pacific coast might have been lost to Russia. It was natural, therefore, that the question of converting the Siberian postal track into a railway should arise shortly after the war. The postal track had been in existence in the 18th century as far as the Amur, and was later extended to the ocean. The great difficulty on the way was Lake

Baikal. This stormy inland sea was 400 miles long and surrounded by high mountains. The road around it was difficult and dangerous and crossing it by ferry was not easy owing to the roughness of the water. Consequently at first the idea of using the Siberian waterways for transportation appeared more plausible. Hence in 1843 the first steamer appeared on the Ob and twenty years later on the Yenissei. But as these rivers all flowed north it was necessary to use the tributaries which were joined by the Ob-Yenissei Canal, in order to make progress from east to west. By 1895 there were some 120 steamers on these rivers and prior to the railway they became the main trade arteries and mail routes. But the drawbacks resulting from the slowness of this traffic and the vast curves of the rivers were so obvious that already in 1875 a scheme was proposed for a railway from Nizhni Novgorod on the Volga to the Pacific Ocean.

The author of this plan, an English engineer, suggested, oddly enough, a horse-drawn tramway, and considering that there were some four million horses in Siberia, the idea was not so strange as it may appear. A number of plans followed, mostly for local stretches. By 1890 the Russian railway system had reached the Urals with three lines, to Tiumen, Zlatoust-Miassa and Orenburg. After careful consideration it was decided to extend the central line from Zlatoust to Cheliabinsk in Siberia. An imperial rescript issued on March 17, 1891, announced the decision of building the Transsiberian Railway, and the issue was immediately given priority over all other state affairs. A special committee was created for the purpose, and at the suggestion of Witte, at that time Minister of Communications, the heir to the throne (the future Emperor Nicholas II) was appointed head of the committee. This appointment guaranteed the rapid overcoming of all bureaucratic obstacles. The Cesarevich Nicholas undertook his notable journey around Asia to Vladivostok for the purpose of laying the first stone of the Vladivostok-Khabarovsk sector of the projected railway on May 19, 1891. To hasten the progress of the construction it was decided to divide the line into seven administratively independent sectors and to carry on work simultaneously in the various sectors. According to the priority of work to be carried out, these sectors were divided into three groups. Group 1 was composed of Sector 1—Western Siberia, Sector 2—Central Siberia, and Sector 7—from Khabarovsk to the Pacific coast. Next in priority came Group 2, composed of the Transbaikal and north Ussuri sectors, and finally Group 3 to be completed last around Lake Baikal and along the Amur River.

The natural difficulties to be overcome were very considerable. The line climbs on the Yablonoi range to 3,400 feet and thence begins a slow descent to the Pacific. On this crest the climatic conditions form the greatest difficulty, the temperature in July ranging from 77 degrees in the day time to 23 degrees at night. Owing to the bitterly cold winters and the absence of snow on account of high winds, the ground is frozen all the year around. In the region of Chita, the ground is frozen in winter to the depth of twenty-four feet and in summer twelve feet. The next difficulty was the great rivers to be crossed; the bridge over the Yenissei has a span of 930 yards, over the Ob 840 yards, over the Irtysh and the Selenga 700 yards.[47] And finally, the floods resulting from the overflow of these rivers in spring were a constant menace. The work was carried on simultaneously in Groups 1 and 2 with the result that these were opened in 1898, the first train going as far as Irkutsk from Russia and as far as Khabarovsk from Vladivostok. The through service along the whole line was inaugurated in 1903. The total length of the railway from Moscow to Vladivostok amounts to 5,542 miles and its cost exceeded 200,000,000 dollars.

When the railway reached Lake Baikal, the tracing of the railway line beyond became the subject of hot discussions and several variations of the original plan were proposed. The Buriat, Badmaiev, court physician, who acquired unexpected influence, suggested the abandonment of Vladivostok as the terminal and the deviation of the line via Kiakhta and Mongolia to Peking. Witte opposed this project violently, on the ground that it would meet with opposition from other powers. He stressed the point that the railway had not been constructed for military or political purposes, but was primarily aiming at economic considerations. However, he took Badmaiev's idea of passing through Chinese territory and offered the suggestion of avoiding the great curve of the Amur by cutting

[47] Vladimir, Russia on the Pacific and the Siberian Railway, pp. 292, 300.

straight across a part of Mongolia and North Manchuria, to reënter Russian territory not far from Vladivostok. He gives his views on the subject in his
"Memoirs":

"I calculated that this direction would shorten the line
considerably and facilitate its construction. Considering the
enormous length of the Transsiberian it was natural to try to
shorten the route. From the technical standpoint the Amur
region presented considerable difficulties. Besides, the line
running along the River Amur would have competed with
the steamship companies operating on the river. The Manchurian route economized 514 versts [about 450 miles]. In
comparison to the Amur region this province [Manchuria]
offered the advantages of a more productive soil and a milder
climate. The problem therefore consisted in obtaining from
China the permission for carrying out this plan by peaceful
means, based on the community of commercial interests." [48]

Unexpected developments in the Far East facilitated
the obtaining of this concession by Russia for the railway, which became known as the Chinese Eastern Railway. Korea, a vassal state of China and a bone of con-
tention between China and Japan for over a thousand
years, was the immediate cause of the trouble. Subjected to westernizing influences by the example of
Japan, that ancient kingdom was torn by political unrest. The liberals were seeking aid and protection from
Japan to carry out reforms, whereas the conservatives
were looking to China in opposing all such innovations.
Thus both China and Japan were involved in Korean
affairs, and an agreement was made between the two
countries by which both sides promised to notify the

[48] Memoirs of Count Witte, p. 74.

other should the sending of troops become necessary. Russia, alarmed by these disturbed conditions on the very border of her Maritime Province, massed troops on the frontier, and England immediately responded by seizing Port Hamilton which she later restored. Thus the circle of powers involved was gradually growing. The unrest led to an open insurrection which broke out in May, 1894, against the King of Korea who appealed for aid to China. Two thousand Chinese troops were landed in Korea on June 10th, the Japanese being notified of this according to treaty provisions. The Japanese, stating that the notification came late, sent twelve thousand men. After several suggestions on the part of Japan for joint action to impose reforms, the Chinese taking the stand that they alone would deal with the situation, war became inevitable and eventually led to a disastrous defeat for China.

We have seen in the Kulja affair that the European nations still believed in the military power of China; now her degradation had been exposed to the world by Japan and she was to pay dearly for her weakness. The Sino-Japanese War ended in 1895 by the Treaty of Shimonoseki, which very materially altered the balance of power in the Far East. The stern conditions imposed by Japan in this treaty were in some respects even more distasteful to Russia than to China, in particular the demand for the cession of the Liaotung peninsula. Japan had not only revealed herself a modern power but was attempting to get a foothold on the continent of Asia in the proximate neighbourhood of the Russian border. At a Council of Ministers in St. Petersburg the affair was discussed, and it was decided that Russia's policy in these new circumstances was to maintain the integrity of China at any cost, and not to allow Japan to take any territory from China. But as Japan had won the war she had to be compensated, and consequently China must be induced to pay her a heavy indemnity. As China could not raise the money, an international loan guaranteed by Russia was to be raised for that purpose. Prince Lobanov now set in motion the play of alliances and friendships, and received the endorsement of this plan by France and Germany, England automatically taking the opposite view. On April 23, 1895, two weeks before the ratification of the Treaty of Shimonoseki, the three European powers made strong representations to Japan, inducing her to give up all claims on Liaotung in return for an indemnity of 230,000,000 taels. Japan was also to get Formosa and the Pescadores Islands. Not being in a position to enter a new war, Japan was forced to accept these conditions, storing her resentment against Russia for another time. As promised, China got her loan of 400,000,000 francs, floated for the most part in France, under Russian guaranty. China, grateful for Russian intervention, sent an embassy under her greatest statesman of the day, Li Hung Chang, to Russia for the coronation of the Emperor Nicholas II. The famous Chinese statesman's opinion on Russia is of peculiar interest:

"I knew," he writes in his diary during his Russian visit, "that Russia was a far reaching Empire, but I had to travel fully to know how immense and solid it is. There are vast plains and tremendous mountains but there are no seas nor oceans coming in between, and I cannot help thinking how much more solid and substantial this Empire must be than the British Empire with its possessions and islands scattered like fowl over a large barnyard. . . . If Russia did not want to control us in all our home affairs what a strong alliance would be possible between us." [49]

The moment was propitious for raising the question of the railway through Manchuria. The result of the negotiations conducted by Prince Lobanov and Mr. Witte on one side, and Li Hung Chang on the other was the secret treaty of 1896 known as the Li-Lobanov Treaty, which caused so much concern and interest abroad that many apocryphal copies are in circulation right up to the present day. General Yakhontov gives the translation of the original in French which he discovered in the Archives of the Soviet Foreign Office in Moscow.[50] Article I declares that in case of aggression on the part of Japan against China or Siberia, both powers were to help each other with all available military resources, and Article II that no treaty of peace was to be concluded by either party without the consent of the other. The Chinese ports were to be open to Russian warships. Finally (Article IV), Russia obtained the right to build the projected railway across Manchurian territory to Vladivostok "in order to facilitate access for the Russian land forces, to the points under menace." This right of transportation of troops is accorded to Russia in peace times as well but "the junction of this railway with the railways of Russia shall not serve as a pretext for any encroach-

[49] Memoirs of the Viceroy, Li Hung Chang, p. 134.
[50] Yakhontov, Russia and the Soviet Union in the Far East, p. 365.

ments on Chinese territory." The railway was to be constructed and exploited by the Russo-Chinese Bank. This last clause concerning the bank was inserted at the insistence of China so that the railway should not be operated by the Russian Government, but Russia evaded the clause by the Russian Finance Ministry acquiring the controlling interest and owning the shares of the bank.

In conformity with this treaty, the contract for the construction of the railway was signed in the following September. The Chinese Government participated in the expenses to the amount of 5,000,000 kuping taels. The railway was to be completed in six years and to be of the Russian gauge. The land over which the railway was to pass would be furnished by the Chinese Government and the railway was to have the complete right of administration of this territory including erection of buildings and establishment of telegraph lines. Through merchandise from one Russian station to another was to be exempt from duty and Russian troops being transported on the line were not to be stopped on the way. The railway was to be constructed and operated by the Chinese Eastern Railway Company, established by the Russo-Chinese Bank, and the president and deputy presidents of this company were to be appointed by the Chinese Government. The duty of the president was to see that the Company fulfilled scrupulously its obligations to the Chinese Government. By repaying in full the capital invested in this railway, the Chinese Government reserved the right of buying back the line after thirty-six years.[51]

[51] Yakhontov, ibidem, p. 367.

The railway was completed in 1903. So far we have seen that Russian diplomacy had obtained and combined the two major purposes it was pursuing in the Far East, namely the exclusion of Japan from the continent and the extension of the Transsiberian Railway through Chinese territory. But presently a new issue arose contradictory to the policy mentioned, and Russia started trying to achieve this third aim also, thus revealing how wayward her policies were becoming. The evil after-effects of the Sino-Japanese War had not been confined to the Treaty of Shimonoseki alone. The weakness revealed by China was too patent not to tempt other powers to meddle in China. The extracts given in an earlier chapter, of the reports of the French Minister in Peking during the Kulja crisis, revealed that German diplomats were hoping for a war which would allow them to fish in troubled waters. They had been restrained thus far by an exaggerated opinion of Chinese power. Now the war had come, not with Russia but with Japan, and the resistance of China was broken. To a Germany which, with the fall of Bismarck, had just "dropped the pilot," and with a young and ambitious ruler eager for colonial expansion, the chance appeared too tempting. Profiting by the murder of two German missionaries, Germany launched the "Grab and Take Policy" towards China, which was eagerly followed by other European powers and forms one of the most disgraceful chapters in history. Though the missionaries were killed by bandits who had attacked a village and killed many Chinese, the German Government held China responsible and four days after the murder was known, the port of Tsingtao was seized.

The demand for reparations included the lease for ninety-nine years of the bay and port of Kiachow (Tsingtao), and railway and mining rights in the province of Shantung. Within a week Russia took similar action, and this was followed by the seizure of Wei-Hai-Wei by the British. France followed with a demand for a ninety-nine year lease on Kuan Chan Wan. Even Italy who had no interests in the Far East, demanded the Sanmen Bay on the Chekiang coast, but China opposed a firm refusal to the Italian ultimatum.

The new imperialist policy thus hastily inaugurated by Russia, was in contradiction to her previous policy and to her new treaty. The reason for this was that with the death of Prince Lobanov, the direction of Russia's foreign policy fell into weak hands and was reflecting the contradictory influences of Court circles. From now on we must visualize the chart of Russia's foreign policy not as a continuous curve as heretofore, but as a series of broken lines. The weak Nicholas II had come under the influence of the Kaiser, and at a meeting at Peterhof had heartily endorsed the latter's Kiachow policy. Tempted by this example on the part of Germany, the Czar embarked on a personal policy carried out mostly by secret orders, which completely disrupted the official policy of his government. In this he was supported by his subservient new Foreign Minister, Count Muraviev, and by the Minister of Marine who insisted that a warm-water base on the Pacific was indispensable in view of the growing power of Japan. After first envisaging a port in Korea, it was decided to occupy Port Arthur on the Liaotung peninsula, the

very port that Japan had been forced to evacuate after
the peace of Shimonoseki. Witte, seeing the danger of
this move and rightly considering it a breach of faith
with regard to China, opposed this policy violently,
but was confronted by the Czar with a fait accompli.
"You know," the Czar told Witte, "I have decided to
occupy Port Arthur; our troops and squadron are already en route . . . if we do not do it the British
will do it." [52] In what a state of chaos Russian diplomacy was plunged by this double policy may be judged
by the views expressed in a letter of the Russian Ambassador in London written to Prince Lobanov two
years earlier, October 29, 1895:

"The telegram of Your Excellency dated last Friday most
opportunely dissipated the anxiety created in the British public
opinion by a cable from Hongkong published by *The Times*
giving the news of a treaty concluded between Russia and
China, granting to the former power the right of anchoring
in Port Arthur, as well as the permission to extend the Transsiberian Railway to this city by passing through Manchuria.
. . . I was not duped by such strange information, emanating
from a suspicious source. . . . The disinterested spirit of our
policy towards the Middle Empire precludes any idea of such
an invasion. . . . It will be curious to observe the evolution
of public opinion when the truth will be known about the
fabrications of Hongkong The whole artificial structure
built by the press on a false assumption will crumble like a
house of cards." [53]

When two years later Staal saw his fears becoming
a reality, he appeared completely bewildered, notwith-

[52] Witte, Memoirs, p. 86.
[53] Meyendorff, Correspondance Diplomatique du Baron de Staal,
Vol. II, p. 283.

standing the reserve of a professional diplomat. The useful practice of keeping all Russian ambassadors abroad posted on the general developments of Russia's foreign policy by circular letters and copies of reports of the ambassadors in other countries sent out regularly by the Foreign Office, had now been abandoned.

Following the entry of the Russian squadron into Port Arthur, Russia demanded a lease for twenty-five years on Port Arthur and the neighbouring city of Talienwan, and the right to construct a branch of the Chinese Eastern Railway southward to these two cities. Li Hung Chang who at the time of the conclusion of the treaty of 1896 warned Russia of the danger of going south in Manchuria, opposed these new demands strenuously. According to Witte's "Memoirs," the resistance of the Chinese statesman was overcome by a bribe of half a million roubles, but the story has been denied by several subsequent writers. One way or another, China gave in, and Russia secured these new concessions by an agreement signed on March 15, 1898.

The next phase of this partition of China, in which Russia now took the lead, was the securing of special zones of interest. This new partition of China resulted in France acquiring special interests in the provinces bordering Tonking, Germany in Shantung, Japan in the Province of Fukien opposite Formosa, Great Britain in the valley of the Yangtse and Russia in Manchuria and generally north of the Great Wall. With regard to this point, Russia came to an agreement with Great Britain in 1899, in which Russia promised not to seek any railway concessions, or to interfere with

British railway projects in the basin of the Yangtse, whereas England promised the same to Russia with regard to that part of China north of the Great Wall. The fact that Japan also had interests in these regions and ought to have been a factor to be taken into consideration, was consistently overlooked in St. Petersburg. Japan felt this attitude bitterly, and moreover she had further reasons to worry over Russia's policy in Korea. The severing of Korea from China only made that country nominally independent. The Japanese were dominating it and their rule proved extremely vexatious, with the result that an anti-Japanese faction headed by the queen became very active at Seoul. The assassination of the queen by a Japanese agent and the flight of the king, Li Hsi, from his palace to seek refuge in the Russian Legation (February 11, 1896) gave Russia the desired opportunity to oppose Japanese influence in Korea. Russian diplomacy felt that it was of no use to get the Japanese out of the Liaotung peninsula if they acquired a strong foothold in neighbouring Korea. The King of Korea, from his safe retreat, now issued a scheme of reforms inspired by Russia, and cancelled the vexatious police measures of the Japanese. Japan receiving a second snub from Russia, decided to come to terms for the time. The Convention of Seoul, dated May 14, 1896, confirmed by the Lobanov-Yamagata Agreement, established a condominium of Russia and Japan over Korea. They were to recognize the independence of Korea, help Li Hsi in his reforms, and share equally in the construction of railway and telegraph lines. But difficulties started. A

Russian military mission appeared in Korea in 1897 and a financial adviser, Mr. Alexeiev, was appointed to the king. By a decree, all railways built in Korea had to be of the same gauge as the Russian railways. However, with the occupation of Port Arthur, Russia's interest in Korea lessened and, as the result of a new agreement with Japan in 1898, the military and financial missions were recalled and Japan was left free to develop her own policy in Korea.

These events, particularly the partition of China, were to have a deep reaction on the feelings of the Far Eastern peoples. The Chinese, seeing their country more and more encroached upon by foreigners, responded by the formidable general rising known as the Boxer Movement. This insurrection played into the hands of Russia. A revolt in Manchuria and the destruction of a part of the railway, led to the military occupation of Mukden and Newchwang. When the legations were in danger Russia moved her forces rapidly from Port Arthur to Peking, thus acquiring prestige, and the European powers were now eager to encourage Russia in her advance in China, in view of the menace to the lives of Europeans in that country. In December, 1900, an agreement was signed between General Kostorovich and the Manchurian authorities in accordance with which the Chinese disbanded their forces in that province and gave up all military posts and arsenals. A Russian Resident was appointed to live in Mukden and had charge of all important affairs. Manchuria was rapidly becoming a Russian province. Port Arthur was transformed into a great naval base and fortress, with docks and a breakwater, and a special artificial harbour in an inland lake was connected with the sea by a canal. Talienwan was transformed into a garden city, a great commercial center, and was renamed Dalny. Later on it was further developed by the Japanese and has become the third port in Asia. The Chinese Eastern Railway was completed, the main line east-west from Pogranitchnaya to Manchuli being 920 miles long and the southern branch to Port Arthur 621 miles. Harbin had grown into an important city. The French writer, M. Cheradame, who visited Port Arthur and Dalny at the time, was surprised to see how quickly the Russian atmosphere pervaded these new cities. Their resemblance to Moscow was striking.

With the settling of the Boxer crisis came the question of the evacuation of the regions in Manchuria occupied by Russia during the emergency. Russia promised to do so by zones, and the first zone was duly evacuated in 1902, but the evacuation of the second zone was deferred. By a treaty signed with China in April, 1902, Russia consented to reëstablish Chinese rule in Manchuria, and promised to return to China the sovereign rights in that province and to evacuate the entire region beyond the leased areas if there was no trouble and no interference from any foreign power. It was this last clause which served as pretext for deferring the evacuation. On May 17, 1902, Russia decreed the establishment of a customs barrier between Korea and Manchuria. The following year a vice-royalty was established for the Amur and the Kuantung regions (the Liaotung peninsula) and the new viceroy, Admiral Alexeiev, was given supreme power over military and civil administration and the right to conduct foreign negotiations. In September, 1903, Russia promised to evacuate Newchwang first, Kirin and the city of Mukden in October and the remaining part of Manchuria within a year.

But Mukden was presently reoccupied because of troubled conditions. At the same time a most dangerous group of financiers and speculators had won a dominating influence at Court and were to be responsible for a reckless adventure. A company known as the East Asiatic Company for Exploitation of Timber in Korea and Manchuria, was formed by the two most prominent members of this group, a captain of cavalry, Bezobrazov, and Admiral Abaza. Bezobrazov's influence over the Czar grew and the latter ordered that 2,000,000 roubles should be placed at his disposal. The Ministers pointed out the extreme danger of this policy and a reactionary journalist, Prince Meshtchersky, wrote a personal letter of warning to the Emperor, who replied: "You will have my answer on the 6th of May," and on that day Bezobrazov was appointed Secretary of State. It was Bezobrazov who secured the appointment of Admiral Alexeiev to the new viceroyalty, a man in no way fitted for such a responsible post. The East Asiatic Company started exploitation of the timber along the river Yalu, forming the frontier between Korea and Manchuria. It is odd to find that Russia with perhaps the richest timber areas in the world should require any further forests in a region obviously dangerous as a source of international complications.

Exploiting a concession granted by the King of Korea in 1896, the company started work on the left bank of the Yalu, that is to say on Korean territory, and early in January some Russian troops came to guard this concession. Japan, who had been negotiating for a long while with Russia without making any progress, now suddenly, without any declaration of war, attacked the Russian fleet in Port Arthur and the war started.

No more disastrous and badly conducted war could be found in the whole of Russia's history, and it was a clear evidence of the complete moral breakdown of the régime. Russia did not score a single victory. It is true she was labouring under exceptional handicaps. First of all, the front was practically 6,000 miles away from the base, with one single track railway connecting it. Then revolution was rife and broke out during the war. Public opinion was practically unanimously opposed to this war and consequently the country was morally disunited, this alone preparing for disaster. Furthermore, Russia completely underestimated Japan and considered her on the same level as China, over whom she had scored such easy successes in the Boxer Rebellion. Hence the war was fought at first with only local units, and the error of the Boer War was repeated, i.e. the sending of too small contingents. Lastly, the extremely inefficient leadership of General Kuropatkin revealed that a man who earned a brilliant reputation as Chief of Staff may lack the qualifications of a Commander in Chief.

With Port Arthur taken after a long siege, the Russian field army having been pushed back beyond Mukden in successive battles, the fleet sunk at Tsushima and the country aflame with revolution, Nicholas II, discouraged, sued for peace the very day that the new Commander in Chief reported that the army was ready for an advance. Indeed, after several months of reorganization during the winter, the army, now under General Linevich, was again in good fighting order whereas the Japanese were showing signs of a near breakdown after a year and a half of continuous warfare. General Linevich therefore asked to wait a few weeks more for spring before starting a counter-offensive, and his message was endorsed by all the commanding generals. But Nicholas II was not a Peter the Great; hence the armistice was signed at an extremely disadvantageous moment. It required all the skill of Witte and the mediation of President Roosevelt to secure exceptionally advantageous peace conditions. The Treaty of Portsmouth, signed on September 5, 1905, recognized the special interests of Japan in Korea, and Russia and Japan promised to evacuate Manchuria simultaneously except for the leased Liaotung peninsula, where Japan took over Russia's rights. The southern branch of the Chinese Eastern Railway between Changchun and Port Arthur with all mining and other rights was handed over to Japan. As for purely Russian territories, Russia ceded half of the island of Sakhalin along the 50th degree parallel, and further, Russia granted special fishing rights to Japan in the seas of Okhotsk and Behring. No contribution was paid but an amount was charged to Russia for the upkeep of prisoners of war.

Witte deserved the title of Count given to him in recognition of his services.

CHAPTER XI

FROM THE RUSSO-JAPANESE WAR TO THE WORLD WAR

THE Russo-Japanese War had tremendous after-effects in Asia. For the first time since the 16th century, an Asiatic power had been victorious in a struggle against a major European power. Asia thrilled and took note of the lesson; Japan's method of using European technique to fight Europe proved correct. Hence an enormous stimulus was given to the awakening of Asia all over the continent; the Asiatic revolutionary movements were encouraged and the attitude of the coloured races towards the European colonizers stiffened. As for Russia, for the first time since the days of John the Terrible, her continuous expansion had been checked and she was aware that this might mean the beginning of a new wave in the opposite direction. Once more Asia, as in pre-Muscovite days, was attacking, and though so far limited to the action of a distant island realm, the movement might swell again into a new tidal wave in a not too distant future. Faced with this situation, Russian diplomacy showed a realistic attitude, and with that continuity of purpose which had marked its action except for the wild gamble preceding the war, it started picking up the threads where they had been severed.

The loss of the war had resulted in a tremendous lowering of Russian prestige, which reacted all over the continent, from the Far East to Persia and Asia Minor. Hence abandoning all ideas of revenge, Russia worked for the conservation of the new status quo which would enable her to regain full hold of those regions where her influence had been weakened. To achieve this it was necessary to create friendly relations with her former foes in Asia—Japan and England, now blended into one by their alliance. This result was obtained barely two years after the war by the two conventions of 1907, the net result of which was to define Russia's sphere of influence in Asia and leave her a free hand to intensify her drive within that zone. The convention with Japan settled the outstanding issues in the Far East, and the one with England those in Central Asia and the Near East. Never had Russia's position been so clear, and once this new orientation of policy became a reality, circumstances irresistibly drove Russia to a closer coöperation with her new friends, leading in a few years to virtual alliances. In the Near and Middle East this was caused by the increasingly menacing rôle played by Germany, a newcomer in Asia, and England and Russia now joined hands to meet this competition. The same happened in the Far East, where the increasing interest shown by the United States in China and Manchuria and in particular the proposal of neutralization of Manchurian railways, brought Russia and Japan closely together. The stage was thus set in Asia for the combination of alliances which existed during the Great War.

These two conventions therefore mark a turning point in Russia's policy and from the historical angle their interest is of equal importance. The Russo-Japanese Convention of 1907, signed by Iswolsky and Baron Motono, put as object the desire "to consolidate the relations of peace and neighbourliness which have happily been reëstablished between Japan and Russia." Accordingly, "Each of the High Contracting Parties engages to respect the present territorial integrity of the other and all the rights accruing to one and the other Party from the treaties, conventions and contracts in force between them and China." [54] Article II guaranteed the integrity of China and the principle of equal opportunities for all nations in that country. However, of far greater importance was the secret convention, delimitating the mutual spheres of interest in Manchuria, Korea and Mongolia. According to this document Russia promised not to interfere in Japanese activities in Korea, and Japan promised the same for Russian interests in Outer Mongolia. Manchuria was divided into respective spheres of influence by a line starting from the frontier of Russia and Korea to Hsiushuichan, thence along the Sungari River and the Nunkiang River to its junction with the river Tolaho, from which point it followed the course of the last-named river up to the 122nd meridian east. In this way Russia reserved for herself the northern part of Manchuria through which passed the Chinese Eastern Railway, and the adjoining Outer Mongolia. Japan

[54] Yakhontov, Russia and the Soviet Union in the Far East, appendices, p. 374.

was left a free hand in South Manchuria which she immediately started developing by investing about two billion yen, and by building in addition to the South Manchurian Railway the vitally important Mukden-Antung Railway which connected the capital of Manchuria with Korea. But above all, she was now in a position to annex Korea to her empire, and this event followed in 1910.

Russia, on her side, consolidated her position in the zone of the Chinese Eastern Railway which was occupied by a strong corps of about thirty thousand men of all arms, camouflaged as frontier police and customs guards (Pogranichnaia Straja). She then undertook to make the best of the privileges of the railway contract of 1896 which remained hers after the Portsmouth Treaty. She reasserted her rights with regard to administration of the cities and localities in the railway zone. Foreigners living in the zone were taxed on equal terms with Russian subjects, the money to be used for the needs of the zone. They were further subjected to disciplinary measures by the Russian police in case of breach of the peace. An agreement signed in 1914 with most of the powers with the exception of the United States, confirmed this status. Harbin, which was a Chinese hamlet in 1896, was deliberately planned by its constructors as the future headquarters of the railway, and became the metropolis of Northern Manchuria with a population of several hundred thousand. New Harbin, or the adjoining Russian city, had a white population of some forty thousand. The economic value of the railway proved to be of great im-

portance to Russia as may be judged by the following
figures: When the traffic was opened in 1902 there
were fourteen million poods or approximately a quarter of a million tons of merchandise transported. By
1912 the figure had risen to sixty-eight million poods
or approximately one million tons. This led to the settling of some two hundred thousand Russians in the
zone and resulted in the springing up of various industrial and commercial enterprises, including thirty-three
mills. Furthermore, by two agreements between the
Russian Government and the Chinese provincial administration of Heilungkiang and Kirin in 1907, details were worked out for the exploitation of coal mines,
gold mines and forests in the regions traversed by the
line, and effectively the railway was duly provided
with coal from the Dalai Nor coal fields.

However, although the work of exploitation of the
railway zone and its colonization was sponsored practically entirely by the Government, it met with comparatively little response on the part of private Russian enterprise. Such private traders and settlers who
had ventured there had had an uphill and often losing
battle against Chinese commercial enterprise. This
has been the subject of bitter criticism on the part of
many Russian writers prone to criticize if brilliant results were not immediately available. What these
writers had overlooked was that the colonization and
development of Northern Manchuria was of secondary
importance. Just as in the case of the Canal Zone, with
which this railway may be compared in so many respects, the important feature was the Canal and not the

American colonization of Panama, so here the paramount issue was to hold the railway and not to allow it to fall into alien hands. Running parallel to the Siberian frontier for approximately one thousand miles, it made possible the rapid concentration of an enemy army at any most vulnerable point. Furthermore, the railway flanked the Maritime Province with Vladivostok, and its seizure would actually have led to the isolation of this rich province and the only stretch of open seacoast Russia had, because it would make the roundabout traffic along the Amur virtually impossible. Just because this railway formed an intrinsic part of the Russian railway system and was built to suit Russian strategic and economic requirements, its permanent passing into other hands would be particularly dangerous.

Another criticism often brought up by foreigners, is based on the results obtained by Japan and Russia in their respective zones in Manchuria. It must however be remembered that Japan had concentrated all her energies on the exploitation of Manchuria and Korea, whereas Russia as we have seen in the past and will see in this chapter, had diffused her energies over practically the whole map of Asia. This has been the fatal mistake of the Czarist policy.

A criticism much more to the point was made by Mr. Ostroumov, a former manager of the railway, who was quoted as saying that Russia had spent eight hundred million roubles to settle on this railway two hundred thousand Russians and fifteen million Chinese. This was indeed the problem which was to cause infinite trouble in the future. The Chinese Eastern Railway served as a powerful attraction for Chinese immigration. The Chinese introduced intensive agriculture and were instrumental in making the formerly deserted Northern Manchuria one of the most flourishing regions in the Far East. In place of wandering Manchu nomads, a highly skilled agricultural population settled down more and more densely. The crops introduced by them were essentially for exportation, hence these settlers had to be in the vicinity of a railway. This was particularly true of the main industry of these regions, the soya bean. It attracted yearly from China a seasonable migration of 150,000 skilled labourers, who for this reason established themselves in the zone of the Chinese Eastern Railway. They were followed by permanent settlers who started moving more and more northward into the still comparatively deserted parts of Manchuria, beyond the railway zone in the vast bow formed by the Amur, and were penetrating dangerously into the region which formed an incurvation of China into Siberia. Russia had thus created for herself a problem of extreme gravity.

These considerations must be born in mind to understand Russia's reaction to the Knox proposal for the neutralization of Manchurian railways, advanced in November, 1909, at the same time as an Anglo-American consortium under J. P. Morgan and Kuhn, Loeb & Co., had obtained a concession from the Chinese Government for a railway cutting clear across the Chinese Eastern Railway to Aigun on the Amur at the northernmost section of the bend of the river opposite the

Russian city of Blagovieschensk. The American interests, to which E. H. Harriman must be added, were also considering the ultimate purchase of the Chinese Eastern Railway and the South Manchurian Railway. These suggestions interfered with Russia's interests as much as a proposal for the neutralization of the Panama Canal or the formation of a European consortium for the construction of the Nicaraguan Canal and the purchase of the Canal Zone would affect American interests. This menace induced Russia to come closer to Japan, equally affected by these schemes. The Russo-Japanese Convention of 1910, to which a secret convention was joined, was the result. In these treaties the maintenance of the status quo as fixed by the Agreement of 1907 and the promise of mutual non-interference was stressed with great vigour, and a new important clause was added:

"To insure the working of their mutual engagements the two High Contracting Parties will always enter frankly and honestly into communication in all matters of common concern to their special interests in Manchuria. In case these special interests should be threatened, the two High Contracting Parties shall agree on the measures to be taken in regard to common action, or the support to be accorded for the protection and defence of these interests." (Article V of the Secret Convention.)[55]

This agreement blocked foreign intervention in Manchuria and Russia now felt secure to turn her attention in the Far East to Mongolian affairs. But she still was not immune from underhand attempts of the Japanese

[55] Yakhontov, ibidem, p. 378.

to overflow into the Russian zone, and to get a commercial control of the affairs by a planned invasion of Japanese business firms. Japan also began expanding into Inner Mongolia and this required a new convention between the two powers for the settlement of their respective positions in Mongolia. In the meanwhile, in 1911 the Chinese Revolution broke out, the third in Asia, having been preceded by those of Persia and Turkey. This great wave of revolutions which was the dynamic outcome of contact of the crumbling Asiatic civilizations with Western materialism, was still only in its early stage. Consequently at the time, European powers derived benefit from the weakening of the established order in Asia, and did not see lying ahead the tremendous challenge to their power as a result of the revitalizing effects of this new quest for life amongst Asiatic peoples. The Chinese Revolution was a boon to Russia in Manchuria and particularly in Mongolia.

It will be remembered under what circumstances the Mongolians were conquered by the Chinese in the 18th century. A century and a half of Chinese domination did not bring the two races any closer. The Mongolians looked upon the Chinese as alien conquerors and the Chinese considered Mongolia as a colony. It was ruled from Peking by a special colonial department and it was considered by the Chinese solely as a colony for exploitation, presenting opportunities to get-rich-quick. Only some one hundred thousand Chinese had settled in this vast country covering over one million square miles. They formed distinct colonies of their own, living in separate quarters in the rare cities such

as Urga, Kobdo, Uliassutái and Maimachin. But as
elsewhere, they achieved complete control over the
economic life of the country. Twenty-five Chinese
firms ruled the Mongolian market, and the leading
Chinese bank, Da Shen Kun, with a capital of fifteen
million dollars had an annual turnover of one million
dollars. Particularly distasteful to the Mongols was
a method widely employed by the Chinese, of selling
the scant necessities of life on credit under the joint
guarantee of the Khoshun, or the clan. This method
ruined the individual debtor, who was faced with either
repaying his debt under pressure and most onerous
conditions or with being ostracized by the clan.

As for the rest, nothing had changed much since the
days of Chengiz Khan. The Khoshuns were still ruled
by princes claiming to be of the blood of Chengiz, and
feudal conditions still prevailed with a large propor-
tion of the population in serfdom. The Mongols remained the primitive nomads migrating with their
Yurtas (huts) from place to place in search of pastures.
Barely one per cent of the population was estimated
as literate, though a habit of consecrating the second
son of the family to religion made forty-four per cent
of the population Buddhist lamas. These possessed a
certain oral tradition and knowledge imported from
Tibet, covering in a primitive way astrology, astron-
omy, medicine and demonology. Russian explorers
had been interested in Mongolia all through the 19th
century. Gradually a small infiltration of Russian settlers took place across the Siberian border, and like the
Chinese, they settled in the cities in separate quarters.

Prior to the Chinese Revolution some five thousand
Russians were to be found in Mongolia, and had succeeded in capturing from the Chinese one-third of the
trade. They introduced Western methods and started
the industrial development of the country. Gold was
discovered and this led to the formation of an important mining concern, the Mongolor. Also, some twenty
leather factories were established.

After the Russo-Japanese War and as a result of
taking stock of her position in Asia, the Russian Government began giving support to Russian enterprises
in Mongolia. When the Chinese Revolution broke out,
it was easy to flame up the discontent of the Mongols
and foster a separatist movement. Hence Mongolia
separated from China and became once more an independent theocracy under the Khutukhta, or the Bobdo
Gegen, residing at Urga. The latter claimed to be the
twenty-third and last reincarnation on earth of Djebt-
sun Damba Khutukhta, a disciple of Buddha, and this
fact was to be of paramount importance later. Apart
from this constitutional change, the social structure of
Mongolia remained untouched. The hated joint guarantee of debts by Khoshuns was immediately abolished
and resulted in the loss of seventy-five per cent for the
Chinese trade. Now the Russians conquered the market. Russian currency ousted Chinese notes, the only
previous currency except for the local means of exchange, sheep, tea and silver. The Siberian Commercial Bank in 1915 opened a subsidiary bank named the
National Bank of Mongolia. A Russian financial adviser, S. Kozin, was appointed to the Khutukhta's court,

to put order in Mongolian finances, which was done with the aid of a loan of four million roubles granted by the Russian Government. During the Great War, huge purchases of cattle were made in Mongolia by a Russian commission, named the Mongolian Expedition; some two hundred and fifty thousand head of cattle were driven into Siberia. Mongolia was gradually becoming a Russian colony.

The international aspect of this new situation had to be regularized and this was done in a series of agreements of which the first was the Convention of 1912 with Japan. China being absorbed in her revolution and Japan being the only other power directly concerned with Mongolia, the matter was settled by a secret convention with that country, signed on July 8, 1912, which extended the line of demarcation of respective zones of interest indicated in the Convention of 1907. This new line of demarcation started from the point in Manchuria on the 122nd meridian east, which was the limit of the previous line, followed the borderline of the province of Heilungkiang and Inner Mongolia to "the furthest point on the border of Inner and Outer Mongolia." [56] As for Inner Mongolia it was to be divided by a line running north-south through Peking. To the west of that line was the Russian sphere of influence and to the east the Japanese. This question being settled, a further step consolidating Russia's position in Mongolia was undertaken by negotiations concerning the respective status of China and Russia in the contested territories. By a tripartite agreement be-

[56] Yakhontov, ibidem, p. 379.

tween Russia, China and Mongolia, signed in 1915,
nominal Chinese suzerainty over Mongolia was acknowledged, but the effective power over the country
went to Russia. The Chinese governor-general who
represented the Peking Colonial Office was to be recalled and replaced by Chinese consular officials. Mongolia was given full autonomy including the right of
negotiating commercial treaties with foreign powers.
Both Russia and China guaranteed the neutrality of
Mongolia and undertook to keep no armed forces in
the country. The Chinese influence was effectively
wiped away, but the Chinese never relinquished their
claim and waited for the opportunity finally given them
by the World War and the Russian Revolution to win
back as much as possible.

While these developments were occurring in Mongolia, Russia, in the initial stage of her activities there,
was faced with a delicate problem which linked her
Mongolian pursuits with the fate of Tibet. It will be
recalled that the Dalai Lama of Tibet had to flee to
Urga when the English Expeditionary Force occupied
Lhasa. He sought refuge at the Russian Consulate
General in Urga. The Consul General received him
amicably but did not commit himself in any way, asking the Foreign Office for further instructions. In St.
Petersburg a thorough study of the Tibetan problem
was taking place and specialists, orientalists from the
Academy of Sciences, were invited to take part in the
deliberations concerning Russia's position in this question. It was decided that Russia was in no way interested in Tibet except as a valuable bargaining card in

any negotiations with Great Britain. Russia would prefer that the Dalai Lama should return to Lhasa and restore the status quo ante, but Britain being opposed to this, the matter was quietly dropped. Later, towards 1912 there even developed a point of view that any aggressive policy on the part of the British in Tibet might be welcome, for it would correspondingly give Russia a free hand in Mongolia.

The Dalai Lama, with his scheme of opposing Russia to England for his own benefit, had come too late. He could not know that in view of the rapidly rising influence of Germany in the Near East, both Russia and England were eager to bury the past and come to an understanding so as to oppose a common front against this serious menace to their interests. Indeed, the first time Germany appeared as a possible competitor in Asia was in connection with the scramble for railway concessions in Asia Minor. Since then her progress, particularly in Asiatic Turkey and Persia, had been amazing. Various suggestions had been made in Russia for building a trunk line to connect Europe with India. The Russian diplomat and engineer, Lessar, worked out a project for a railway from Krasnovodsk and Merv via Kouchka and Afghanistan to Karachi in India, which would make the latter city 174 hours from London. Another suggestion by Mr. Siromiatnikov was to extend the Transcaucasian Railway across Persia to Bander Abbas or Bushir on the Persian Gulf, but these plans remained on paper mainly because of Anglo-Russian jealousies. In the meanwhile the Germans had forged ahead with a scheme of their own which became famous as the Bagdad Railway. A Sultan's Irade gave the concession in 1902 to a German company; the railway was already completed through Konia and Eregli as far as Bulgurli by 1904. The original scheme of bringing the railway down to a point on the Persian Gulf was cleverly outmanœuvred by British diplomacy which succeeded in inducing the Sultan of Koweit to withdraw his consent to the railway on his territory. The alternative scheme of a branch line from Bagdad to Khanikin near the Persian frontier was equally distasteful to Britain and to Russia, particularly in view of the fact that German commercial travellers had already invaded the Persian market in anticipation. The Anglo-Russian rivalry had become obsolete under these circumstances, and the only way for an understanding lay in the clear delimitation of mutual zones of interest.

This was achieved by the Convention of August 31, 1907, signed by Sir Edward Grey and Iswolsky. According to this agreement the two governments undertook to respect the strict independence and integrity of Persia, and promised not to seek concessions in those regions of Persia bordering the sphere of influence of the other party. These were determined as follows: for Russia, northwest of a line from Kasr i Sirin on the road to Bagdad to the point where the frontiers of Persia, Russian Turkestan and Afghanistan meet; for England, from the Afghan frontier near Birjand to Kerman and Bander Abbas. The intermediate zone was to be neutral. A glance at the map reveals that Russia got the lion's share, with the capital Teheran, and the cities of Tabriz, Isfahan, Yezd, Kermanshah and Meshed. England got a virtually desert region, but in return Russia gave up all claims on Tibet and Afghanistan. Particularly valuable for Britain were the clauses concerning Afghanistan. Article I declared that Great Britain promised not to alter the political conditions in Afghanistan and not to encourage any hostile measures of Afghanistan against Russia. In Article II she further promised not to annex or occupy any territory in Afghanistan and not to interfere in the administration of the country as long as previous treaties and agreements were respected; and finally Article III granted Russian frontier authorities the permission to get into touch with border authorities in Afghanistan at special localities designated for the purpose, for the settlement of local questions of a non-political nature. With these reservations Russia was to keep entirely out of Afghanistan and have no relations whatsoever with that country. In this way the chain of buffer states covering the Indian northwestern "scientific frontier" was finally established and all causes of disagreement between Great Britain and Russia vanished so completely that King George V found it possible to make his historic naval visit to Reval for the purpose of cementing the entente cordiale between the two countries.

But the difficulties in the Near East did not diminish for Russia, due not only to the German menace which was soon to become the all-absorbing issue for Russian diplomacy, but also because a wave of revolutions was sweeping across these Asiatic countries and required careful handling. The first revolution occurred in Persia in 1906, caused in great part by the resentment of true Persian patriots against their country's being trampled upon by powerful neighbours. The autocracy of the shahs had reached such absurd limits that according to a Persian poet, if the Shah stated that day was night there remained nothing else to say but "behold, I see the stars." A group of nobles educated along western lines started a constitutional movement which rapidly became revolutionary. The Shah Muzzfar u Din was forced to grant a constitution and died shortly after opening the first parliament. He was succeeded by Mohammed Ali Shah who was bitterly opposed to reforms, and attempted to close the National Assembly by force. The liberal minister Nazir ul Mulk was imprisoned, but the Shah's armed coup failed in view of the state of public opinion. Civil war followed, and the plight of the country was made worse by a desperate financial crisis. A violent rebellion in Tabriz made Russian intervention a matter of course. The city was blockaded by the Shah's forces and the European colony there was endangered. A Russian force under General Baratov marched on Tabriz, broke the siege after severe fighting and introduced supplies into the city. Persia was now seething and Russia landed one thousand men at the port of Enzeli on the Caspian Sea. Finally the Shah became frightened and sought refuge at the Russian Legation in Teheran. He accepted a pension of seventy-five thousand dollars from Russia and went to finish his days in Odessa. The Russian expeditionary force then withdrew.

In the meanwhile the Persian patriots were attempting to interest a third foreign power in Persian affairs, so as to offset the absolute domination of Russia and England. The able Persian representative in the United States, Mr. Ali Kuli Khan, succeeded in interesting American capitalists in the natural riches of Persia, and the Persian Government following his advice, invited Mr. W. Morgan Shuster as financial adviser to restore Persian finances. This nomination was obviously unwelcome to Russia, and Mr. Shuster refusing upon his arrival in Teheran to make a call of courtesy at the Russian Legation, relations became strained from the beginning. Mr. Shuster worked energetically to restore Persian finances, throwing in his lot with the democratic party. When, however, he created a treasury military police and gave the command to an Anglo-Indian officer known for his anti-Russian feelings, the Russian Legation objected and this officer was sent back to India. But the final quarrel came when the treasury police clashed with Russian guards over the property of a Persian prince which was mortgaged to a Russian bank. Following this incident, the Russian Government delivered an ultimatum to Persia demanding the annulment of Mr. Shuster's nomination and the latter left Teheran.

In the meanwhile the Turkish Revolution of 1908 had strengthened tremendously Germany's position in the East. The Young Turks and particularly the man of the day, Enver Pasha, were all friends of Germany, and most of them had been educated in Germany. An opportunity to discredit the German Government as being too friendly with the fallen Abdul Hamid, was lost by the diplomacy of the Entente Powers. The German Ambassador, Marshal von Bieberstein, became all powerful in Constantinople and the Deutsche Bank opened a magnificent branch office in the very heart of the native part of the city, Stamboul. It was becoming apparent that Germany at the height of her power and prestige was intent upon using the Bagdad Railway for the purpose of carving out in the East a colonial empire which she had failed to gain elsewhere. The so-called formula of the three B's, Berlin, Byzantium (Constantinople), Bagdad, was being given an enlarged interpretation by enthusiastic pan-Germanists, as meaning Germany's domination of Asiatic Turkey and possibly Persia, where German commercial activities were rapidly increasing. At the same time Austria had annexed Bosnia-Herzegovina and was starting a drive on Salonica which would link Bagdad and Persia with the allied Central Powers. Russia was watching with the utmost concern this gradual encircling of her southern border. But worse was to come. We have seen all through history how jealously Russia had fought any one attempting to get control of the Bosphorus and the Dardanelles. Now Germany was to achieve military control in addition to political influence. Following the Turkish disasters in the Balkan War of 1912, the Turkish Government asked Germany to reorganize the Turkish Army. A German military mission headed by General Liman von Sanders was sent to Constantinople in August 1913 and Liman von Sanders was appointed Commander of the crack First Constantinople Corps of the Turkish Army. Russia was deeply stirred by this nomination and protested violently. As a result of protracted negotiations, the Turks gave way and Liman was made Inspector-General instead. But the incident flared up with renewed violence when in January, 1914, he was appointed Commander of the Turkish Third Erzerum Corps. This meant German command and increased fighting efficiency of the Turkish forces gathered in the great fortress menacing the Russian Caucasian frontier. It might be said that as far as Russia was concerned, a war with Germany became inevitable from that day. It happened to break out as a result of the Serajevo murder.

The Russian diplomatic activities in Asia during the World War were naturally conditioned by the development of hostilities, but mention must be made of them. Russia was allied with both her former foes in Asia: England and Japan. The alliance with Japan was sealed by the two conventions of 1916. In the first of these Russia and Japan promised not to be a party to any political combination directed against the other, and to support each other should the interests of either party be menaced in the Far East. The secret convention attached, stipulated that both parties should act together so as to keep any third power from gaining supreme influence in China, and that should a war break out between one of the parties and the third power in question, the other should come to the aid of its ally. In the same year the Russian Government was working out its desiderata in Asia in the eventuality of a victorious peace. A confidential report to the Czar written in 1916 by the Governor-General of Turkestan, Kuropatkin, and published by the Soviet Government, reveals the innermost thoughts of Russian statesmen concerning what may be called the maximum program of Russian ambitions in Asia. General Kuropatkin, better known as the Commander in Chief of the Russian Army in the Japanese War, was rightly considered a great authority on Central Asian problems. He first made his name under Skobelev in the expedition against the Tekke Turkomans, by the conquest of Askhabad. Later, as Administrator of Central Asia he showed brilliant qualities, which however he sorely lacked as Commander in Chief. His opinion therefore had great weight. He writes:

"I take the liberty of expressing the opinion that the necessity of making secure the enormous state border of Turkestan after the end of the Great War . . . will demand a definite decision with regard to Persia which should be equal to the greatness of Russia. It appears to me that the return to Russia of the provinces of Astrabad, Gilian and Mazanderan, the heritage of Peter the Great, is imperative, as well as the establishment of a Russian protectorate, with British consent, over Northern Persia with Tabriz, Teheran and Meshed.

With regard to Afghanistan, there appears to be no necessity for an alteration of the existing border, but an alliance with England enduring also in peace, ought to enable us to modify the attitude of Afghanistan and the Afghan Government, which has been hostile and undignified for Russia, and open the Afghan market for us. At present Afghans have free access across the Russian border, whereas Afghanistan is closed to Russians. Apart from this, Russia ought to secure full control over the waters of the Amu Darya, the Murgab and the Tedjen within Afghanistan, and finally with British consent, Russia ought to connect by railroad through Afghanistan with India.

As for China, the danger menacing Russia in the future from that Empire of 400,000,000 people is not to be doubted. The most vulnerable point on the Russian border, as 800 years ago, will be the Great Gateway of the Nations, through which the Hordes of Chengiz Khan invaded Europe. So long as Kulja will remain in Chinese hands, the protection of Turkestan against China will be a matter of great difficulty and will require considerable military force. It is impossible to leave this gateway in the hands of the Chinese. The alteration of our frontier with China is absolutely imperative. By drawing the border line from the Khan Tengri range (27,000 feet high and the highest in the Tian Shan Mountains) in a direct line to Vladivostok, our frontier will be shortened by 4,000 versts and Kulja, Northern Mongolia and Northern Manchuria will be included in the Russian Empire." [57]

This program has been partly carried out by the Soviet Government.

[57] Ryskulov, The Khirgiz Rebellion of 1916, The New East, Vol. VI, p. 270.

CHAPTER XII

THE REVOLUTION AND THE CIVIL WAR

The most striking outcome of the troubled decade after 1914 was the practically total obliteration of the borderline between Asiatic Russia and the bordering countries. During the Great War, the crushing defeats sustained by the Turks at the hands of the Russian Caucasian Army resulted in the occupation by Russia of Turkish Armenia, including Trebizond and Erzerum. Persia became a battlefield for the Russian, British and Turkish armies. Mongolia was virtually merged with Russia in so far as her resources were concerned, and Manchuria became the channel through which flowed the much required military supplies from Japan. But when the Revolution came and resulted in a bloody civil war between the "Whites" and the "Reds," after the triumph of the Communist Party in Moscow, the bordering regions were drawn into this gigantic struggle, and the contending forces swept freely over them with a complete disregard for national frontiers.

The very character of the populations of Asiatic Russia made the struggle against Communism at first particularly bitter. The Siberians being descendants of a pioneering stock or themselves pioneers were more energetic, more independent and more tenaciously individualistic than the peasants of European Russia;

257

they also had a greater regard for private property and liberty than the long-submerged Russian moujiks, accustomed to the semi-Communistic land system of the "Mir" which was in force in Russia prior to the Revolution. On the other hand, vast regions of Asiatic Russia had been given over by the colonizing policy of the Czarist Government to Cossacks, and the latter clung desperately to their rights and privileges. All over Russia, it was the Cossacks who put up the sternest fight against Soviet forces. Lastly, the alien minorities particularly important in Siberia and Central Asia had no direct interests in the great social convulsion taking place in Russia except in so far as it could give them possibilities for the fulfillment of national aspirations.

The situation was further complicated by allied intervention. Under pretence of helping Russia to rebuild a fighting front against Germany, these foreign armies with the sole exception of the United States Expeditionary Force were in reality pursuing their own private aims at the expense of Russia. Important Japanese contingents had occupied the whole of Eastern Siberia up to the Baikal and the Japanese Government was studying the question of how far this region was suitable for Japanese colonization. The British had occupied parts of Turkestan and the Caucasus, Baku and Batum. The Anglo-Indian Government was openly hoping to drive Russia out of Central Asia, while the rich oil fields of Baku were tempting for London. Finally, the Czechs, who had formed a national army out of Czech prisoners taken by the Russian Army in Galicia and Poland, were completely under the influence of the French, and their activities in Siberia were dubious, not to say treacherous. Russians will certainly have no reason to keep a happy memory of their doings, and this first contact between them and their Western Slav brethren from Bohemia, was more than unfortunate. As a result of all these conflicting influences, Asiatic Russia was plunged into a complete state of chaos, and it looked as if Russian domination in Asia was to be completely wiped out.

The confused events in Siberia can only be dealt with briefly. In April, 1918, the Union for the Regeneration of Russia was created in Moscow for the purpose of fighting Communism and coördinating the struggle against the Germans with the Allied Powers. The Volga region and Siberia being freed from Bolshevist rule, provisional governments were set up by the moderate parties participating in the work of the Union, at Samara on the Volga and Omsk in Siberia. In July, 1918, the first contingents of the Czech formations retreating eastward under the pressure of the Reds, arrived on the Volga and were instructed by the Allied Powers to coöperate with the new government.

But this government was weak, owing to internal dissension caused by the fact that it was formed of too many diverging parties. This led to its overthrow by a military dictatorship under Admiral Kolchak, who proclaimed himself Supreme Ruler and extended his rule over the whole of Siberia. Kolchak was a man of remarkable energy and power who, still a young man, had made his way up to the post of Commander in

Chief of the Black Sea fleet, by sheer determination and genius. He issued a manifesto from the seat of his government at Omsk, stating that he would tolerate no reactionary policies or party spirit, but was pursuing solely the struggle against Communism. He restored discipline and his armies met with conspicuous success at first, rapidly advancing into European Russia and pursuing the Reds. It was during this advance that the retreating Reds killed the Czar and his family at Ekaterinburg, for fear that he might be liberated by Kolchak's forces. But the Czechs refused coöperation as their mood became increasingly radical. This fact is one of the important contributory causes of Kolchak's defeat and the turning point in the campaign came in the summer of 1919. In November Kolchak was forced to evacuate Omsk and transfer his government to Chita in Eastern Siberia. He was finally compelled to put himself under the protection of the Allied High Commissioners who turned him over to the radical revolutionary committee at Irkutsk who in their turn gave him over to the Bolsheviks. Admiral Kolchak, most of his ministers and members of his staff were executed by the Reds on February 7, 1920. There is no denying that this is a black spot on the conscience of the Allied representatives in Siberia, particularly in view of Kolchak's outstanding achievements in the Great War and the zeal with which he had fought their cause. The responsibility for this treacherous act, when it would have been so easy to evacuate Kolchak's government abroad, seems to fall upon the French High Commissioner, General Janin and on the Czech Legionaries.

The Soviet Government was now virtually in control of the whole of Western Siberia. Not wishing to antagonize the Japanese, the Red forces did not advance beyond Lake Baikal, and in Eastern Siberia four independent republics emerged from the chaos into which the country had been plunged after the death of Kolchak. These were the Republics of Verkneudinsk, Chita, the Amur and the Maritime, the last named having its capital at Vladivostok. These new governments were extremely weak as the real power was in the hands of the Japanese. Moreover they all had different political colourings. At Verkneudinsk, the government was shared by Mensheviks and Bolsheviks and consequently was leaning towards Moscow. Chita, on the contrary, was held by the notorious Ataman Semenov, a bitter foe of the Soviets, deriving his power from the Japanese. The Amur Republic never emerged from a state of chaos, whereas Vladivostok was in the hands of democratic elements and Socialist Revolutionaries, the party of Kerensky. Under these circumstances, the policy of the Soviet Government was naturally to use Verkneudinsk as a lever to gain control of Eastern Siberia. A Red force was created there and invaded Chita, while a pact of coöperation was signed between the Soviets and the Vladivostok Government. Pressed from both sides, Semenov was forced out of Russia into Manchuria and Mongolia, where his forces disarmed. The Maritime Republic now annexed both the Amur and the Chita Republics and formed a larger state known as the Far Eastern Republic. Here the Communists, in view of the presence of Japanese forces, had to act warily. They gradually got the upper hand in the government and prepared for the ultimate reunion with Moscow.

As a result of these events, a colourful episode which cannot be overlooked occurred in Outer Mongolia. A growing nationalist movement amongst the Buriats or that branch of the Mongols living around Lake Baikal, was noticeable prior to the Revolution. They had resented the confiscation of their lands as a result of Russian colonization and the building of the Transsiberian Railway. When the Russian Revolution broke out in 1917, a Buriat Congress met, demanding autonomy, but in the turmoil of the civil war their claims were overlooked. Presently a leader appeared from a most unexpected quarter. One of the White generals, associated with Ataman Semenov was driven with his forces into Mongolia. This was Baron Ungern Sternberg, a most romantic personality. After having been expelled from the Naval School in St. Petersburg, he joined the Siberian Cossack Force, the abode of all adventurers or those who for some reason or other were trying to forget the past. In the Revolution, he emerged as an empire builder, blending medieval and feudal conceptions inherited from his German ancestry with a mystic fear of Bolshevism as the emanation of evil forces ruling the world. Having embraced Buddhism, he secured a hold on the Mongol populations and began dreaming of following the example of Chengiz Khan and recreating a great Mongol Empire to include Mongolia and the regions of Siberia inhabited by the Buriats.

Meanwhile, profiting by the breakdown of the Rus-

sian influence in the East as a result of the anarchy following the Revolution, the Chinese had made a bold
attempt to regain their hold over Mongolia and had
actually captured Urga. Ungern, coming with his
White force into Mongolia, issued a proclamation stating that he was fighting for the independence of Mongolia, and met with a most enthusiastic response. Forming a mixed Russian and Mongolian army, he attacked
the Chinese and drove them out of Urga. Now Ungern
was master of Mongolia and on one hand he started
modernizing the country, building roads and establishing a powerful electrical plant in Urga, a telephone
exchange, newspapers, hospitals and laboratories. On
the other hand he showed subservience to the Buddhist
lamas, and took stringent measures to protect the Mongols in any conflict with the Russians. Ruthless cruelty
marred his otherwise noble endeavours to create justice.
Having firmly established his rule in Urga, he started
upon his great venture of fighting the Reds and carving
out his empire at the expense of Russia. But here luck
turned against him. Defeated at Troitskosavsk in
August, 1921, he was captured by the Soviet forces
and shot.

At about the same time another remarkable personality, Enver Pasha, was attempting to create a great empire in Central Asia, this time following in the footsteps
of Tamerlane. Central Asia was plunged into even
greater anarchy by the civil war than was Siberia.
Trouble had started with an insurrection of the Khirgiz
in the northern steppes in 1916, still during the World
War. It is interesting to note that with the exception

of a small rising of mountaineers in 1898 in a distant part of Ferghana, really of a religious nature, being led by a fanatical Muslim mullah and which was easily suppressed, absolute peace had reigned in Central Asia from the time of the Russian occupation. This was due to the policy of Russian colonization which left local customs and institutions unimpaired and even protected unless there was a special reason for not doing so. Perhaps of all the European colonizing states, Russia's rule was the least heavy, for it did not interfere with the life of the natives. No attempt at forceful Russification was made in Asia. And a proof of this statement lies precisely in the fact that the moment Russia did begin to interfere with native affairs as a result of the situation created by the Great War, the natives took up arms. The insurrection of the Khirgiz was caused by a decree of the Imperial Government ordering the mobilization of the natives of Central Asia for work in the rear of the German front. This order affected some two hundred thousand Khirgiz who rebelled and the insurrection spread rapidly all over the Samarkand and Ferghana regions. When the Revolution broke out in 1917, Turkestan rapidly became a hotbed for revolutionary agitation, and local Soviets were formed which virtually detached themselves from the Central Government in Petrograd and became independent. But the fever spread only amongst the Russians residing in Central Asia. The natives watched the events passively, bewildered and not understanding what was taking place.

With the war between the Whites and the Reds, a

period of utmost confusion started. Each side controlled the region in turn, the Reds under the command of an Austrian war prisoner, Vitchich, alternating with Admiral Kolchak's forces and the Cossacks under Ataman Dutov, whereas Bokharian regulars were making war on bands of brigands. The complete disorganization of supplies resulting from this state of anarchy led to a dreadful famine which took a toll of some thirty per cent of the population, the Uzbegs suffering most. The following figures will give an idea of this economic breakdown: In 1917, Bokhara exported to Russia two million poods of cotton in return for wheat and other products; in 1921 the export figure had fallen to 142,000 poods. With the overthrow of Kolchak, the Soviet Army automatically gained control of Turkestan and Soviet agents immediately capitalized an agrarian movement which had been developing in Bokhara against the Ameer, the begs (feudal landowners) and the wakufs (clergy). A revolution was staged in Khiva and Bokhara and the rulers of these states, the nobles and the Muslim clergy were obliged to flee to Afghanistan where they immediately started stirring up trouble against the Communists. On the 14th of September, 1920, a Soviet emissary, Lubimov, made an announcement to an assembly of awe-stricken Bokharians for the first time admitted to the forbidden palace of the Ameer, that independence had been granted to Bokhara by Moscow, and that all previous treaties binding Bokhara to Russia were cancelled. A similar announcement was made in Khiva.

Meanwhile a formidable counter-revolutionary

movement was launched by the Muslim émigrés who had found refuge in Afghanistan, with the connivance and later with the active help of the Afghan Government. This movement, known as the Bassmatchi Rising, started as a guerilla warfare of bands of mountaineers fighting on their own against the Soviets, but was rapidly coördinated into a formidable insurrection. The movement attracted widespread attention over the whole East. Not only Afghans but many Turkish staff officers unemployed in Turkey, took a hand and gave to it the character of a Muslim struggle against European imperialism. A Holy War was declared against the Jadids (the Bolsheviks), and the movement was also in protest against the forcible confiscation of land which was being carried on by the Soviet Government. The insurrection became a regular war when the former dictator of Turkey, Enver Pasha, took the leadership. Enver, after having been ousted from the position of virtual ruler of Turkey by Kemal Pasha, quarrelled with the latter and was obliged to leave his country after being condemned to death in 1919. He fled to Russia seeking a new field for his boundless energy. He appeared in Moscow, was then traced in Crimea, still at that time in possession of the Whites, and finally emerged in Baku. He first thought of giving his services to the Soviet cause, and was well received though not without caution. The Kemalist sympathies of Moscow made Enver pass into the opposite camp, and the Bassmatchi Movement induced him to select Turkestan as the fitting place for the realization of a great dream he had been cherishing for a long while, that of build-

ing up a vast pan-Turanian Empire of which he would
be the ruler.

He arrived in Bokhara in November, 1921, and
under the pretence of going to a hunting party he
joined the Bassmatchi rebels. He was received with
suspicion and even imprisoned, but he managed to get
into touch with the Ameer of Bokhara in Afghanistan,
who appointed him "Commander in Chief of the Muslim Army." With his military training he had received
in Berlin and his innate sense of leadership he became
a most formidable opponent to the Soviet forces. In a
vigorous offensive he drove them out of Turkestan and
in January, 1922, he sent an insolent ultimatum demanding the total abandonment by Russia of the whole
of Central Asia. Now the fugitive native administration was returned from exile and restored to its duties,
and Enver issued a program revealing his ideas. He
was aiming at the creation of a vast empire to include
Turkestan, Persia, Afghanistan and eventually even
Turkey, the union of all the Muslims and the final
liberation from European domination. Thoroughly
alarmed, Moscow replied to the ultimatum by sending
large forces against Enver. The latter suffered his
first defeat in an attack on Derbent on June 14, 1922,
where he was repulsed by the superior forces of the
Soviet General Kakurin. The latter pursued him and
eventually drove him into the mountains where in the
narrow passes a fierce struggle between small bands
took place. In one of these encounters, Enver with a
small force was surrounded by the Reds and after a
desperate hand-to-hand fight the Bassmatchi fled leav-

ing their dead. Among the corpses the body of Enver was discovered and identified owing to letters from Berlin and a notebook found in his coat pocket (August 4, 1922).

After his death the spirit of the Bassmatchi Rebellion was broken and though it still smouldered for a while causing some further trouble to the Soviet Government, Central Asia had been reconquered by Russia and was again well in hand. In the Caucasus and in Transcaucasia the general movement for independence on the part of the natives (though at first they voted for a federation with Russia) assumed a much more definite and clear character. The situation was complicated by the presence of the White forces of General Denikin, the British Occupationary Force, and at one time the Turks who tried to regain Batum and Baku. However, already in December, 1917, a National Assembly meeting in Tiflis proclaimed Georgia an independent republic and in April, 1918, a Federative Transcaucasian Republic came into existence, uniting the major nationalities of the Caucasus under the leadership of Georgia. But a strong Communist movement disrupted this federation and by May, Georgia, Azerbaijan (the Baku region) and Armenia notified the European powers of their separate existence. At the same time, the numerous peoples of the northern range formed a loose federation and proclaimed their independence. The Communists regained power at Baku, but later the city was occupied by the Turkish army and afterwards by the British. The British policy in the Caucasus was confused, due to the conflicting interests of London, thinking in terms of a struggle with Communism, and of the Anglo-Indian Government at Delhi wanting to humiliate Russia. The latter course seems to have triumphed, for by a secret treaty General Denikin was bound in return for financial help not to allow the Russian fleet to operate in the Black Sea, and not to allow Russians to go to Batum, though it was oddly enough still a Russian city.

The year, 1919, was one of utmost confusion. Having gained their independence, the Georgians and Armenians gave vent to their perennial mutual hatred resulting in war between the two newly born republics, and the ultimate defeat of the Georgians. With the overthrow of General Denikin by the Reds in March, 1920, and the end of the White Russian movement, the divided nations of the Caucasus were defenceless before the invading Soviet forces. After a stubborn struggle and the suppression of a great insurrection in Georgia, the Moscow Government forced a federation upon the three Caucasian republics, and on March 12, 1922, they were merged into the Soviet Socialist Republic of Transcaucasia which was attached to the Soviet Union. The tendency on the part of the Caucasian peoples to quarrel amongst themselves made their independence short lived.

We see therefore that out of the tremendous turmoil of the five years following 1917 which plunged Russia into a state of chaos verging on a complete breakdown, there emerged a new Russia. If we now compare the map of the former Russian Empire in Asia with that of the Soviet Union, we are surprised to see that except

for a small loss of territory in Transcaucasia where the
region of Kars was regained by Turkey, the border-
lines of the Russian dominions remain the same. All
the territories which had detached themselves during
the period of anarchy were again reunited, order re-
emerged and to the mind of the writer this is a conclu-
sive proof of the extraordinary stability of the work accomplished in Asia by the Russian nation during four
centuries. No more acid test of such stability can be
found in the history of any nation than those fateful
first years of the Russian Revolution. However, the
structure of Asiatic Russia underwent a momentous
change; from having been a united Empire it became
a Federation of Soviet Republics. As in so many other
questions, the Revolution merely brought to fruition
a change which had been maturing for some time. With
the enormous expansion of Russia in the 19th century
and the rapid growth of Asiatic Russia both in population and economic importance, the excessive centralization of the Czarist régime had made administration too
cumbersome. The issue had been raised as early as the
beginning of the 19th century when the Emperor Alexander I became so interested in the possible application
of the federal principle to Russia that he thought of
getting some advice on the matter from President Jef-
ferson. The issue was later shelved but the Government was obliged, as we have seen, to resort to the
dangerous expedient of granting sovereign powers to
the Russian viceroys in the East, to Muraviev and
Kauffman and in the beginning of this century, in a
lesser degree, to Admiral Alexeev, the Viceroy of

Liaotung and to Count Vorontsov Dashkov, the Viceroy of the Caucasus. The federal issue was becoming more and more a matter of public discussion.

There were, however, factors pertaining to the Soviet régime which influenced this reform and these must now be examined. The celebrated Declaration of November 15, 1917, issued by the Second Congress of the Soviets, immediately after Lenin had gained power in Russia, embodied the new principles in the question of alien minorities in the Empire, which were to form the basis of Soviet policy. According to this declaration, all the nationalities within the former Russian Empire were declared equal and sovereign. All religious, national or other privileges or limitations were suppressed and the alien minorities were given the right to dispose of themselves to the extent of constituting independent states. Though later, during the civil war the spirit of this declaration was violated in certain cases, particularly in the case of Georgia, it nevertheless formed the official basis of the new status of the alien minorities in the Soviet Union. Furthermore, the mere fact that the outlying regions had to be reconquered brought about an overhauling of the previous status of these regions; the reincorporation of the independent republics into the Soviet Union was effected by the signing of special treaties with the Soviet Government, and here it must be pointed out that the word "Soyuz" in Russian means both alliance and union, and thus was open to the most elastic interpretation by both contracting parties. Theoretically the Soviet Union must be regarded as a free partnership of equal nations bound together by treaties.

In reality, because the task of coördinating the efforts of building a new socialist society lies with the Communist Party, which has its headquarters in Moscow, the centralization of the Soviet Union is at least as great as that of any other federal republic in the world. Indeed, according to the treaties mentioned above and the Constitution of 1923, the competence of the Central Government in the Federated Republics extends over:

"the diplomatic relations of the Unions with foreign powers, questions of boundaries between the Soviet Republics, the incorporation of new republics, declaration of war and conclusion of peace, foreign loans and ratification of treaties, control of foreign trade, establishment of basic principles and of a general plan of national economy, post, telegraph, and communications, naval and military forces, a general state budget and determination of general taxes, currency and credit system, waterways, the exploitation of mineral wealth and natural resources, colonization and migration, civil and criminal legislation, labor laws, national education, weights and measures, rights of foreigners in the Union, adjudication on disputes between republics, and the right to veto any measures infringing on the constitution." [58]

Limited by these clauses the sovereign rights of the Federated Republics assume the aspect of a local autonomy.

Particularly illuminating were the reforms undertaken in Central Asia by the Soviet Government after the Bassmatchi Revolt, which clearly indicate the general trend of the policy of Moscow and the power it kept in hand with regard to the affairs of the outlying

[58] Haden Guest, The New Russia, p. 63.

parts of the Union. Having learned the bitter lesson of the Bassmatchi Revolt, the Soviet Government, when it felt it had sufficient hold on Turkestan again, proceeded to abolish all existing national entities and to reorganize that region according to the ethnographic principle. Accordingly in a series of decrees dating from September, 1924, to May, 1925, the states of Khiva and Bokhara were abolished as well as the Turkestan Soviet Republic created earlier, and in their place were formed the Uzbeg Soviet Socialist Republic with its corollary the Autonomous Soviet Republic of the Tadjiks, the Turkoman Soviet Socialist Republic with the autonomous provinces of Kara Kalpak and of Kara Khirgiz, and to the north in the great steppe the Khirgiz Soviet Republic. These republics were informed that they might apply for membership in the Soviet Union, and this was granted by the Central Executive Committee in October, 1925. The borderline of these republics cut clear across Khiva and Bokhara and the obvious idea therefore was to stamp out all associations with the past. The Soviets were deliberately stimulating the feebly developed nationalistic feelings of the natives of Central Asia in the hope of obliterating any dynastic, feudal or religious attachments. Of particular interest was the creation of the Tadjik Republic. Following a method employed on the Finnish and the Roumanian borders where the Karelian and the Moldavian Republics were created to attract the inhabitants of the border regions of these neighbouring states, the Tadjik Republic was to serve as a focus of attraction for the discontented populations of Afghan Turkestan, alien to the Afghans and of the same racial stock as the inhabitants of Tadjikistan. Later, some further re-shuffling took place and these republics were once more reorganized, but as on the whole the general scheme of the reforms was maintained, we need not go into these details.

At the same time an important aspect of the Soviet policy was to give the widest cultural autonomy possible. In this field a great deal was accomplished. Not only has education been spread amongst the primitive races, but also efforts have been made to develop local cultures and to bring to life certain local native languages which were so primitive that they did not possess a written alphabet. Alphabets and grammars had to be created, and the efforts of Soviet scientists to equip the primitive Asiatic races with the cultural means for further development without infringing upon their individuality, has been highly creditable. An important step in the direction of cultural unification has been the Latinization of the Turkish alphabet. First discussed at the Baku Congress in 1920 the reform was introduced by decision of the All-Union Central Executive Committee in 1927.

We have here what may appear two contradictory policies. The tendency to develop cultural autonomy and to foster a national consciousness among races which had scarcely any at all, seems to contradict the strong political centralization of the Soviet Union. It must be pointed out that both pursue the same aim. The goal of the Soviet régime relegates Russian nationalism or racial feeling to the second rank; indeed, the very name of Russia has been officially abolished. On the other hand, the aim being to create a Communist society, this implies that every citizen irrespective of race, nationality or creed must be brought to a uniform level of cultural development at which he can consciously participate in the task and understand the Communist doctrines. The ultimate aim is to achieve this all over the world, but pending that time when according to the belief of the Soviet leaders this may become a reality, they are carrying out the program within the territories they control. And here comes the dominating factor which makes for the unity of the component parts of the Soviet Union: the strong party discipline and the absolute loyalty to party interests within the Communist Party itself, and its absolute domination over the mass of the population. No national development must interfere with the will of the governing elements of the Communist Party, and as a measure of precaution it is curious to observe that the regional Soviets or other directing party organs in the Federated Asiatic Soviet Republics, are practically always headed by Russian Communists or Communists imported from the neighbouring region and of a different race. Thus the hold over the whole Union by the Central Government, though based on a different principle, remains very much the same as under the Czarist régime. But as we have seen, it takes for granted the maintenance of the dictatorship of the Communist Party. Should that fail, the cultural autonomy developed by the Soviet Government may result in separatism, or at least will require the establishment of a new principle to keep the component parts of the Union together.

There is, however, at present another perhaps dominating factor which is working as a unifying force, particularly in Asiatic Russia. This is the economic development of the country under the Five Year Plan. Though giving a great deal of attention to regional development and particularly to Asiatic Russia, this plan was conceived by the Gosplan in Moscow as making the Soviet Union into one economic whole, and making the component parts of the Union so interdependent as to kill their economic life if they segregate themselves from the greater body politic. This will probably be the determining factor in the conservation of Russian domination over Siberia and Central Asia, whatever the changes may be in the future. The most important achievements of the plan to date, influencing the life of Asiatic Russia, are the Turkestan-Siberian Railway, the industrialization of the Kusnetsk region, irrigation and cotton development in Central Asia, and the enormous increase of oil production in the Caucasus.

The Turkestan Siberian Railway, commonly known as the Turksib, is of very great political importance. This line, 1,442 kilometers long (about 900 miles), connects the two great trunk lines of Asiatic Russia, the Transsiberian and the Transcaspian railways, running in a northeasterly direction along the frontier of Chinese Turkestan. It opens up to colonization the rich plains of Kazakstan (former Semirechie), which promises to become one of the world granaries. Before the

War, a fairly extensive colonization of the northern part of this plain had started, the colonists making their way south from the Transsiberian Railway. Consequently the Turkestan-Siberian Railway had already been planned and a part of the preliminary work accomplished, but it was completed by the Soviet Government and opened for traffic in April, 1930. Its further mission is to serve as an additional outlet for the Turkestan cotton and to facilitate the importation of Siberian grain into that region. Last but not least, being the only railway in the vicinity of Chinese Turkestan it assures Russian economic domination of that enormous area. As far as Turkestan itself goes, the railway plays an important rôle by directing the overflow of Russian colonization from Siberia towards this region. It is a delusion to consider Siberia, particularly Western Siberia, so far underpopulated. The most fertile lands have already been distributed amongst emigrants from European Russia and the pioneer is now tempted to turn south along the tracks of the new railway into the lands of the Khirgiz instead of penetrating into the great virgin forests of the Taiga region. This tends towards an increase of purely Russian stock in Central Asia, with the consequent important political results. Furthermore, from the military angle, the railway serves as the third link with Russia, permitting rapid transportation of troops. The Bassmatchi Revolt showed clearly that the control of Central Asia depends on holding the railways, and this is an important factor to be considered in case of war in Afghanistan or in China. The Anglo-Indian Government has been rightly disturbed about the potentialities of this railway for increasing Russian power in Turkestan.

The industrialization of the Kusnetsk region is also an event of tremendous, one might even say revolutionary importance. Here in the foothills of the Altai range, virtually on the border of Jungaria, are to be found the richest coal deposits in the Soviet Union. High grade coal is lying near the surface of the earth in strata of varying thicknesses ranging from two to sixteen meters with an estimated total of four hundred billion tons. The erection of steel plants in this region is not only creating the first industrial region in Siberia with the consequent attraction of population, the growth of cities and generally speaking boom conditions which usually follow such developments, but it is enormously increasing the potentialities of Russian action all over Asia. It will be remembered that one of the most important handicaps in the Russo-Japanese War was the tremendous distance separating the front from the source of supplies at home. With powerful steel plants erected half way between the Ural Mountains and the Pacific Ocean, Russia will be in a position to tackle her Far Eastern problems with much more vigour.

Generally speaking, one of the most important results of the Five Year Plan will be precisely the strengthening of Russia's position in the East. As a result of the experience gained in the Great War which revealed that the Russian industrial plants were located in many cases too near the border, the Soviet Government has decided to erect the most ambitious industrial plants in a region safe from any invasions from the

West or from the East, namely in the very center of the Eurasian plain, on both sides of the Ural Mountains. This new center now coming to life, extends roughly from the Volga River to the Yenissei. Here on the Volga have been erected the great Stalingrad tractor and Nizhni Novgorod automobile plants, and the Magnitogorsk iron foundries in the Urals, to name only the most important. The inevitable result will be the increase of population in this part of the Soviet Union and consequently the general shifting of Russia's center of gravity eastward. Thus the rôle played by Asiatic Russia in the future history of Russia, looms as more and more important, and conversely the rôle played by Russia in Asia.

CHAPTER XIII

SOVIET POLICY IN ASIA

WITH the advent of the Soviet power, a new principle was established in Russia's Asiatic policy. Instead of pursuing the sole aim of Russian imperialism as heretofore, the new policy aimed at using Asia as a lever for overthrowing European capitalism. With the ultimate goal of world revolution as the reason for the existence of the Communist Party in Russia, it was obvious that Soviet Russia should look upon Asia as the most propitious field for action, particularly after the illusion nurtured by so many Soviet leaders, that a Communist Revolution would be possible in Europe immediately after the War, had been dispelled.

In Asia the flames were already burning and needed only to be fanned; indeed, revolutions in China, Turkey and Persia had preceded the advent of Soviet power. India, French Indo-China and the Dutch East Indies were seething with unrest; Afghanistan was in the throes of a rampant civil war and court revolutions, and Japan was unbalanced by a severe economic crisis and by the rapid advent of democracy, marked by universal suffrage. Hence this great unrest affecting some eight hundred million people was to be capitalized and, if possible, brought under the direction of the Third

International in Moscow, which had been created by Lenin to fight Europe.

This policy was made clear at the Second Congress of the Third International held in July and August, 1920, which formulated the general points of the Soviet Asiatic policy along the following lines: since the colonies constitute the main force of European capitalist powers, the overthrow of European capitalism can be best achieved by the overthrow of European power in Asia, and this can be brought about by vigorously supporting the revolutionary and nationalist movements in Asia.

Consequently the two bodies which derive their power from the Political Bureau, the supreme organ of the Communist Party, i.e., the Soviet Government itself and the Executive Committee of the Communist International (the Komintern), so coördinated their policies as to carry out this plan jointly. Lenin, who was conducting the discussions of this fateful Second Congress, at which delegates from thirty-four countries were present and in which the foundations of the organized Communist action throughout the world were established, directed its main attention towards Asia by laying down his views in twelve points. His main arguments were that the Treaty of Versailles representing a product of bourgeois ideology must be nullified, and that this could be done by the alliance of the Asiatic revolutionary movements with Russian Communism. The destructive force of this alliance would lie in the fact that the strength of the European powers was based on the exploitation of Asia as a market for its finished products and a field for raw materials required in European industries. Lenin went so far as to state that the European bourgeois, feeling himself insecure before the onslaught of Socialism in Europe, was investing his money in colonial enterprises. He concluded by stressing the necessity of severing the ties between the two continents as a preliminary move, before the overthrow of capitalism in Europe.

Following out this new policy, a pan-Asiatic Conference convened in Baku in September of the same year, and 1,891 delegates, representing thirty-seven Asiatic countries, were present. The task of coördinating the revolutionary movements of Asia under the guidance of Moscow was undertaken; "The Soviet of Action and Propaganda of Baku" was founded as a permanent body for linking all Asiatic organizations. The activities of the congress resulted in a noticeable increase of Soviet propaganda and also of Soviet prestige throughout Asia.

An important factor with regard to this increase of Soviet influence was the impression produced amongst the Asiatic nations by the Declaration of 1917 mentioned in the previous chapter, granting, to all races within the former Russian Empire, absolute equality and the right to secede. Therefore what Asia saw in the advent of Bolshevism in Russia was that one of the great European imperialistic powers was reversing its policy and was now favouring the Asiatics. This belief was coupled with the fact that as the civil war was still on in Russia, her power in Asia was at its lowest ebb. The terror that Imperial Russia had inspired was gone, and the Asiatics ceased to look upon Russia as a menace. The Soviet policy in its turn was now governed by both these factors. On one hand was the realization of inherent weakness which had made Russia abandon practically all her previous positions in Asia, and on the other hand the men guiding the destinies of the Soviet Government were still in the stage where practical politics had not shattered their belief in the power of abstract principles.

But when the period of reconstruction in Russia opened and Soviet Russia reëmerged as a powerful nation, and also when the ideological revolutionists who had seized power in Russia were confronted with the everyday practical problems of government, Soviet diplomacy began to slip back more and more into the grooves made by centuries of Russian action in Asia, and the new principles laid down by the Revolution gradually receded into the background. As this process developed, the Asiatics began to find it more and more difficult to differentiate between the new and the old Russia, and the consequence was the vanishing of their friendly feelings towards the Communists. It is important to trace the various stages of this development.

The opening period of Soviet relations with Asia may be termed the period of renunciation. The Soviets made a clean sweep of all rights and privileges secured by the treaties made by Imperial Russia in Asia, and were anxious to secure new relations with the neighbouring Asiatic powers on a basis of friendliness and equality, so as to start upon the vast scheme worked out by the Third International. (Of these friendships only one has survived to date, that with Kemalist Turkey.) This period began when the Red Army was marching into Siberia, with a note sent by the acting Commissary of Foreign Affairs, on July 25, 1919, in the form of a declaration to the Chinese people and to the governments of Southern and Northern China:

"We are bringing to the people," says the note, "their liberation from foreign bayonets, from the yoke of the foreign gold which is strangling the enslaved peoples of the Orient, and first among them the Chinese nation. We are bringing relief not only to our labouring classes but to the Chinese people as well." [59]

The note declares that in consequence Soviet Russia is willing to annul the Treaty of 1896, the Peking Protocol of 1901 and all the agreements with Japan from 1907 to 1916. The Soviet Government further refused to receive the indemnity for the Boxer Rebellion and "abolishes all the special privileges and all the concessions to the Russian merchants on Chinese soil." A year later, on October 27, 1920, Karakhan sent a new note with the basic suggestion for the conclusion of a treaty, but the response of China to these overtures being, for reasons which will be examined later, not what the Soviet Government had expected, negotiations dragged on till 1924, when an agreement was finally concluded. Soviet diplomacy, however, was not dismayed at these disappointing results and made similar offers to the three Near Eastern powers, Af-

[59] Yakhontov, Russia and the Soviet Union in the Far East, appendices, pp. 381-384.

ghanistan, Persia and Turkey, scoring here the desired success.

The position of Kemal Pasha, the future dictator of Turkey, was at the time somewhat similar to the position of the Soviet Government in Russia. He was hard pressed by the Greek Army supported by the Allies, and had to face the opposition of the pro-Ally party in Turkey, which in effect played the rôle of the Whites in the Russian civil war. This similarity of position and a common foe, the Allied Powers, brought about close coöperation between Moscow and Angora.

But upon the demand by Kemal for an alliance, which would have meant participation in the war against the Greeks, Chicherin, the Soviet Commissary for Foreign Affairs, in his note of June 2, 1920, suggested the resumption of diplomatic relations. Nevertheless, the Soviet Government helped Turkey "with much cannon, money, arms and military advice." [60] For a time, however, the occupation of Batum by the Turkish Army on March 11, 1921, remained a hindrance to closer relations. But when the Turks agreed to restore Batum in return for Kars and Ardagan, a treaty with the Grand National Assembly of Turkey could be signed on March 16, 1921.

This treaty stipulated that the contracting parties would not recognize any international agreements imposed upon either of them by a third party. Article VI cancelled all previous treaties or agreements concluded by Czarist Russia with the Turkish Empire. The capitulations were abolished, and the outstanding indem-

[60] Fischer, The Soviets in World Affairs, Vol. I, p. 391.

nity due from Turkey as a result of the War of 1877-1878 and all other debts were cancelled (Article VII). The treaty further regulated the new Caucasian frontier and mentioned the solidarity between the two nations in their struggle against imperialism.

This treaty gave Soviet Russia a preponderating influence in Turkey and Kemal started organizing his own Communist party. When the Commander-in-Chief of the Soviet Ukrainian Armies, Frunze, visited Angora in December, 1921, to settle remaining questions, he was met with such signs of friendship that he could make rapid headway. The first Soviet envoy in Turkey, Aralov, became a persona grata with Kemal and played a part in Turkish affairs far beyond the rôle assigned to a foreign ambassador. He visited the front with Kemal, took the salute at parades and exhorted the Turkish soldiers to carry on the struggle with the Greeks.

In Persia the breakdown of Russia had at first played into the hands of the British, as might have been expected. The Anglo-Persian Agreement of 1919 virtually excluded Russia as a factor in that country's affairs. By that treaty Britain was to supply experts and advisers to the Persian Government, the army was to be officered and equipped by Great Britain, a joint Committee of Experts was to elaborate a new customs tariff favourable to the English, and a loan of two million pounds at seven per cent was made in London. In return the Anglo-Persian Oil Company, controlled by the British Admiralty, secured the extremely valuable Persian oil fields. Characteristically, the agreement was not submitted to the Persian Assembly and met with violent opposition in public opinion. Persia had become an extension of British India.

Unfortunately for British interests, Russia came back in the form of an invasion of the Red Army pursuing the remnants of General Denikin's White forces. In the spring of 1920, Soviet forces bombarded Enzeli, entered Persia, occupied Resht and formed a Soviet Government under Kuchik Khan, which lasted until October, 1921. A hurried evacuation of the former Russian zone by the British forces and the Cossack Brigade, now in British pay, was followed by a revolution in Teheran. A period of confusion ensued, and the Anglo-British Agreement was virtually annulled except for the ground gained by the Anglo-Persian Oil Company. The way was again clear for new negotiations with Soviet Russia, the outcome of which was the treaty signed at Moscow on February 26, 1921.

According to this treaty, Soviet troops were to evacuate Persia when the British departed. As in the treaty with Turkey, Russia promised to abandon all "imperialistic encroachments," to cancel all existing treaties and agreements, and not to recognize any other treaties detrimental to Persia. Article IX cancelled all debts and financial advantages, and gave the Discount Bank over to Persia. All concessions were returned on condition that they should not be granted to anyone else (Article XIII). More important was a virtual military alliance provided by Articles VI and VII, which stated that the two countries would take joint measures of defence against any third power attacking Persia or the Caspian coast. Lastly, the frontier was established according to the line of 1881, and the Ashurada Islands in the south Caspian and the little city of Firuze were returned to Persia.

Soviet influence now became very powerful, particularly with the overthrow of feudal landlords in Persia who had pro-British sympathies out of fear of the Reds. Economically, Northern and Central Persia remained under Russian dependence, and with the rise to power of the trading middle class in Persia, this economic factor became very important. But when in 1925 the national hero of Persia, Riza Khan, made himself Shah on what may be termed the "Fascist" program of nationalism and centralization, Soviet political influence suffered a staggering blow.

More spectacular were the gains of the Soviet policy in Afghanistan. It will be remembered that by the Anglo-Russian Convention of 1907, Afghanistan was made into a British preserve, forbidden to Russia. During the Great War a German-Turkish military mission played a conspicuous rôle in Kabul, and after the War a period of court revolutions started, finally bringing to power Amanullah Khan, the nephew of the dethroned Nasrullah Khan. He started a period of modernization by sending a party of one hundred Afghans to study in Europe. But his pan-Islamic sympathies brought him into a war with British India, a war favourable to Afghanistan at least in one respect: it restored the complete political independence of that buffer state.

According to well-established traditions of Afghan

policy, Amanullah immediately turned to Russia. The resulting treaty, signed in Moscow on February 28, 1921, was most favourable to Russia. Diplomatic relations were established, and the Russians obtained the right, for the first time in history, to establish consulates in Herat, Meimen, Mazar-i-Sherif, Kandahar and Ghazni. Afghanistan acknowledged the independence of Khiva and Bokhara, whatever form of government might be in existence there. In return Russia granted free transit to Afghan exports and promised financial and technical help.

Under this clause a powerful Russian radio station was established at Kabul, and a telegraph line was built between Kouchka on the Russian border and Kabul and Kandahar. Russian engineers were engaged for road building and Soviet instructors worked on the creation of an Afghan air force, after a Soviet squadron had made a spectacular flight across the Hindu Kush from Turkestan to Kabul. This was followed by the establishment of a regular Tashkent-Kabul air line. The Anglo-Indian Government, being powerless to stop the conclusion of the treaty, tried to obstruct its working out, capitalizing the Afghan support given to Enver Pasha in the Bassmatchi Rising. In fact, this incident strained Soviet-Afghan relations to the breaking point, but after the Afghan Government issued an order forbidding the border populations to participate in the Turkestan rebellion, the treaty was revived in 1922.

The list of Soviet agreements concluded with Asiatic neighbours in this important year 1921 would not be complete without the mention of a treaty with Mongolia, granting mutual recognition, and containing a clause of non-interference in each other's affairs.

A second phase in the Soviet policy in Asia began to shape itself about 1923-1924, that is, after the Soviets had succeeded in regaining full control over the whole of Russian territory, and after the destructive period of the Revolution had come to an end. The Soviet Government now began to manœuvre to regain the Russian zones of influence in the Far East, possibly with the aim of using them as convenient channels for spreading the Communist gospel.

Since at this time the main effort of proselytizing was directed against China, which was still not responding to Soviet advances, the question of Mongolia and of the status of the Chinese Eastern Railway assumed a particular importance. The Chinese themselves were responsible for the coming of the Red Army into Outer Mongolia, for they had secretly appealed to the Soviets to help them to fight Baron Ungern Sternberg. The Red Army having captured Urga, the Soviet agents then formed a Mongolian People's Revolutionary Party and a Red force. When the last remnants of the Whites were wiped out, the People's Party set up a puppet government in Urga under Soviet guidance.

The Soviet policy was to antagonize the poor downtrodden native against the Mongolian princes and the lamas. This first government, however, was by no means Communistic and limited itself to calling the so-called Small Khuruldan, or a preparatory council for the convocation of a Constituent Assembly. Some radical measures of this body, nevertheless, antagonized the princes and lamas to a point where the latter got into touch with the Japanese and formed a conspiracy for the overthrow of the Reds. The Central Executive Committee of the People's Party discovered this conspiracy, and on the grounds that the Prime Minister Bodo and several members of the Government had participated in it, had them executed. The next government, formed by a lama, Djakhandzi Khutukhta, and his Minister of Interior, Prince Tzetzen Khan, was of distinctly pro-Soviet tendencies and appealed to the latter to regulate the relations between Urga and Peking.

In September, 1922, an exchange of memoranda between Moscow and China on the question of Mongolia revealed an opposition of views. The Chinese stubbornly refused to yield their rights over Mongolia, and this question became the stumblingblock in the negotiations for a treaty between China and Russia. Meanwhile, in May, 1923, a Mongolian embassy was received in Moscow with great honours, and shortly after that the Soviet envoy, Lubarsky, reached Mongolia.

Now events favoured the Soviet scheme. In 1924 the Great Khutukhta, Bobdo Gegen, died. As he had been in his last reincarnation and had completed the cycle of lives on the earth, no successor could be chosen. Hence the Great Khuruldan, or Constituent Assembly, was faced with the problem of establishing a new régime. Under Soviet advice, a Soviet Republic was proclaimed in August, 1924, and the hold of Moscow over this new state, though unofficial, was practically complete. From a military point of view Mongolia was divided into districts after the Russian pattern, and a Red force was raised and equipped by Russia. Economically the country became a dependency of Siberia.

A year earlier, in 1923, the Uriankhai region had detached itself from Mongolia and notified Moscow of its independence. This mountainous but fertile region, covering the northernmost part of the former Jungaria, was beginning to be colonized by Russian settlers even before the War. Now the new state, which took the name of the Tanu Tuva People's Republic, was, like Mongolia, patterned on Soviet Russia, with a Council of Commissaries, a Red Army, and a new capital which was named, significantly, Krasnoye (in Russian, Red City).

Thus oddly, the great imperialistic dream of General Kuropatkin, who visualized after the Great War a Russia absorbing all the territories north of an ideal line from the Tian Shan range to Vladivostok, with a straight borderline shortened by several thousand miles, was being realized through the policy of the Soviet Government, by setting up puppet states in this region. There remained Manchuria.

The problem of the Chinese Eastern Railway was difficult, for it had in the meantime assumed an international character. The Japanese Government had profited by Allied intervention in Siberia to try to lay its hand on this valuable railway. But after the American Government protested, an agreement, drawn up on January 9, 1919, established an inter-Allied Technical Board for the control of the railway, with the American engineer J. F. Stevens as chairman. This status produced further friction with the result that the railway was handed back to China but operated by White Russians under inter-Allied control. The Russo-Asiatic Bank, in which France was interested, was to be the link through which this control was effected. This anomalous situation lasted until 1922.

Along with the question of the status of Mongolia, the Soviets were now also interested in regaining possession of this all-important railway. In China, meanwhile, an ever-increasing number of public men were favouring an understanding with Soviet Russia. Most influential amongst these were Sun Yat Sen, the Father of the Chinese Revolution, and General Wu Pei Fu, then at the height of his power. The first direct contact with the Soviet Government was established through a representative of the Far Eastern Republic, Mr. Yurin, who went to Peking. Shortly afterward, a Soviet official envoy, Mr. Joffe, made his appearance, and at a banquet given in his honour was greeted by the words, "Young China will be a disciple of the Great Russian Revolution." [61] He was succeeded in 1923 by Mr. Karakhan, who brought the negotiations to a successful conclusion. On May 31, 1924, the agreement was secretly signed by Mr. Karakhan and Mr. Wellington Koo, and was followed by an immediate resumption of diplomatic relations between the two

[61] Yakhontov, ibidem, p. 135.

countries. Thereupon, the Soviet Government transformed the Peking Legation into an embassy.

The agreement itself was composed of a treaty settling in principle the questions pending between the two parties, a separate agreement concerning the Chinese Eastern Railway, and various declarations. On the Soviet side, all privileges were renounced in accordance with the Declarations of 1919 and 1920, as well as extraterritoriality and consular jurisdiction. Both parties promised not to permit in their territories any activities hostile to the other party, and the thorny question of Mongolia was settled by the acknowledgment that Outer Mongolia was an integral part of China, and by a promise on the part of the Soviets to withdraw their troops from that region. As for the Chinese Eastern Railway, it was declared a commercial enterprise to be managed jointly by China and Russia to the exclusion of all other powers, pending the time when China should be in a position to repurchase it.

The agreement concerning the railway, however, was necessarily only theoretical, because the actual power in Manchuria was in the hands of Chang Tso Lin who was virtually independent of Peking. Therefore a separate agreement had to be concluded with the Manchurian War Lord, which became known as the Mukden Agreement of September 20, 1924. It confirmed the previous convention with slight modifications of a technical nature.

The great popularity which the Soviets enjoyed in China as a result of these agreements gave the Communist leaders the idea that their main effort in Sovietizing Asia ought to be directed toward winning over the Chinese revolutionaries. In this they were greatly encouraged by Sun Yat Sen, whose word in China was as powerful as Lenin's in Russia. As far back as 1907, Sun Yat Sen in a speech published by the Chinese newspaper *Min Bas,* had set forth the program of the nationalist party he was founding, later known as the Kuomintang. He laid down three principles: 1. race warfare, or the struggle against Manchu predominancy; 2. overthrow of the Empire and establishment of a democratic republic; 3. social and agrarian reforms.

This relatively mild program was extended when Sun Yat Sen came under Soviet influence, and at the Kuomintang Congress of 1924, a new interpretation was given to the three points already mentioned. Race warfare was now translated into a struggle against the imperialistic designs of foreign powers. As for point two, the final constitution was to be drafted only after a complete victory over the various war lords or Tuchuns. The program of social and agrarian reforms became much more drastic, including redistribution of land, limitation of private capital and nationalization of large enterprises. This new interpretation fits in with the stipulations of the Baku Congress, and reveals the influence of Russian Communists.

Furthermore, on his deathbed, Sun Yat Sen sent a message to the Central Executive Committee of the Communist Party in Moscow, which has been regarded as a political testament.

"You are heading the Union of Free Republics," he writes. "I am leaving behind me a party which will work in conjunction with you for the liberation of China. Bidding you farewell, I hope the day will come when the Soviet Union will find in a powerful China, a brother and an ally, and that both will move hand in hand in the struggle for the liberation of nations." [62]

With the successors of Sun Yat Sen following blindly these precepts of the great Chinese leader, Moscow's hold on the Kuomintang Party became complete.

But here arose a serious geographical difficulty. The Kuomintang controlled only Southern China with the great commercial city of Canton as its center. Northern China, feudal, militaristic and traditionally different from the south, was hostile to the Cantonese, and eventually the rift widened into a war. Under these circumstances, the policy of the Soviets was clear. It consisted in helping the South to create a military force sufficiently powerful to overcome the resistance of the North, with the hope that with the advance of the Kuomintang forces the Soviet doctrines would sweep the North, and eventually in this way China and Soviet Russia would merge into one vast political combination under the directing hand of Moscow.

The Cantonese, eager for technical assistance, accepted these suggestions readily and a Soviet mission was enthusiastically received at Canton in the autumn of 1923, that is to say, at the time when Peking was still reluctant to sign the Sino-Soviet Agreement. Invited by Dr. Sun Yat Sen, the mission, composed of

[62] Pavlovitch, Sun Yat Sen, The New East, Vol. VII, p. 20.

military and civil experts under the leadership of Michael Borodin, started reorganizing the Kuomintang along the lines of the Russian Communist Party. The mission's influence reached its zenith after the death of Sun Yat Sen, which occurred on March 12, 1925. Borodin was looked upon as the executor of the political program of the deceased leader, and Communists, both Russian and Chinese, secured entire control of Kuomintang affairs, to the dismay of a more moderate section headed by Chiang Kai Shek.

The Soviet mission did efficient work. It cleaned up the city of Canton and reorganized its administration, but above all it built up a good army, good according to Chinese standards. The officers' corps in the new Chinese Army was founded by the Soviet instructors. The army did well in the first campaign, and by December, 1926, the Canton Government was able to transfer its seat to Hankow, renamed Wuhang. But the very success of the Soviet mission was the cause of its undoing, and here the inherent weakness of the Soviet position in Asia became apparent.

Indeed, the case is typical of what occurred all over Asia. The Asiatic Nationalist Revolutionary movements, after some oscillation, came under the leadership of relatively moderate elements representing the middle-class intelligentsia. These were eager to secure the technical aid of the Soviets, but on the other hand were fully aware of the danger of anarchy resulting from the penetration of Communist ideas amongst the illiterate masses of their peoples. Consequently, seeing that Soviet aid meant also a dangerous undermining of the social structure of their countries, they eventually turned against the Communists.

This happened in China. By the success of his arms, Chiang Kai Shek, the moderate leader of the Kuomintang and now Commander-in-Chief of its forces, acquired sufficient following to attempt to overthrow the domination of the left wing of the party, which was servile to the Soviets. He accused the Soviets of "intriguing and using China for their own end of fostering a world revolution"[63] and staged a bloody coup against the Communists on December 15, 1927.

Relations with Soviet Russia were severed, and all Soviet citizens expelled from Southern China. The Soviet Consul General was arrested and the Vice-Consul shot. Similar action was taken in Northern China. On April 6, 1927, a raid on the Soviet Embassy in Peking occurred. The buildings were ransacked, archives seized and persons arrested in connection with the raid were put to death. Thus the whole Soviet structure so laboriously built up in China was crumbling.

In the meantime, having concentrated their efforts on China, in the Near East the Soviets had adopted a passive policy. The disappointing results of the great drive on China, coupled with the increasing seriousness of the economic crisis in Russia itself, became responsible for the extension of this passive attitude all over Asia. From 1926 on, a general receding of Soviet influence in Asia is noticeable. In Afghanistan and Persia as well as in China, there occurred events unfavour-

[63] Yakhontov, ibidem, footnote p. 168.

able to the Communists: the fall of Amanullah in Kabul, and the emergence of the Pahlevi dynasty under Riza Khan in Teheran. At the same time the economic reconstruction of Russia became a matter of life and death for the Soviet régime, hence the Five Year Plan.

Under these circumstances, Soviet policy in Asia entered a third phase, which may be termed "defensive." The attack on Europe through Asia was abandoned just as the direct attack on Europe had been abandoned earlier by Lenin. The new idea was to concentrate all efforts on the creation of an economically powerful Soviet Union and to demonstrate the workability of a socialist state. The Asiatic countries would follow suit if they saw a Soviet success. With this new policy, the main object to be pursued was security from outside aggression in order to be able to work peacefully at home, and the acquisition of markets for goods exported under the Five Year Plan in return for the cash required for the capitalization of the plan. It is in pursuance of these two aims that the Soviet diplomacy in Asia is now working.

With Turkey a treaty of neutrality and non-aggression was signed on December 17, 1925, just two days after the League of Nations issued a decision unfavourable to Turkey on the Mosul question. This treaty was renewed in 1929, and both parties have made demonstrations to stress the closeness of their relations on more than one occasion.

With Afghanistan also there has been no difficulty. As a result of the Treaty of 1921, King Amanullah had been receiving a regular subsidy from the Soviets, sometimes in cash, but mostly in goods and armaments. Even without this, Soviet Russia could count upon his sympathy. Consequently there was no difficulty in the signing of a treaty of non-aggression on August 31, 1926.

But with Persia, things did not go as smoothly, particularly after the advent of Riza Khan, and a pact was concluded only on October 1, 1927, after all outstanding economic questions, such as fishing rights, the use of the port of Enzeli, transit of Persian goods through Russia, etc., had been solved in separate agreements.

On the whole, however, the relations of Soviet Russia with her three Near Eastern neighbours remained very friendly, and Soviet diplomacy was even instrumental in the conclusion of treaties between Persia and Turkey and Persia and Afghanistan. The fall of King Amanullah, punished for proceeding too rapidly with his reforms, was a set-back for the Soviets, but when in November, 1929, Nadir Khan came to the throne, Moscow was reassured. Nadir Khan had no more reason for liking the British than had Amanullah.

More and more absorbed in the Five Year Plan, the Soviet Government was eager to extend this chain of protective treaties to the Far East, but on account of the strained relations which followed the Borodin period in China, the Chinese Eastern Railway became a constant source of trouble and a serious menace to good neighbourly relations. The condominium over the railway could not work without constant friction. The Chinese had obtained an important advantage by securing the right to police the railway. The technical management remained in Russian hands, though the number of directors on the board representing each country was equal.

On this basis, conflicts were inevitable, and grew in seriousness. The Manchurian War Lord, Chang Tso Lin, had been openly coveting the railway, and was impatient with Russian management, particularly after transit for his troops was refused. In 1926 he had the Soviet manager arrested but was obliged to release him after an ultimatum had been sent by the Soviet Government. In 1929 Chang Tso Lin's son, Chang Hsueh Liang seized the railway by having the Russian staff arrested. The reason given was that the Soviet Government had been using the railway as a channel for Communist propaganda, but the evidence presented by the Manchurian authorities was very slim.

This open aggression compelled the Soviet Government to employ force. Red Army detachments invaded Manchuria and carried on a desultory war with the Chinese troops, easily defeating the latter. On November 27, 1929, Chang Hsueh Liang capitulated completely, accepting all Soviet conditions. The Red Army retired back into Siberia, but the impression produced on the Chinese was such that Soviet prestige again rose very high, and Russia became undisputed master of the railway and the Russian sphere of influence. A final settlement of the status of the railway was left to negotiation, but while this dragged on interminably in Moscow, the Soviets were masters of the situation.

This very success, however, proved a boomerang

to the Soviet position in the Far East which was
menaced from a new and much more dangerous
quarter. The seeds of Japanese Imperialism went
far back into the past and were nurtured gradually through the period of the rise of Japan as a
great power. Already, Hideyoshi had suggested
the creation of a Japanese Empire on the mainland of Asia.

In the 1850's these ideas were taken up by
Yoshida Shoin, whose writings had a great influence on Japanese minds. He advocated the
creation of a continental empire extending from
Kamchatka to Korea and including Manchuria.
The Soviets had plenty of warning that the plans
of Japanese imperialists and militarists involved
the conquest of Manchuria and of Eastern Siberia.
However, when the hour struck, they were found
unprepared to meet this danger. Tension between
Japan and China had been building up during
the summer of 1931 as a result of clashes between
Chinese landholders and Koreans in the province
of Kirin, and the execution of a Japanese officer,
Major Nakamura, by Chinese troops. On the
night of September 18-19, 1931, the officers of the
Japanese troops guarding the South Manchurian
Railway at Mukden launched upon their own
initiative an attack on the Chinese garrison and
took possession of the city, following which the
Japanese heavily reinforced from Korea, occupied
the whole of southern Manchuria. A new chapter
in the history of the Far East and, as later events
were to prove, in the history of the world was
opening. Faced with this serious menace to its
own position in Manchuria, the Soviet Govern-

ment adopted a policy of strict non-interference in this conflict and merely protested the appearance of Japanese gunboats on the Sungari river. The Russian offer of a non-aggression pact was demonstratively turned down by the Japanese Government. That the Russians were well aware of the gravity of impending developments may be seen by Molotov's statement to the Central Executive Committee of the Soviets that the Far Eastern crisis had absolute priority in Soviet foreign policy. The crisis came when in November 1931 the Japanese forces crossed the Chinese Eastern Railway at Tsitsikar, thus impeding the operations of the system, even though the railway administration announced its strict neutrality in the conflict. Furthermore, the Japanese were now penetrating into a region of Manchuria which had been regarded as of great strategic import since it menaced the Russian cities on the Amur and the main line of the Trans-Siberian running close to the river. This was the area within the bend of the Amur and north of the Chinese Eastern Railway. By the spring of 1933, the operations of the Chinese Eastern Railway had come to a complete standstill. Furthermore, coupled with this aggressive military policy, the Japanese pursued an equally provocative diplomatic campaign. In 1932 they sent Russia a bristling note demanding the extradition or internment of the Chinese General Su, who had retreated into Siberia. To these obvious provocations, the Soviets replied by a show of extraordinary patience and moderation, which only proved that they were not yet ready to face an open conflict and wanted to avoid war at all costs. Furthermore, the coming to power of Hitler in Germany at this time placed Russia in the difficult position of facing two rising and aggressively imperialistic dictatorships on both her Asiatic and European borders. Russia was further faced with the fait accompli of the establishment in February 1932 of the puppet state of Manchukuo under the regency of the former Chinese Emperor Pu Yi, and with the occupation in the opening months of 1933 by the Japanese armies of the province of Jehol east of the Great Khingan Mountains. The new state was thus composed of four provinces, Fengtien, Kirin, Heilungkiang, and Jehol, two of which (Kirin and Heilungkiang) had been in the Russian zone of Manchuria. Facing the situation realistically, the Soviet Government decided to write off its interests in Manchukuo and announced its readiness to negotiate the sale of the Chinese Eastern Railway. The first conference met on June 26, 1933, the Soviets announcing that the railway had cost 411,600,000 gold rubles and the representatives of Manchukuo countering with an offer of 50,000,000 yen. After 15 months of bargaining, the railway was sold for the nearly nominal sum of 180,000,000 yen. The main purpose of Soviet diplomacy, that of gaining time, had been achieved and during this period Russia had been feverishly preparing for war in the Far East. Not only were the Red army forces in Eastern Siberia increased and brought to fighting trim, but the Trans-Siberian railway was double tracked and a major trunk line north of Lake Baikal to Komsomolsk was projected.

The second phase of the acute conflict between Russia and Japan was opened in 1935 with the Japanese penetration into Inner Mongolia and the raising by Japanese agents of Pan-Islamic slogans in Sinkiang. Thus a Japanese master plan menacing the great industrial centers of western Siberia in the Stalinsk and Kuznetzk basins was shaping itself with a flanking advance through the Gobi desert, around the Siberian border. Directly in line of this advance was the Mongolian Soviet or People's Republic. A serious incident occurred around Lake Khalkha. The Japanese wished to have the borders between Manchukuo and Mongolia delimited and their demand was countered by a Soviet announcement that the border had been fixed. The Mongolian Soviet Republic appealed for aid to Moscow announcing that the Japanese were aiming at the creation of a second Manchukuo in Mongolia. A Soviet-Mongol mutual assistance pact concluded over the protest of China resulted in the arming of the Mongol Red Army by Russia with the latest weapons of war. This, coupled with increased border clashes, with seizure of small Russian river craft by the Japanese and the penetration of Japanese destroyers beyond the 12 miles limit in Kamchatka waters heightened the tension between the two countries. The following year occurred the Amur islands incident. Opposite Blagavieshchensk the Amur is separated into two channels by some islands. The Soviets established frontier posts on these islands which Japan claimed to be a part of Manchukuo. The Japanese sunk a Soviet patrol boat and occupied the islands with their troops.

It was, however, in 1938 that hostilities flared up on a larger scale in what amounted to a veritable undeclared war. This was the so-called Chanku-feng incident near Lake Hasan, where, owing to the fact that the frontier had not been clearly delimited, a dispute arose over the possession of a hill which had some religious significance for the Manchus. The rejection of the Japanese demand for the evacuation of the hill by the Soviet forces led to the Japanese attack on Russian positions which developed into a violent ten-days battle (July 31-August 10th). The issue was eventually settled by mediation, but the Russians retained the hill. A similar incident flared up in 1939 in the Nomonhan area along the Mongol border. After several weeks of fighting, a truce was arranged on September 16th, but not before the Japanese had lost around 20,000 men and the Japanese general staff had acknowledged the superior mechanization of the Soviet-Mongol forces. Once more the Soviets retained the territory they were holding.

With the outbreak of World War II, both sides became anxious to compose their difficulties and in 1941 a Soviet-Japanese non-aggression pact was signed on April 1, guaranteeing the territorial integrity of Manchukuo and of Mongolia. When Hitler's invasion of Russia was followed by Pearl Harbour, both countries found themselves fighting for survival with Germany and the United States, respectively, and an uneasy peace prevailed along the Manchukuo and Mongolian borders.

The relations between the Mongolian People's

Republic (Outer Mongolia) and Soviet Russia followed closely the pattern of the larger framework of events we have just examined. After a violent phase of socialization in Mongolia, which ended in 1932, a new policy was opened with the Mongolian Prime Minister Gendung's visit to Moscow in 1934. The industrialization of Mongolia was started by the construction of machine shops, printing presses, large wool-washing plants, and the establishment of motor transport, to be followed, after World War II, by a railway line from Choibolsang in Mongolia to a point on the Trans-Siberian Railway. With Soviet credits and loans extended and a vast number of Russian technicians and advisors flooding the country, it is not surprising to find that by 1934 already 91% of all Mongolian trade was with Russia as compared to only 34% in 1927. Notwithstanding this economic, cultural and, to some extent, military control by Russia, it must be pointed out that though a Soviet Republic, Outer Mongolia has not been integrated into the Soviet Union, and has maintained a somewhat precarious independence which, prior to 1945, had been only recognized by the Soviet Union. The recognition of this independence by China in 1945 has somewhat strengthened this independence, even though the annexation of neighboring Tannu Tuva by the Soviets may be construed as a handwriting on the wall. In the fluid condition existing at present in the Far East, the future alone will answer this question.

In contrast to the high priority given by the Soviets to the Far East during the decade preceding World War II, the Near East occupied a relatively secondary place in the preoccupations of Soviet diplomacy. This was due to two reasons — first, the Japanese war menace coupled with the rise of Hitler Germany was an immediate threat to the very existence of the Soviet Union and, secondly, the Near Eastern countries, Afghanistan and Persia (Iran) in particular, were safely anchored to the British orbit, after their earlier oscillations, and to some extent this applied to Turkey, too.

It was only with the early military disasters sustained by the Allies in the War, and the falling of British prestige and influence in the Near East, that this area once more attracted the attention of Soviet diplomacy. Indeed, during the period of the Russo-German rapprochement under the Ribbentrop-Molotov agreement, Molotov in November 1940 seems to have agreed to a joint four-power pact which designated the areas of territorial aspirations of Germany, Italy, Japan, and Russia, as well as the delimitations of spheres of influence. The Soviets reserved for themselves a line from Transcaucasia across Persia to the Persian Gulf, and the right to lease a naval base on the Bosphorus and the Dardanelles, thus reverting back to the traditional policies of Imperial Russia. However, when on April 14, 1941, the pro-German Rashid Ali Bey Gailani overthrew the pro-British Government in Iraq all German efforts to induce Russia to give military aid to the rebels failed and the Kremlin did not go beyond establishing diplomatic relations with the new government. But with the involve-

ment of Russia on the side of the Allies in the
World War, the exigencies of the military situation gave Russia the opportunity to advance into
Persia and the Red Army entered Iran on August
26, 1941. In Persia itself, Riza Shah Pahlevi was
forced out of power by British action and replaced
on the throne by his son, Mohammed. Both the
newly built railway across Persia and the motor
roads served as one of the main arteries for the
penetration of lend-lease supplies to Russia, and
Persia signed a tri-partite Treaty of Alliance with
the Soviet Union and Great Britain. For a brief
moment Persia became the focal center for world-
shaking developments with the Teheran Conference in November 1943.

It is now necessary to give an over-all survey
of the position of the Soviet Union in Asia, as she
emerges, victorious from the holocaust of the
World War and to draw a balance. As a result of
the Yalta agreement and after her victory over
Germany, Soviet Russia pledged herself to enter
the war against Japan in August 1945, in return
for the acknowledgment of her claims in the Far
East. Accordingly, the Red Army conducted a
lightning campaign against the Japanese army in
Manchuria. To what extent this campaign con-
tributed, as the Soviets claim, to the capitulation
of Japan is, in view of the Hiroshima explosion, a
problem for future historians to decide. What is
certain is that at the end of the hostilities Russia
found herself in the most advantageous position
she has ever occupied in the Far East. The Treaty
of Portsmouth and even the agreement of 1875
concerning the Kurile islands were written off.

In accordance with the terms of the Yalta agreement, Russia regained possession of the lower half of Sakhalin and of the Kurile archipelago. She regained control over Port Arthur and Dairen, and over the whole network of the Chinese Eastern Railway. In addition, the Red Army occupied the northern half of Korea up to the 38th parallel, and in evacuating Manchuria Russia dismembered the industrial plants built by the Japanese, the machinery going to replace what had been destroyed by the German advance in Russia. However, these very successes carried in them the seeds of the "Cold War" with the United States, the first signs of which appear shortly after the conclusion of the hostilities with Japan.

There remained also the problem of the relations with China. During the World War, so far as is known, the Russians refrained from giving aid to Chinese Communists, and sent their supplies to the Chungking Government. For this purpose, a military motor road had been developed from the Sinkiang border across the Gobi desert to Lanchow. Sinkiang itself came more and more under Russian economic and political domination, and for a while portions of it were under Russian military occupation. Thus a wide range of issues had arisen between China and Russia, and after rather protracted negotiations these were settled by a treaty signed on a quid pro quo basis with the Kuomintang Government in 1945. In return for Russian non-interference in Sinkiang, the Chinese Nationalist Government renounced all claims to Mongolia and acknowledged the independence of that country. In Manchuria, the former Chinese

Eastern Railway, to be renamed the Changchung Railway, and the treaty ports (Port Arthur and Dairen) were to be administered jointly by Russians and Chinese on an equal basis and for "joint utilization" by both parties. However, the Cold War with the United States and the Communist victory in China have now invalidated this treaty by the elimination of the government of Chiang Kai Shek and opened a new and unpredictable chapter in the Far East. A Russo-Chinese treaty recently negotiated with the Communist Government in Peking pledges Russia to return to China all possessions in Manchuria by 1952 and establishes a new military alliance between the two countries.

In the Near East the events did not shape themselves as favorably for the Soviet. The occupation by the Red Army of the provinces of Azerbaijan, Khorasan, Mazanderan, and Kurdistan in Northern Persia fostered an autonomous movement among the local population against the rule of Teheran. The Iranian Government in turn refused the Soviet demand for oil concessions in this area and the increased tension produced border incidents. In November 1945, accusing the Soviet Government of having violated article 4 of the treaty of alliance, the Persians sent two infantry brigades, a tank force and a brigade of gendarmerie to crush the autonomous movement in Azerbaijan, but these forces were halted at Sharifabad by the Russian troops. Persia, backed by the United States and Great Britain, appealed to the Security Council of the United Nations, and after much wrangling and inconclusive actions, the

Russians evacuated Northern Persia. Similarly in Turkey, the demand for a base in the Straits and the cession to Russia of the districts of Kars and Ardahan met with no success and was not pressed further by the Soviets. The results of these moves has been that both Persia and Turkey have aligned themselves with the western powers and form strategic outposts against Russia in the "Cold War"

The Soviets as a result of these developments seemed to have adopted a "wait and see" policy with reference to the Near East as a whole. Cognizant of the strategic importance of these areas, they seem to limit themselves to a policy of strengthening their hold on the Communist movements and of supporting and fostering the racial and religious minorities in these countries. Thus, by a circuitous route they have come back to the policies elaborated at the Congress of Baku in 1920.

CONCLUSION

WHITHER is Russia going? What are the future potentialities for Russian action in Asia? These two questions are of paramount importance for the future destinies of the world. It is still too early, however, to answer with any certainty, for both Russia and Asia are at present in the play of dynamic forces which make for rapid evolution. The pace of this movement and its directions are so divergent as to make any attempt to coördinate or compare the trend of development of Russia and Asia well-nigh impossible. What can be done is to submit to critical analysis some conceptions which have at present received wide circulation, concerning the inter-relation of the Soviet Union with Asia.

Indeed, two ideas seem particularly popular at the present time. The first is, that the Soviet Revolution has resulted in the return of Russia to Asia, thus definitely frustrating the attempt of Peter the Great to make the Russian Empire a European country; and the second is, that the Russians are not a nation but a medley of races with a powerful ingredient of purely Asiatic elements.

Before we discuss these arguments one thing must be remembered: all great revolutions produce a set of ideas or a mode of life which diverges from the ruling

313

concepts of the day, and consequently antagonizes and shocks the community of nations. Such was the case with Puritan England of the Commonwealth, the France of the Jacobins, and is with Communist Russia to-day. Nobody thought of calling Cromwell or Robespierre Asiatic for this reason.

As for the first point, the return of Russia to Asia, how can one say that the Russians are returning to Asia when they never came from there, as the great French historian Leroy Beaulieu once put it? It will be remembered that originally the Slavs migrated into Russia from Central Europe. If on their way they had to fight and at times were submerged by waves of Asiatic nomadic invaders, these nomads, it must be remembered, splashed over the rest of Europe as well, during the period of Great Invasions. It is curious to notice that the Hunnish invasion of Attila reached Orleans in its westernmost push, while the Arabs coming from Asia through Africa and Spain reached Tours. Thus it was in France that the two great currents of Asiatic intrusion coming from east and west nearly touched each other at several centuries' distance. It is known that the modern European nations represent the blending of these invaders with the original stock, hence the fate of the Russian Slavs would hardly differ greatly from the other branches of Caucasian stock in Europe.

Strictly speaking, Europe as a whole ought to be considered a mere extension of Asia. It is difficult to understand why India, a sub-continent separated from the rest of Asia by the highest mountains on the earth, and by a great ocean, should be considered an integral part of that continent, while Europe with no appreciable geographical frontiers is detached into a separate continent.

Coming to more recent times, we have in Russia the Tartar domination which corresponds to the Moorish yoke in Spain. But for reasons which we have already examined, the influence of the Tartars must not be overestimated. The racial admixture of blood was relatively insignificant, and culturally, Russia was not absorbed because she had already crystallized her own cultural personality four centuries before their coming. What the Tartars undoubtedly did was to magnify certain existing tendencies which were in harmony with Asiatic ideas. Here Eastern influence did exert itself on Russia. It must be remembered that Russian life and culture were of Byzantine origin, and in so far as Byzantium may be regarded as an Eastern state, Russia must be considered the same. But Rome was the model upon which the Eastern Roman Empire was moulded, and consideration of the Oriental ingredients must not obliterate this fundamental fact.

Broadly speaking, Russian history follows in its main lines the development of other European nations. The Kiev period with the democratic basis for the authority of the Prince was followed by the splitting of Russia into small units, just as was the case in feudal Europe, though it must be said that the resemblance of the Russian institutions to feudalism was superficial. The rise of united Russia into one powerful nation coincided with a similar process in Spain, France and elsewhere, and likewise the advent of the autocracy of the Czar coincided with the growth of absolutism in Western Europe. John the Terrible has his counterparts in Henry VIII of England and Philip II of Spain, Peter the Great in Louis XIV and Frederick William, the King Sergeant of Prussia, who, as much as the Great Czar, enjoyed personally caning his subjects for disobedience. Catherine II may be compared to Maria Theresa or Joseph II, and so forth.

Every one of these characters, however, mentioned in Russia exaggerated either the autocratic power or the cruelty of his European counterpart, and in this exaggeneration the Eastern influence appeared again. Another characteristic, due possibly to the same reason, is that this evolution of Russian history lagged a generation or two behind the similar process in Western Europe, and this lag accounts for the impression that Russia was at a standstill, when actually if we look at her alone, we find her progressing steadily. For instance, the abolition of serfdom in Prussia in 1807 and Hungary in 1848 followed in Russia only in 1861, and Russia had to wait till the beginning of the 20th century for a timid constitutionalism of the type introduced in Prussia in 1851 and in Austria in 1861.

It must also be noticed that Russia expanded into Asia proper at the very time when colonial expansion in Western Europe was taking place. Furthermore, the success of the Russian advance in Asia was due to the superiority of European technology over that of the natives, and the movement was accelerated when Peter the Great's Westernizing reforms gave Russia adequate military power. Thus, paradoxically, Russia could become an Asiatic nation only by becoming European.

The Soviet Revolution, by its new policy of fostering the cultural autonomy of the Asiatic minorities in the Union, and by the economic development under the Five Year Plan, has given a new importance to Soviet Asia. Under the Czarist regime the alien minorities were submerged and unconspicuous in Russian life. Russia had an atmosphere comparable to that of the United States alone in sameness and absolute predominancy of one culture. In crossing the vast Eurasian plain, one was struck with the identical pattern and general Russian atmosphere in cities separated by thousands of miles; we pointed out the observation of a French traveller who was surprised to see the newly acquired territories in Manchuria become so quickly pervaded with this atmosphere. Just as in the United States, where the important alien and even coloured minorities cannot affect the aspect of the cities, which are essentially American, one used to feel in the remotest Asiatic corners of the great Slav Empire, the cultural domination of the Russian. To-day the formerly submerged minorities have arisen to a new life of equality and partnership in the affairs of the Soviet Union. Hence the ubiquitous presence in Soviet Russia of various Asiatics has produced the impression among foreign observers that the Soviet Republics are a medley of Eurasian races.

The following figures according to the 1939

census in percentage totals give the truth of the
relative importance of the various races residing on
the territory of the Union. [1])

Russians (Great Russians Ukrainians,
   Byelorussians)............................. 78.68%
Georgians...................................... 1.33%
Armenians..................................... 1.27%
Tartars....................................... 2.54%
Uzbecks....................................... 2.86%
Jews.. 1.78%
Kazaks.. 1.83%
Azerbaidjanians............................... 1.34%

and all the other races inhabiting Asiatic Russia
below 1%.

Even if heeding the claim of some rabid Ukrainian & Byelorussian Nationalists, we leave out
of consideration these two branches of the Russian
people closely related as they are by blood and
language ties, still we find that the Great Russian
stock exceed 58% of the total.

There remains the question of racial intermarriage. The infusion of Tarter blood as a result of
the invasion was comparatively insignificant, as we
have seen. During the colonization of Siberia,
however, the Russian emigrant did mix with the
native, particularly the Siberian Cossack, but here
an effective bar was found in the religious issue.
The Russian had no strongly developed racial
feeling, but his religious sentiments segregated him
very effectively from the natives. Marriage with a
non-Christian was forbidden in old Russia, both by
law and by custom, and the cases of conversion

[1]Sir Bernard Pares, A History of Russia
  Appendix p. 551 it. y. 1949.

being proportionately rare among the natives, the obstacle was very real.

With these facts in mind it is possible to discuss the so-called return of Russia to Asia as a result of the Revolution. The Soviet Regime has aimed at and succeeded in stamping out the Byzantine elements which formed the foundation of old Russia. The two most important pillars, namely, autocracy and orthodoxy, have either disappeared or been badly shattered. Byzantium being the first source of the Eastern influences in Russia, it would appear therefore that the process is developing in the opposite direction. More plausible would seem the hypothesis that the Soviet Revolution is the last stage of the revolutionary process initiated by Peter the Great. Indeed, just as Peter introduced Western culture to the top layer of Russian society by spreading technical knowledge, so to-day the Soviet regime, after having destroyed these higher strata, is introducing technical education in the lower classes. The object is the same: teaching self-help and building up efficiency. It is only in the number of people affected and the classes affected that the experiment differs. Just as Peter took his ideas from abroad and adapted them to the Russian conditions, so did Lenin transplant German Marxism onto Russian soil.

We have to examine now the position of Russia with respect to Asia, as emerging from the Second World War. The cleavage between East and West caused by the Cold War seems to have brought Russia and Asia closer together and there exists a real fear that a gigantic Russo-Asiatic Empire extending over the greater part of the continent may come in to being. The idea antedates the Soviet Revolution and at the turn of the century, a writer, Mr. Ular, envisioned the blending of Russia and China into one Great Empire. However the prophets of this extension of Russia's power overlook the fact that the Soviet Revolution and the great revolutionary and nationalist tides sweeping over Asia, even if under the cloak of Marxism, are related but certainly not entirely identical: — Their points of contact are a common ideology and the technological drive which confronted and confronts both Russia and Asia to a varying degree. If from the point of view of Western democracies the Soviet way of life appears as a regression, to the Asiatics in the early throes of an industrial revolution it appears as the shortest way to achieve economic power and to obtain the industrial and other weapons with which to successfully confront the West. Precisely for this reason we are faced with the paradox that the apparent spread of Sovietisation in Asia strengthens the rise of nationalism which basically remains antagonistic to Russia. It was this paradox which apparently caused the failure of the Soviet drive in Asia in the 1920's and though today the pull towards Moscow is very much stronger — it is due to a certain extent to the postponement and not the settling of problems in the areas of conflict between Russian interests and those of the neighboring Asiatic countries. So long as this basic contradiction exists the Soviet influence in Asia will be more or less of a temporary nature and only real to a degree. The second factor to be considered is that after the flush of victory of a revolutionary ideology, the basic forces of the past which formed the national culture of a given people begin to reassert themselves and show their inherent vitality. If this was true in Russia, where after the period of integral Communism there appeared to be a readmission of certain historic traditions, of religion, of art and of other basic factors of Russian national life, one may expect the same thing to happen in those countries, like China, which have a back log of millenary cultural and historic traditions which can hardly be eradicated in so short a time. It is therefore necessary to make a distinction between the immediate prospects of the extension of Soviet power in Asia and the long range view.

BIBLIOGRAPHY *

(Works available in English, French and German)

AMANN, GUSTAV—The Legacy of Sun-Yat-Sen; Canada, 1929.

BADDELEY, J.—Russia, Mongolia, China 2v.; London, 1919.

BALFOUR, J.—Recent Happenings in Persia; London, 1922.

BLISS, E. M.—Turkey and the Armenian Atrocities; London, 1896.

BRYAN, J. INGRAM—A History of Japan; London, 1928.

BRYCE, J.—Transcaucasia, with Supplement on the Armenian Question; London, 1896.

CAHEN, G.—Histoire des relations de la Russie avec la Chine sous Pierre le Grand; Paris, 1911.

CAHUN, L.—Introduction à l'histoire de l'Asie; Turcs et Mongols, des origines à 1405; Paris, 1896.

CHARYKOW, N. V.—Glimpses of High Politics; New York, 1931.

CHERADAME, A.—Le monde et la guerre Russo-Japonaise; Paris, 1906.

COXE, W.—Account of the Russian Discoveries between Asia and America; London, 1787.

CURTIN, J.—The Mongols in Russia; Boston, 1908.

CURZON, BARON G.—Russia in Central Asia in 1889 and the Anglo-Russian Question; New York, 1889.

D'AVIGDOR, D. C.—La Sibérie Orientale et le Japon; Paris, 1922.

DENNIS, A. L. P.—The Foreign Policies of Soviet Russia; New York, 1924.

* Consulted by the author at the time of writing.

DRIAULT, E.—La Question d'Orient depuis ses origines jusqu'à nos jours; Paris, 1912.

FISCHER, L.—The Soviets in World Affairs 2v.; New York, 1930.

GERARD, A.—Nos Alliés d'Extrême Orient; Paris, 1918.

GIBBONS, H. A.—The New Map of Asia 1900-1919; New York, 1921.

GOLDER, F. A.—Russian Expansion on the Pacific, 1681-1850; Cleveland, 1914.

GUEDALLA, P.—Palmerston; New York, 1927.

GUEST, L. H.—The New Russia; London, 1925.

HOLLAND, T. E.—The European Concert in the Eastern Question; Oxford, 1885.

INDIAN OFFICER—Russia's March toward India, by an; London, 1894.

KLUCHEVSKY, V. O.—A History of Russia 4v.; New York, 1911-26.

KRIEGER, B.—Die ersten hundert jahre russich-chinesicher politik; Berlin, 1904.

KUROPATKIN, GEN.—The Russian Army and the Japanese War 2v.; New York, 1909.

LEBEDEV, V.—Vers l'Inde; Paris, 1900.

LEROY-BEAULIEU, P.—La Rénovation de l'Asie; Paris, 1900.

LI HUNG CHANG—Memoirs of the Viceroy; London, 1913.

MALCOLM, SIR J.—History of Persia; London, 1829.

MALLESON, G.—The Russo Afghan Question ^nd the Invasion of India; London, 1885.

MEYENDORFF, BARON A.—Correspondance Diplomatique du Baron de Staal 2v.; Paris, 1929.

MARCO POLO—Travels of; New York.

MILLER, W.—The Ottoman Empire; Cambridge, 1913.

MORFILL, W. R.—A History of Russia from the Birth of Peter the Great to the Death of Alexander II; London, 1902.

MORFILL, W. R.—The Story of Russia; New York, 1893.

NORTON, H. K.—The Far Eastern Republic of Siberia; New York, 1923.

OWEN, D. E.—Imperialism and Nationalism in the Far East; New York, 1929.

PARES, SIR BERNARD—A History of Russia; New York, 1926.

PASVOLSKY, L.—Russia in the Far East; New York, 1922.

PERRY-AYSCOUGH, H. G. C.—With the Russians in Mongolia; New York, 1914.

PINON, R.—La Lutte pour le Pacifique; Paris, 1906.

PINON, R.—L'Europe et l'Empire Ottoman; Paris, 1909.

POKROVSKY, M. N.—A History of Russia from the Earliest Times to the Rise of Commercial Capitalism; New York, 1931.

RAMBAUD, A.—Histoire de la Russie depuis les origines jusqu'à nos jours; Paris, 1914.

ROSTOVTSEV, M. T.—Iranians and Greeks in South Russia; Oxford, 1922.

SCHUYLER, E.—Peter the Great, Emperor of Russia 2v.; New York, 1890.

SCHUYLER, E.—Turkistan 2v.; New York, 1877.

SKRINE, F. H.—Expansion of Russia; Cambridge, 1904.

SOOTHILL, W. E.—A History of China; London, 1927.

SYKES, SIR PERCY—Persia; Oxford, 1922.

TONG, H. R.—Facts about the Chinese Eastern Railway Situation; Harbin, 1929.

THOMPSON, E.—A History of India; London, 1927.

TREAT, P. J.—The Far East; New York, 1928.

ULAR, A.—Un Empire russo-chinois; Paris, 1903.

VÁMBÉRY, ÁRMIN—Western Culture in Asiatic Lands: a Comparison of the Methods Adopted by England and Russia in the Middle East; London, 1906.

VANDAL, A.—Napoléon et Alexandre Ier, 3 v.; Paris, 1891-96.

VERNADSKY, G.—A History of Russia; Yale, 1930.

VLADIMIR—Russia on the Pacific and the Siberian Railway; London, 1899.

WALISZEWSKI, K.—Ivan the Terrible; Philadelphia, 1904.

WALISZEWSKI, K.—Le Régne d'Alexandre Ier (1818-1828); Paris, 1925.

WEIGH, K. S.—Russo-Chinese Diplomacy; Shanghai, 1928.

WHEELER, J.—A Short History of India and of the Frontier State of Afghanistan, Nipal and Burma; London, 1894.

WITTE, Memoires du Comte; Paris, 1921.

YAKHONTOV, V. A.—Russia and the Soviet Union in the Far East; New York, 1931.

YOUNG, C. WALTER—The International Relations of Manchuria; Chicago, 1929.

INDEX